The Meditations of the Emperor Marcus Aurelius Antoninus

NATURAL LAW AND
ENLIGHTENMENT CLASSICS

The Meditations of the Emperor Marcus Aurelius Antoninus

Translated by Francis Hutcheson and James Moor

Edited and with an Introduction by James Moore And Michael Silverthorne

The Collected Works and Correspondence Of Francis Hutcheson

GYAN

ISBN : 978-81-212-1495-7(HB)

Published, 2018

Published by

Gyan Publishing House
5, Ansari Road
Daryaganj, New Delhi-110002
Phone: 011-47034999, 9811692060
www.gyanbooks.com
E-mail: books@gyanbooks.com

Printed at: G. Print Process, Delhi.

CONTENTS

INTRODUCTION

On May 31, 1742, Francis Hutcheson in Glasgow sent to Thomas Drennan in Belfast some copies of *The Meditations of the Emperor Marcus Aurelius Antoninus. Newly translated from the Greek: With Notes, and an Account of his Life* (Glasgow: Printed by Robert Foulis and sold by him at the College: 1742).[1]

The letter that accompanied the dispatch of the books contained the following intriguing account:

> The bearer Mr. Hay takes over some copies of a new translation of Antoninus, the greater half of which and more, was my amusement last summer, for the sake of a singular worthy soul one Foulis;[2] but I don't let my name appear in it, nor indeed have I told it to any here but the Man concerned. I hope that you'll like it; the rest was done by a very ingenious Lad one Moore.[3] Pray try your critical faculty in finding what parts I did & what he did. I did not translate books in a suite, but I one or two, & he one or two. I hope if you like it that it may sell pretty well with you about Belfast I am sure it is doing a publick good to diffuse the Sentiments & if you knew Foulis you would think he deserved all incouragement.[4]

1. *The Meditations* were reprinted in Glasgow by Robert and Andrew Foulis in 1749 (2nd ed.), 1752 (3rd ed.), and 1764 (4th ed.). Another "4th ed." was printed in Dublin for Robert Main in 1752.

2. Robert Foulis (1707–76) was appointed printer to the University of Glasgow in 1743. In partnership with his brother Andrew, he was responsible for the publication of many attractive and accurate editions of classical texts.

3. James Moor (1712–79) was appointed university librarian of the University of Glasgow in 1742 and professor of Greek in 1746. He edited many of the classical texts published by Robert and Andrew Foulis. Robert Foulis married Moor's sister Elizabeth in September 1742. Moor and the Foulis brothers witnessed Hutcheson's will on June 30, 1746.

4. Letter of Francis Hutcheson to the Reverend Mr. Thomas Drennan in Belfast, Glasgow, May 31, 1742. MS: Glasgow University Library, MS Gen 1018 no. 11.

Hutcheson's letter raises a number of questions: (1) Which books of *The Meditations* contain Hutcheson's translations and notes and which books should be attributed to Moor? (2) What considerations prompted Hutcheson to undertake this translation and edition, apart from his announced desire to be of assistance to Robert Foulis and the Foulis press? (3) What might be the significance of Hutcheson's notes to the text? Do they make up a coherent set of ideas concerning human nature, morals, politics, and religion? And what may be the relevance of these notes for our understanding of his other writings? (4) Why was Hutcheson determined that his name should not appear in the volume and that no one in Glasgow and its environs apart from Foulis should know the identity of the persons responsible for the translation and the notes? (5) And, finally, what was the significance of Hutcheson's adaptation of *The Meditations* for the Enlightenment in Scotland?

1. Hutcheson and Moor: The Division of Responsibility

There is a prima facie problem concerning the respective contributions of Hutcheson and Moor to *The Meditations.* There are three pieces of external evidence, and they do not agree. The first is Hutcheson's letter to Drennan, with his claim that he had done "the greater half . . . and more"; a claim complicated by the circumstance that Hutcheson originally wrote "the first half and more" and then struck through "first" and substituted "greater." Clearly Hutcheson was reluctant to be specific and preferred to make a game of it with Drennan. The second bit of evidence is found in *The Foulis Catalogue of Books* (Glasgow, 1777), where it is reported that the first two books were by James Moor and the remainder by Hutcheson.[5] This record of the matter has been accepted by many later scholars.[6] It has the merit of consistency with Hutcheson's claim that he had done "one or two books," and Moor, "one or two"; and it leaves Hutcheson with responsi-

5. Duncan, *Notices and Documents,* 49.

6. Scott, *Francis Hutcheson,* 144; Hutcheson, *On Human Nature,* 176.

bility for the "greater half," although not for the "first" half, as he had originally written.

There is another account of the matter. Thomas Reid entered the following note in his own copy of the 1764 edition of *The Meditations:* "Dr. Moor translated the 9th and 10th books. Dr. Francis Hutcheson the rest. Dr. Hutcheson wrote the Preface and Dr. Moor collected [*sic!*] the Proofs. This information I had from Dr. Moor."[7] We believe that Reid's note is the most authoritative of the three versions of this matter. Books IX and X differ from the other books. The style of the translation of books IX and X lacks the characteristic flow of Hutcheson's prose. These two books also contain a number of phrases not found elsewhere in the text. "Nature" or "the nature of the whole" is referred to as "she" (for example, bk. IX, art. 1, pp. 107–8)—the Greek *phusis* is a feminine noun—whereas elsewhere in *The Meditations* nature is referred to as "it."

In the notes for books IX and X there are a number of references to Greek terminology and to Thomas Gataker's translation of *The Meditations* from the Greek into Latin. A preoccupation with the original Greek of Marcus and with the quality of the translation by Gataker is not a conspicuous feature of the notes found in the other books. It is a concern, however, that might be expected of someone like Moor, who was renowned for the accuracy of his command of ancient Greek. In every one of the other books there are extensive notes that expand upon and interpret the philosophy of the Stoics, with the exception of the first book, which is concerned not with ideas but with individuals who influenced Marcus (many of them Stoics). The term *Stoic* is never used in books IX and X. Finally, in books IX and X, there is an abundance of citations to writers of the New Testament: fourteen in all; twice as many as are found in the notes to all of the other books combined. In light of these considerations, we conclude that Reid's record of his conversation with Moor may be taken as the most authoritative of the three pieces of external evidence: books IX and X by Moor; the rest by Hutcheson.

7. Bodleian Library, Oxford, Vet A4 f. 505 (9). See Stephen, "Francis Hutcheson and the Early History of the Foulis Press," 213–14. The editors are grateful to Dr. Daniel Carey for bringing this item to their attention.

2. The Glasgow Edition in Context: Other Editions and Influences

What prompted Hutcheson and Moor to undertake this translation and edition of *The Meditations*? One of their expressed motivations was stylistic. They were dissatisfied with the two translations then available in English. One was the translation by Meric Casaubon (1599–1671) published in 1634,[8] described by Hutcheson as "the old English translation": it "can scarce be agreeable to any reader; because of the intricate and antiquated stile" ("Life of the Emperor," p. 3). The other translation, published in 1701 (and reissued in 1714 and 1726), was by Jeremy Collier (1650–1726), a nonjuring Anglican clergyman best known for his attack on the English stage.[9] This edition was described by Hutcheson as an exercise that "seems not to preserve the grand simplicity of the original." Hutcheson tells us that his translation is "almost intirely new" and has been made "according to Gataker's edition of the original, and his Latin version" ("Life of the Emperor," p. 4). Thomas Gataker (1574–1654) was an Anglican clergyman with Puritan sympathies, who maintained good relations with Presbyterians and was a member of the Westminster Assembly. Gataker's edition of *The Meditations*[10] in Greek, with a translation and commentary on the text in Latin, has been described by a modern classical scholar as "a monument of vast and fastidious erudition," which "has long been and will always remain, the principal authority for any one undertaking to study or edit the *Meditations*."[11] An enlarged version was published in London in 1697,[12] with a dedication by George Stanhope (1660–1728) to Lord John Somers and a translation into Latin by Stanhope of a life of Marcus Aurelius, composed in French, by André Dacier (1652–1722).

It is this 1697 edition of *The Meditations* that Hutcheson and Moor used as the basis for their edition. Hutcheson informs the reader that the "short abstract" of the life of the emperor prefaced to his edition is "taken from

8. *Marcus Aurelius Antoninus the Roman Emperor, His Meditations Concerning Himselfe.*

9. *The Emperor Marcus Antoninus His Conversation with Himself.*

10. *Markou Antoninou tou Autokratoros tōn eis heauton biblia 12* (1652).

11. *The Meditations of the Emperor Marcus Antoninus,* ed. Farquharson, xlvi, xlix.

12. *Markou Antoninou tou Autokratoros tōn eis heauton biblia 12* (1697).

the collections made by Dacier and Stanhope." The "Maxims of the Stoics," appended to the Hutcheson and Moor edition, was excerpted from Gataker's "Praeloquium":[13] it had been included in the 1697 edition and, in English translation, in the 1701 edition. An abbreviated version of the 1697 edition was published in Oxford in 1704, with emendations by R. I. Oxoniensis (thought to be Richard Ibbetson).[14] This edition, with the Greek text and Latin translation by Gataker on facing pages, was republished by Robert and Andrew Foulis, in Glasgow, in 1744.[15] It was one of a dozen classical texts, published by the Foulis Press, that Hutcheson donated to the University of St. Andrews in 1746.[16]

While Moor's particular talent was his mastery of ancient Greek, Hutcheson was also sensitive to the challenge of translating the technical Stoic vocabulary employed in *The Meditations:* such terms as *hegemonikon* ("ruling principle") and *hypexairesis* ("reserve clause") were part of this vocabulary.[17] Hutcheson called attention to the difficulty of finding English words that would convey the meaning of these terms. He translated *hegemonikon* as "the governing part," and in a note to bk. IV, art. I, p. 47, he wrote of the term *hypexairesis:* "The word here translated reservation, is a noted one among the Stoics, often used in Epictetus, Arrian, and Simplicius." As Hutcheson explained it, the governing part of the mind may exercise a reservation upon desires for external things and then redirect the mind to the pursuit of "our sole good," which "is in our own affections, purposes, and actions."

It will also be evident that the language of Hutcheson's translation remains very much his own. A. S. L. Farquharson, the editor of *The Medi-*

13. In Jeremy Collier's English translation (1726 ed., pp. 1–30) the title of Gataker's "Praeloquium" reads: "Gataker's Preliminary Discourse, In which the Principles of the Stoics are compared with the Peripateticks, with the Old Academicks, and more especially, the Epicurean Sect: The remaining Writings likewise of the Stoick Philosophers, Seneca, Epictetus, and particularly those of our Emperour Marcus Antoninus, are briefly examined."

14. *Markou Antoninou tou Autokratoros tōn eis heauton biblia 12* (1704).

15. *Markou Antoninou tou Autokratoros tōn eis heauton biblia 12* (1744).

16. See Moore and Silverthorne, "Hutcheson's LLD," 10–12.

17. Hadot, *The Inner Citadel,* 52, discusses the significance of these technical terms in the vocabulary of the Stoics.

tations,[18] renders the first sentence of bk. II, art. 1, as follows: "I shall meet today inquisitive, ungrateful, violent, treacherous, envious, uncharitable men."[19] Hutcheson translates the same sentence in his own idiom: "to day I may have to do with some intermeddler in other mens affairs, with an ungrateful man; an insolent, or a crafty, or an envious, or an unsociable selfish man" (p. 33).

As Hutcheson presents *The Meditations,* Marcus's reflections are designed to directly affect the sensibility of the reader and excite a desire to contribute to the happiness of others. Marcus's soliloquies, he tells us, "contain some of the plainest, and yet most striking considerations, to affect the hearts of those who have any sense of goodness"; they cannot fail to inspire in us "a constant inflexible charity, and good-will and compassion toward our fellows, superior to all the force of anger or envy, or our little interfering worldly interests" (p. 3). Marcus's language, in short, posed no obstacle to Hutcheson's discovering in *The Meditations* a moral philosophy very much congenial to and in harmony with his own. His reading of *The Meditations* may also have been influenced by the recognition that moralists whom he very much admired had discovered in the reflections of Marcus Aurelius insights of great relevance for themselves.

Shaftesbury declared that he had discovered the proper meaning of *sensus communis,* as that phrase had been used by Roman moralists and satirists, in the notes and commentaries on *The Meditations* by Meric Casaubon and Thomas Gataker.[20] It was in the glosses of those commentators on the term translated by Hutcheson as "an unsociable, selfish man" that Shaftesbury recognized that *sensus communis* had been used by Juvenal, Horace, and Seneca "to signify sense of public weal and of the common interest, love of the community or society, natural affection, humanity, obligingness, or that sort of civility which rises from a just sense of the common rights of mankind, and the natural equality there is among those of the same species."[21] In the same essay, Shaftesbury went on to account

18. See n11, above.

19. *The Meditations of the Emperor Marcus Antoninus,* ed. Farquharson, vol. 1, p. 21.

20. Shaftesbury, "Sensus Communis, an Essay on the Freedom of Wit and Humour," in *Characteristics of Men, Manners, Opinions, Times,* 48–49, n19.

21. Ibid., 48.

for the origin of families, societies, clans, and tribes in a manner similar to Marcus (bk. IX, art. 9, pp. 109–10). Shaftesbury did not draw the conclusion formed by Marcus, however, that there is a universal happiness or good that all mankind may share. Instead, he thought that "Universal good, or the interest of the world in general, is a kind of remote philosophical object. That greater community falls not easily under the eye."[22] In this respect, Hutcheson's concern for "universal happiness" has more in common, as we shall see, with Marcus and with Stoic ideals. Shaftesbury elsewhere considered Marcus "one of the wisest and most serious of ancient authors."[23] And he cited sayings of Marcus, together with excerpts from the works of Epictetus and Horace, to urge readers to withdraw their admiration and desire from objects that are merely pleasurable and direct them instead to "objects, whatever they are, of inward worth and beauty (such as honesty, faith, integrity, friendship, honour)."[24]

Another moralist whom Hutcheson held in high regard, Henry More, cited sayings of Marcus repeatedly throughout his handbook of morals, *Enchiridion ethicum.*[25] More was particularly impressed by Marcus's concept of the rational soul, of the idea that there is a divinity within us: "that every Man's Mind is a God, and had its Original from him";[26] that "in the Judgment of that wisest Philosopher . . . to acquiesce in Nature's common Law, is . . . to obey the common Reason, that is in God; nay, which is little less than God himself. For he is the living Law";[27] "that it was highly estimable to live benignly, and to practise Truth and Justice."[28] More, it may be added, was attempting in these citations to reconcile Stoic and neo-Platonic ideas concerning virtue with a reading of Aristotle's ethics in which Right Reason was ultimately nothing more than the promptings of an "Inward Sense."[29]

22. Ibid., 52.
23. Shaftesbury, "Soliloquy, or Advice to an Author," in *Characteristics,* 113.
24. Shaftesbury, "Miscellany IV, Chapter I," in *Characteristics,* 423.
25. More's *Enchiridion ethicum* (1667) was translated in 1690 as *An Account of Virtue: or, Dr. Henry More's Abridgment of Morals.*
26. More, *An Account of Virtue,* II.5.VII, p. 120.
27. Ibid., I.2.VII, p. 95.
28. Ibid., II.8.XVI, p. 143.
29. Ibid., I.3.VII, p. 17.

Hutcheson's earliest reference to the work of Marcus Aurelius appears in *An Essay on the Nature and Conduct of the Passions and Affections with Illustrations on the Moral Sense* (1728) in the course of a response to John Clarke of Hull, who had argued, after Locke, that desire arises from the need to relieve uneasiness of some kind. Hutcheson replied: "the noblest Desire in our Nature, that of *universal Happiness,* is generally calm, and wholly free from any confused uneasy Sensation: except, in some warm Tempers, who, by a lively Imagination and frequent Attention to general Ideas, raise something of Passion even toward *universal Nature.* . . . See Marcus Aurelius, in many places."[30]

A similar appeal to the reader to enlarge the scope of our desires was made in *A System of Moral Philosophy* (1755, but composed in the 1730s), in which Hutcheson explains the diversity of moral judgments by the tendency to confine moral approval to one's own countrymen or, worse, to members of one's own party or sect or cabal. He proposes that "we enlarge our views with truth and justice, and observe the structure of the human soul, pretty much the same in all nations; . . . we must find a sacred tye of nature binding us even to foreigners, and a sense of that justice, mercy and good-will which is due to all. . . . See this often inculcated in Marc. Antonin."[31]

Again, in *A System of Moral Philosophy,* Hutcheson drew upon the work of Marcus to explain the meaning of true piety, as he understood it. True piety was not to be found in the asceticism of the early Christians nor in the perpetuation of their "melancholy notions of sanctity" in the absurd provisions of the canon law: "piety is never more sincere and lively than when it engages men in all social and kind offices to others, out of a sense of duty to God: and just philosophy, as well as religion, could teach that true devotion, tranquility, resignation, and recollection too, may be practiced even in a court or camp, as well as in a wilderness. . . . See Marc Antonin in a variety of passages."[32] In this connection it may be recalled that

30. *An Essay on the Nature and Conduct of the Passions and Affections,* sec. 2, art. 5, p. 44 (1728 ed.) or p. 40 (2002 ed.).

31. *A System of Moral Philosophy,* I.5.VII, vol. I, pp. 93–94.

32. Ibid., III.1.XII, vol. II, p. 182.

Hutcheson was also diffident about revealing his authorship of the *System;* it was circulated only privately in his lifetime.

3. The Significance of the Annotations

How should we understand the significance of Hutcheson's notes to the text? Hutcheson's notes typically provide short explanatory discourses or exegeses of the ideas of the Stoics. It is remarkable that the same notes also illuminate Hutcheson's own moral philosophy. This will become evident as we consider his treatment in *The Meditations* of Stoic theories of human nature, the rational soul, the law, the citizen, God, and divine providence.

A central theme of Hutcheson's moral philosophy, from the earliest to the last of his publications, had been that human nature is so constituted that mankind is naturally sociable. This theme was the subject of his inaugural lecture following his appointment as Professor of Moral Philosophy at the University of Glasgow.[33] It was also the professed position of the Stoics, or so Hutcheson reminds the reader of *The Meditations:* "The Stoics always maintained, that by the very constitution of our nature, all men are recommended to the affectionate good-will of all: which would always appear, were it not for the interfering of falsely imagined interests" (bk. III, art. 5, p. 42, note). In a passage of the text where Marcus writes of "the peculiar structure and furniture of human nature," Hutcheson notes: "This, as it was often mentioned already, is such as both recommends to us all pious veneration and submission to God, and all social affections; and makes such dispositions our chief satisfaction and happiness" (bk. XI, art. 5, p. 134, note).

Hutcheson had maintained, in his inaugural lecture and elsewhere in his writings, that it is the presence of kind affections, a natural desire to perform good offices for others, public spirit—benevolence, in a word—that disposes us to be naturally sociable. He was at pains to remind readers, in *An Essay* and in *A System of Moral Philosophy,* that the Stoics, "the avowed enemies of the passions," had made provision for the passions and affec-

33. "On the Natural Sociability of Mankind," in *Logic, Metaphysics, and the Natural Sociability of Mankind.*

tions, for desire and aversion, joy and sorrow.[34] But the Stoics had also recognized that the lower passions, the appetites of the body, desires for external things, must be subordinated to the more noble desires, the kind affections, etc.[35] Hutcheson found a similar ordering of the passions and affections in the thought of Marcus Aurelius. Marcus had reminded himself not to be misled by the passions: "suffer not that noble part to be enslaved, or moved about by unsociable passions, without its own approbation" (bk. II, art. 2, p. 34).

Hutcheson noted that Marcus was employing "a metaphor from puppets, mov'd by others. Such are men when led by their passions against what their higher faculties incline to and recommend." Marcus invoked the puppet metaphor later in the text (bk. X, art. 38, p. 132; bk. XII, art. 19, p. 148). The "noble part" that must direct the passions and not be enslaved by them was, in Marcus's mind, the intellect, the spark of divinity within us, the rational soul. "Won't you, at last, perceive, that you have something more excellent and divine within you, than that which raises the several passions, and moves you, as the wires do a puppet, without your own approbation? What now is my intellectual part? Is it fear? Is it suspicion? Is it lust? Is it any such thing?" (bk. XII, art. 19, p. 148).

The intellect or the soul was "the governing part," the *hegemonikon.* Hutcheson, too, recognized that there was a governing part in human nature, which he called diversely the moral faculty or conscience but most often the moral sense. Hutcheson discovered this "governing part" in "the heart." And he understood "the heart" to be the moral and spiritual equivalent of "the rational soul."

Hutcheson had been critical in his earlier writings, notably in *Illustrations on the Moral Sense,* of contemporary rationalists who attempted to discover moral good and evil in the relations of things (Clarke), in truth (Wollaston), or in a notion of absolute and infinite perfection (Burnet, Balguy). These efforts were misdirected; they failed to focus upon the only quality in human nature that could properly be considered good: benev-

34. *An Essay* (1728), sec. III, pp. 58–59, or pp. 49–50 (2002); *A System* I.1.V, vol. I, p. 8.

35. *A System* I.4.VI, vol. I, p. 61.

olence or kind affection.[36] There were other rationalists who recognized the fundamental importance of benevolence and sociability in the general scheme of things (Cumberland, Pufendorf), but the reasoning required by these "metaphysicians" was beyond the abilities of many who were undoubtedly virtuous or capable of virtue and goodness.[37]

The Stoic conception of reason and the rational soul was not subject to those objections: it was a faculty capable of immediate perception of virtue and vice, moral good and evil. Hutcheson provided the following note to a reference by Marcus to "that divinity which is within us": "Thus the Stoics call the rational soul, the seat of knowledge and virtue: deeming it a part of the divinity, ever pervaded, attracted, and inspired by it to all moral good, when the lower passions are restrained" (bk. II, art. 13, p. 37, note). The rational soul was conceived by "the Stoics, after Plato . . . to be a being or substance distinct both from the gross body, and the animal soul, in which are the sensations, lower appetites and passions" (bk. V, art. 19, p. 65, note).

This article and note are cited elsewhere (e.g., at bk. VII, art. 28, p. 87, and bk. VII, art. 55, p. 90). The rational soul so conceived was the faculty that distinguished virtue and vice, perceived moral good and evil: considered in this light, "the rational soul" was synonymous with "the heart": "they [the Stoics], and the Platonists too, . . . endeavoured to make virtue eligible, from the very feelings of the heart, . . ." (bk. VI, art. 24, pp. 75–76, the daggered note). Also, "the most important practical truths are found out by attending to the inward calm sentiments or feelings of the heart: And this constitution of heart or soul is certainly the work of God, who created and still pervades all things; . . ." (bk. XI, art. 12, p. 137, the double-daggered note).

Now the Stoics, Marcus Aurelius among them, maintained that there is a law of nature and that this law is known by reason, the intellect, the rational soul. Hutcheson had maintained, in the *Inquiry* and elsewhere, that the perception of moral distinctions, of virtue and vice, of rights of various kinds, did not depend upon a law.[38] But in a note on *The Medi-*

36. *Illustrations on the Moral Sense,* secs. I, II, III.

37. Hutcheson, *Inquiry into the Original of Our Ideas of Beauty and Virtue* (1725; 2004 ed.), sec. I, art. IV, p. 94.

38. *Inquiry,* sec. VII, pp. 176ff. (2004 ed.).

tations, Hutcheson acknowledged that human beings are governed by a law of nature: "all intelligent beings are, by their nature, under the same immutable eternal law of promoting the good and perfection of the whole. This, in the supreme Being, flows essentially from his nature: in created beings, it is a gift from him" (bk. VIII, art. 2, p. 95, note). Moor, too, in his notes on books IX and X refers to the "law of our nature; entire resignation to the will of God in all events, and kind affections to our fellows" (bk. IX, art. 10, p. 110, the double-daggered note); and, at bk. X, art. 13, p. 125, note, Moor refers to the "grand law of promoting the perfection of the whole, obedience to which is the supreme happiness." In Hutcheson's mind, how we come to know the law of nature is not problematic: it is quite simply "the law of God written in the heart."

> It may be remembered here once for all, the life according to nature, in Antoninus, is taken in a very high sense: 'Tis living up to that standard of purity and perfection, which every good man feels in his own breast: 'Tis conforming our selves to the law of God written in the heart: 'Tis endeavouring a compleat victory over the passions, and a total conformity to the image of God. A man must read Antoninus with little attention, who confounds this with the natural man's life, condemned by St. Paul. (bk. VII, art. 56, p. 91, note)

The law of nature is the law of God; indeed, according to Marcus, *the law is God.* In bk. X, art. 25, p. 127, he wrote of "these things which are ordered by him who governs all: Who is the law, appointing to every one what is proper for him." Moor noted that "this passage clears up many others where the same word occurs obscurely. See, [bk.] VII. [art.] 31." He also referred the reader to "the book de Mundo, which goes under Aristotle's name; chap. 6. 'For our law, exactly impartial to all, is God.'" Hutcheson agreed (bk. XI, art. 1, p. 133, note; bk. XII, art. 1, p. 144, note). But Hutcheson had earlier observed that God is also present in every human being: "such is the divine goodness that he is ever ready to communicate his goodness and mercy, in the renovation of the heart, and in forming in it all holy affections, and just apprehensions of himself, to all minds which by earnest desires are seeking after him" (bk. VIII, art. 54, p. 105, note). Hutcheson was employing the scholastic language of the communicable attributes of the deity: that God communicates to or shares with human beings some but not all of the attributes of divinity. He was also contending that the notion that God is present in the heart or soul of everyone who, "by earnest desires," is "seeking after him" is consistent with the Stoic idea that there is a part of God, a spark of the divine fire, that is present in every human being.

Everyone, Marcus declared, "who flies from his master is a fugitive-slave. Now, the law is our master; and so the transgressor of the law is the fugitive" (bk. X, art. 25, p. 127). Marcus also described all who live under the law that is common to all rational beings as fellow citizens of the universe or the world. "We are all fellow-citizens: and if so, we have a common city. The universe, then, must be that city; for of what other common city are all men citizens?" (bk. IV, art. 4, pp. 48–49). Hutcheson endorsed this idea of citizenship and expanded upon its implications for the relationship that should pertain between the citizens of the universe and its ruler:

> This city is the universe. A mind entirely conformed and resigned to God, the great governour of this city, and persuaded of his wisdom, power, and goodness, cannot imagine any event to be hurtful to the universe; and when it is united in will with God, it must acquiesce in all that happens, and can make all events good to itself, as they are occasions of exerting the noblest virtues, which are its supreme good. (bk. V, art. 22, pp. 65–66, note)

Marcus and Hutcheson were in basic agreement concerning the obligations, the sense of duty, or devotion, the piety that should govern relations between citizens and their ruler in the city of God. Marcus had written: "Love and desire that alone which happens to you, and is destined by providence for you; for, what can be more suitable?" (bk. VII, art. 57, p. 91). Hutcheson endorsed this maxim unreservedly:

> For, a man who desires only what God destines him, can never be disappointed; since infinite power, wisdom, and goodness, must always accomplish its designs; and, as he loves all his works, every event ordered by him, must be really best for the whole, and for the individuals to which it happens: An intimate and permanent conviction of this, must be the best foundation for the practice of the maxim here recommended. (bk. VII, art. 57, p. 91, note)

Hutcheson's enthusiastic acceptance of Marcus Aurelius's conception of divine providence is consistent with the views expressed in *A System, A Short Introduction,* and in "A Synopsis of Metaphysics," part III. Hutcheson had not replaced the Stoic doctrine of fate or predestination with benevolence. He thought rather that acting in a manner consistent with the divine plan was the most effective way to promote benevolence. He considered it "an amiable notion of providence, that it has ordered for every good man that station of life, and those circumstances, which infinite wisdom foresaw were fittest for his solid improvement in virtue, according to that original disposition of nature which God had given him" (bk. XI, art. 7, p. 135, note).

One may see in the Stoicism of Marcus Aurelius and Hutcheson's enthusiastic endorsement of it the possibility of a benign redescription of the predestinarian doctrine of Calvinists and the Presbyterian or Reformed Church. The crucial difference between Hutcheson and more orthodox Calvinists did not turn on predestination: it was rather that Hutcheson, unlike Calvin (and St. Augustine and St. Paul), did not think that mankind was naturally sinful. He thought that mankind was naturally kind, benevolent, good. In his inaugural lecture, he had placed particular emphasis on the state of innocence, which Reformed theologians attributed only to Adam and Eve before the Fall. In Hutcheson's mind, this "original disposition of nature" applied to every human being. Insofar as men were presently to be found in a condition of sinfulness and depravity, it was as a result of bad education, confused imaginations, the pursuit of external things, property and riches, love of fame: these were the dispositions, the passions which were productive of moral evil. Marcus had written: "Look inwards; within is the fountain of good; which is ever springing up, if you be always digging in it" (bk. VII, art. 59, p. 91). Hutcheson considered this excellent advice. "The author of this advice, had the best opportunities of trying all the happiness which can arise from external things. The dissipating pursuits of external things, stupify the nobler powers. By recollection we find the dignity of our nature: the diviner powers are disentangled, and exert themselves in all worthy social affections of piety and humanity; and the soul has an inexpressible delight in them" (bk. VII, art. 59, p. 91, note).

4. Hutcheson and Christianity

It is clear then that Hutcheson was refashioning Christian doctrine, notably the Presbyterian or Reformed doctrine of original sin, by substituting for it a particular variant of Stoicism, the version represented in *The Meditations,* in which the original or natural constitution of human nature contains something divine within: a heart or a soul that is oriented toward affection for others, good offices, benevolence. Was it a view consistent with the life and teachings of Christ? Hutcheson and Moor clearly thought so. They celebrated again and again in their notes the exhortation of Christ to his followers to return good for evil. They were also observing, however, in every case, that Marcus had given the same advice to himself and to anyone who might read his *Meditations.* Moor also perceived in Marcus's pleas that we should attempt to imitate the gods "the same with the grand Christian doctrine of the divine life" (bk. X, art. 8, p. 123, note). Hutcheson thought that Marcus's reference to his own "publick service to the Gods" expressed "the same divine sentiment with the Apostle; that whatever we do in word or deed, we should do it as to God" (bk. V, art. 31, p. 68, the asterisked note).

Hutcheson and Moor were pleased to discover in the teachings of Christ expressions of kindness, forgiveness, service to God, piety properly understood as service to God and mankind in general. Their references to the writers of the New Testament typically provide confirmation and endorsement of the Stoic morality of Marcus and Epictetus. They were also pleased to enclose "Gataker's Apology," which similarly discovered an equivalence between the ethical teachings of Christ and the reflections of Marcus Aurelius: "All these same precepts [of Christ] are to be found in Antoninus, just as if he had habitually read them" ("Gataker's Apology," below, p. 162).

At the same time, there is much that Hutcheson found objectionable in the doctrines and in the conduct of Christians. He was unimpressed by the Christian doctrine of repentance after vice. "A continued innocence of manners is preferable to even the most thorough repentance after gross vices. . . . To this refer many thoughts in the former books, about the advantage of 'being always straight and upright, rather than one rectified and amended'" (bk. XI, art. 8, p. 136, note). He was pointedly critical of what he took to be the desire for martyrdom among the early Christians: "It is well known that their ardour for the glory of martyrdom was frequently immoderate; and was censured even by some of the primitive fathers." He goes on to make an apology for their weakness. Christianity could not have been expected to "extirpate all sort of human frailty. And there is something so noble in the stedfast lively faith, and the stable persuasion of a future state, which must have supported this ardour, that it makes a sufficient apology for this weakness, and gives the strongest confirmation of the divine power accompanying the Gospel" (bk. XI, art. 3, p. 134, note).

Hutcheson's most scathing criticisms of Christian practice appear in the closing paragraphs of his "Life of the Emperor Marcus Antoninus." There is no counterpart to these pages (pp. 18–23) in the larger "Life" by André Dacier. Here Hutcheson retorted upon Christians the charge against Antoninus that he had been guilty of persecuting Christians:

> Let none make this objection to Antoninus, but those, who, from their hearts, abhor all Christian persecutions, who cannot hate their neighbours, or deem them excluded from the divine favour, either for neglecting certain ceremonies, and pieces of outward pageantry, or for exceeding in them; for different opinions, or forms of words, about some metaphysical attributes or modes of existence, which all sides own to be quite incomprehensible by us; for the different opinions about human liberty; about which the best men who ever lived have had opposite sentiments: for different opinions about the manner in which the Deity may think fit to exercise his mercy to a guilty world, either in pardoning of their sins, or renewing them in piety and virtue. (p. 21)

The number of churchmen and churches who are included in this indictment of Christian practices and Christian dogmas would appear to be very extensive indeed: ecclesiastics who insist on rituals and pageantry and dissenters who oppose them; scholastics of all denominations who insist on their understanding of the divine attributes, even though one of those attributes of God was widely deemed to be his incomprehensibility; those philosophers who quibble about liberty and predestination and, most seriously, those who would consign their neighbors to eternal damnation for failure to subscribe to the correct dogma concerning sin and redemption. But it was particularly the dogmas and practices of the Church of Scotland, as Hutcheson knew it from direct acquaintance, in its churches and in its universities that appear to have been foremost in his mind as he penned his concluding peroration: "Christians may be ashamed to censure our author on this account; considering how rashly, arrogantly, and presumptuously, they are cursing one another in their synodical anathemas; and in their creeds, pronouncing eternal damnation on all who are not within the pale, or hold not the same mysterious tenets or forms of words" (p. 22).

The concluding paragraphs of Hutcheson's "Life of the Emperor" may be the finest illustration in his writings of his ability to turn his eloquence, usually expended upon extolling the virtues and the goodness of human nature, against ideas and practices to which he was deeply and passionately opposed. Given the force and the directness of his indictment, it is indeed understandable that he should have taken pains to ensure, as he told Thomas Drennan, that he would not allow "his name to appear in it."

5. *The Meditations* in the Scottish Enlightenment

It has been said of Hutcheson and Moor's edition of *The Meditations* that its influence in the Scottish Enlightenment was both great and lasting: "Its educational influence can be judged from the fact that it was reissued three times after his death and that devotion to Marcus became a badge of Hutcheson's followers."[39] David Fordyce (1711–51), a regent, or teacher, of philosophy at Marischal College in Aberdeen, wrote in his *Dialogues Concerning Education* (1745, 1748) a glowing description of Marcus Aurelius as a philosopher, "whose Principles are so sublime, and his Maxims of Virtue so stupendously great and commanding, that no Man can enter into his Soliloquies without becoming a greater and better Man, a Creature more

39. Rivers, *Reason, Grace, and Sentiment,* vol. 2, p. 160. The term *badge* seems particularly apposite in this connection, inasmuch as it indicates a connection between the systems of Hutcheson and Marcus that was rarely made explicit by Hutcheson's followers or by his critics. The reason seems clear: Hutcheson and Moor and the Foulises were careful to preserve the anonymity of the translators and editors of the Glasgow edition of *The Meditations.* Even the Glasgow translator of Hutcheson's *A Short Introduction to Moral Philosophy* (Glasgow, 1747, p. 69) referred to chapter numbers in *The Meditations* (I, 17 and IX, 48) that do not appear in the Hutcheson-Moor translation, although these chapter numbers do appear in Gataker's Latin translation, also published by the Foulis Press in 1744. See also note 47, below.

elevated above the World, and more enlarged in his Affections to Humankind, and the Whole of Things."[40]

It is understandable that *The Meditations,* particularly the manner in which Marcus's thinking had been represented and interpreted by Hutcheson, should have come under forceful criticism from Scots Presbyterians who adhered to a more orthodox, anti-Moderate position in theology and philosophy. John Witherspoon wrote a satirical critique of those who preferred *The Meditations* to the Westminster Confession of Faith: "let religion be constantly and uniformly called *Virtue,* and let the *Heathen philosophers* be set up as the great patterns and promoters of it," particularly Marcus Aurelius, "because an eminent person, of the moderate character, says, his Meditations is the BEST book that ever was written for forming the heart."[41] Witherspoon's satire on all this in *Ecclesiastical Characteristics* (1753, reissued four times in the next ten years) includes "The Athenian Creed": "I believe in the divinity of L. S[haftesbury], the saintship of Marcus Antoninus, the perspicuity and sublimity of A[kensid]e [?], and the perpetual duration of Mr. H[utcheso]n's works, notwithstanding their present tendency to oblivion."[42]

But criticism of Marcus Aurelius and the kind of Stoicism represented by *The Meditations,* in the form in which it had been cast by Hutcheson, was not confined to the theologically orthodox. Hume's depiction of "The Stoic" (1742) was not a description of an ascetic philosopher obsessed by the importance of extinguishing all passion and affection. Hume's Stoic was a "man of action and virtue" like Marcus and Hutcheson.[43] Hume's Platonist (1742) was critical of the Stoic for claiming (like Cato, in Lucan's *Pharsalia,* invoked by Hutcheson) to have a God within him: "Thou art thyself thy own idol," the Platonist complained.[44] Hume was reluctant to

40. Fordyce, *Dialogues Concerning Education,* II, pp. 340–41, and see Rivers, *Reason, Grace, and Sentiment,* vol. II, pp. 181–84.

41. See Rivers, *Reason, Grace, and Sentiment,* vol. 2, pp. 188–89.

42. Ibid., p. 189.

43. Hume, "The Stoic," in *The Philosophical Works,* vol. III, p. 209: "In the true sage and patriot are united whatever can distinguish human nature, or elevate mortal man to a resemblance with the divinity. The softest benevolence, the most undaunted resolution, the tenderest sentiments, the most sublime love of virtue, all these animate successively his transported bosom. What satisfaction, when he looks within."

44. Hume, "The Platonist," in *The Philosophical Works,* vol. III, p. 212.

grant Marcus the title of theist. He was, like all the other Stoics (except for Panaetius, on whose work Cicero's *Offices* was modeled), a believer in lesser gods, in auguries and divinations.[45]

Adam Smith devoted several paragraphs to the Stoic system of Marcus in *The Theory of Moral Sentiments.* Smith identified two basic paradoxes of the Stoics: one, contempt for life and death and complete submission to the order of providence, which Smith found in the fragmentary writings of "the independent and spirited, but often harsh Epictetus"; the second paradox he traced to "the mild, the humane, the benevolent Antoninus." The latter was the paradoxical position that whatever befalls us in life, however painful, appalling, catastrophic, should be regarded as part of the divine plan and should be embraced; whoever wishes otherwise, he declared, "wishes, so far as in him lies, to stop the motion of the universe, . . . and, for some little convenience of his own, to disorder and discompose the whole machine of the world." This second paradox, the paradox of Antoninus, Smith considered "too absurd to deserve any serious consideration. It is, indeed, so very absurd that one can scarce help suspecting that it must have been in some measure misunderstood or misrepresented."[46]

In contrast with David Hume and Adam Smith, their friends William Robertson and Hugh Blair found in Marcus Aurelius's and Hutcheson's ideas of virtue and divine providence an early and, in Blair's case, an abiding source of inspiration. Robertson had begun his own translation of *The Meditations* in the early 1740s. He had completed his translation, from the Greek, up to book VIII; then he abandoned it when Hutcheson and Moor's

45. Hume, "Natural History of Religion," *The Philosophical Works,* vol. IV, p. 350: "Marcus Antoninus tells us that he himself had many admonitions from the gods in his sleep."

46. Smith, *The Theory of Moral Sentiments,* VII.2.1, pp. 288–91 (1982 ed.). This summary dismissal of *The Meditations* is taken from the 6th ed. published in 1790. In earlier editions (from the 2nd ed. published in 1761 to the 5th published in 1784) Smith had concluded his discussion of the Stoics on a more positive note: "Such was the philosophy of the stoics. A philosophy which affords the noblest lessons of magnanimity, is the best school of heroes and patriots, and to the greater part of whose precepts there can be no other objection, except that they teach us to aim at a perfection altogether beyond the reach of human nature" (*Theory of Moral Sentiments,* I.iii.2, p. 60n).

translation was published.[47] In a thesis published in Edinburgh in 1739,[48] Blair had endorsed an understanding of the law of nature based upon the moral sense and the benevolence of human nature. He wrote a generous, not uncritical, review of Hutcheson's *System of Moral Philosophy* in 1755.[49] In his *Sermons,* Blair adumbrated and echoed the main themes of Hutcheson's notes to *The Meditations:* the union of piety and morality, the divine government of the passions, the mixture of bad men with the good in human society, and the compassion and beneficence of the deity.[50]

Hutcheson's translation and edition of *The Meditations* are important, finally, for the light they shed on Hutcheson's other works on moral philosophy. In them we find one of the most forceful statements of one of his most central themes, that "our sole good is in our actions and affections." One may also return to his other works with a deeper understanding of his theory of the soul and the manner in which the rational soul is understood to be synonymous with the heart. Indeed, it may not be fanciful to see in Hutcheson's introduction and notes a way of understanding Presbyterianism, perhaps Calvinism itself, as a religion of kind affection, of public spirit and benevolence, a religion of social virtue for men and women of an enlightened age.[51]

47. Untitled manuscripts: National Library of Scotland MSS 3955 and 3979. Dugald Stewart reported that Robertson had been preparing his own translation of *The Meditations* "when he was anticipated by an anonymous publication at Glasgow." "Account of the Life and Writings of William Robertson, D.D.," p. 106. See also Sher, *Church and University in the Scottish Enlightenment,* pp. 30 and 181.

48. *Dissertatio philosophica inauguralis de fundamentis et obligatione legis naturae.*

49. "Hutcheson's Moral Philosophy," pp. 9–23. The review concludes: "His philosophy tends to inspire generous sentiments and amiable views of human nature. It is particularly calculated to promote the social and friendly affections; and we cannot but agree with the author of the preface, that it has the air of being dictated by the heart, no less than the head."

50. Blair, *Sermons.*

51. The Hutcheson-Moor translation of Marcus Aurelius was reprinted a number of times and retained its reputation into the twentieth century. A late Victorian translator of Marcus, Gerald H. Rendall, described it as "the choicest alike in form and contents" (*Marcus Aurelius Antoninus to Himself,* p. iii); and C. R. Haines, the Loeb translator, in a review of English translations, declared it to be "certainly the best translation previous to Long's, for accuracy and diction, and superior to that in spirit" (*The Communings with Himself of Marcus Aurelius Antoninus,* p. xviii; his reference is to *The Thoughts of the Emperor Marcus Aurelius Antoninus,* translated by George Long, 1862).

A NOTE ON THE TEXT

The translation of *The Meditations of the Emperor Marcus Aurelius Antoninus* that is reproduced here is the first edition published in Glasgow by Robert Foulis in 1742. The 1742 edition was the only edition of the English translation published by the Foulis Press in the lifetime of Francis Hutcheson. The same press in 1744 published the Greek text of *The Meditations* established by Thomas Gataker in 1652, together with Gataker's Latin translation.

The footnotes provided by Francis Hutcheson and James Moor for the 1742 edition remain at the foot of the page and are designated in the text, as they were in eighteenth-century editions, by asterisks, daggers, and similar symbols. Hutcheson and Moor used single square brackets to indicate the insertion of words in the text that were not in the original Greek. The notes to the text and to the footnotes that have been provided by the present editors are marked by numbers and are gathered at the end of the volume. Page breaks in the 1742 edition are indicated by the use of angle brackets (for example, page 112 begins after <112>).

ACKNOWLEDGMENTS

In the preparation of this volume we have enjoyed the cooperation and assistance of many individuals and institutions. David Weston of the Department of Special Collections of the University of Glasgow made available to us the text of the Glasgow edition of 1742. Moira Mackenzie and Elizabeth Henderson, Keeper of Rare Books at the University of St. Andrews, brought to our attention the copy of *The Meditations,* published in Glasgow in 1744, that was presented to the university by Francis Hutcheson, along with other classical texts, "as a testimony of his Regard for the Honour they had done him" in conferring upon him, in 1746, the degree of LL.D. We are also obliged to Raynald Lepage and the staff of the Department of Rare Books at McGill University; to the Special Collections Library at the University of Exeter; and to Judy Appleby, Wendy Knechtel, and the librarians of Concordia University who assisted us in various ways.

A number of our fellow scholars have provided assistance and advice. We are particularly grateful for the contributions of Edward Andrew, Donald Baronowski, Daniel Carey, Aaron Garrett, Frederick Rosen, Sandy Stewart, and Luigi Turco. Finally, we are indebted to Knud Haakonssen for his encouragement and for his sense of urgency, a quality that contributed in no small way to bring our work on this volume to a conclusion.

THE MEDITATIONS OF THE EMPEROR MARCUS AURELIUS ANTONINUS

THE MEDITATIONS

OF THE EMPEROR

MARCUS AURELIUS ANTONINUS.

NEWLY translated from the GREEK:
With NOTES, and an Account of his LIFE.

GLASGOW:

Printed by ROBERT FOULIS; and sold by him at the College; by MESS. HAMILTON and BALFOUR, in EDINBURGH; and by ANDREW MILLAR, over against St. *Clements* Church, LONDON.
MDCCXLII.

INTRODUCTION

Containing some of the

MOST MEMORABLE PASSAGES,

Preserv'd, of the Life of the

EMPEROR

MARCUS ANTONINUS.

The authors of this translation, judging that these divine sentiments of Antoninus,[1] may be of some advantage to many who have not access to them, while they are kept in the learned languages, undertook to make them as plain as the subjects would admit. Some of these meditations cannot well be apprehended, without a considerable acquaintance with the philosophy and stile of the Stoics: Some of them are only memorial hints this great man intended only for him-<2>self, the design of which, the commentators cannot pretend certainly to explain; and the true text of the original is not always certain: but, there are many of them obvious to every capacity; which contain some of the plainest, and yet most striking considerations, to affect the hearts of those who have any sense of goodness, and warm them with the noblest emotions, of piety, gratitude, and resignation to GOD; contempt of sensual pleasure, wealth, worldly grandeur, and fame; and a constant inflexible charity, and good-will and compassion toward our fellows, superior to all the force of anger or envy, or our little interfering worldly interests.

The old English translation[2] can scarce be agreeable to any reader; because of the intricate and antiquated stile. The late translation[3] seems not to preserve sufficiently the grand simplicity of the original. This translation, therefore, is almost intirely new; according to Gataker's edition of the original, and his Latin version.[4]

'Tis quite foreign to our design, either to shew art and ingenuity in drawing a character of this great man; or in making encomiums upon him; or <3> to display our diligence or knowledge, in making an history of his life. His own meditations, to every judicious reader, will present a great soul; adorned with the soundest understanding, the most amiable sweetness and kindness of affections, the most invincible meekness, steddy justice, humility, and simplicity, and the most entire resignation to GOD. And the history of his life, even as 'tis imperfectly preserved to us, will shew his great capacity, and penetration, in public affairs, and his strength of mind, calmness, and intrepidity amidst the greatest dangers.

To give these meditations the greater force upon the mind of the reader; as well as to gratify his natural curiosity; and, to remove what prejudices may possibly occur to him; we subjoin the following short abstract of his life, taken from the collections made by Dacier and Stanhope.[5]

Marcus Aurelius[6] was born in the year of our Lord 121, during the reign of Adrian.[7] By his father Annius Verus, he was of one of the greatest families in Italy, descended, as 'tis said, from Numa.[8] His grandfather had been thrice Consul and Prefect of the city, and sur-<4>vived Annius Verus. His aunt by his father, Annia Faustina, was married to Antoninus Pius the Emperor. Marcus Aurelius's mother was also of an eminent consular family, the daughter of Calvisius Tullus.[9]

Our Emperor's first name was Annius Verus, the same with his father's. Adrian, who had loved him from his infancy, called him Annius Verissimus; probably, from the early appearance of candour and veracity in his temper. When he was adopted into the Aurelian family, he took the name of his adoptive father Marcus Aurelius. He was but a child when his own father died; but was educated by his grandfather; who procured for him the best instructors in pronunciation, music, geometry, Greek, and rhetoric, or, oratory. But his soul was soon intent upon something still greater than these ingenious accomplishments; and he shewed no high taste for them. He was instructed in the Stoic philosophy by Sextus Chaeronensis, Plutarch's grandson,[10] Iunius Rusticus, Claudius Maximus, and Cinna Catulus; and in the Peripatetic, by Claudius Severus.[11] Philosophy was his favourite study. <5>

He shewed his perpetual gratitude to these good men; not only by promoting them in the world, to dignity and wealth; but by a continual respect for them, even when he was in the highest elevation of fortune. And, in the very beginning of his meditations, he has perpetuated their memory, his own gratitude, and his honest humility, in ascribing all his virtues to their instructions, and nothing to himself; in a manner truly original, and peculiar to him. He studied also the laws of his country under Volutius Mecianus, the most celebrated lawyer of that age.[12]

He was dear to Adrian, so early, that he was advanced to the equestrian dignity at six years of age; and made one of the priests of Mars at eight. He was even intrusted with some great charges, before he was twenty; and acquitted himself with as great decency and dignity, as any of the old magistrates. He had some taste for painting, in his youth, and practised it for some time. But he more admired wrestling, racing, tennis, and hunting, as the natural means of health and vigour, for the discharging all honourable offices. <6> He often encountered the fiercest boars, with safety and honour.

But, his chief delight was in the Stoic philosophy; and that in practice, as well as speculation. He lived up to all their austerities, in spare diet, plain dress, and abstinence from all softness, effeminacy, and luxury; even from his being twelve years of age. Nature had formed him for the greatest dignity and constancy; with a singular firmness of soul; not to be moved by any accidents; so that most of the historians assure us, that scarce ever did joy or grief make any change in his countenance; and this gravity was ever easy to others; being free from all moroseness or pride.[13]

He gave up all his father's, and his mother's estate too, to his sister Annia Cornificia, who was married to Numidius Quadratus.

A.D. *139.* Adrian, upon the death of his former adoptive son Cesenius Commodus, inclined to have adopted Marcus Aurelius to be his successor, then about 18 years of age; but deeming him too young, he adopted Antoninus Pius, on condition that he should immediately adopt Marcus, and L. Verus, <7> the son of the same Commodus. 'Tis said that Marcus had dreamed, the preceeding night, that his shoulders and arms were of ivory, and that he found them much stronger than formerly. The news of his adoption seemed to afflict him; and he spoke a great deal, on that occasion, about the evils and dangers which always attend supreme power.

A.D. *140.* Upon Adrian's death, Antoninus Pius his successor betrothed his daughter Faustina in marriage to Marcus Aurelius, and raised him to the consulship; and, soon after, conferred on him the honours of the successors to the empire. These things increased his keenness in the study and practice of philosophy; and Antoninus Pius brought Apollonius the Stoic from Athens, to assist him.

About this time, Marcus's old tutor died; who had had the constant charge of him from his infancy. On this occasion, he could not refrain from tears; and when some about the court, put him in mind of his usual constancy and steddiness, Antoninus Pius replied in his defence, "You must give him leave to be a man: neither philosophy nor im-<8>perial dignity can exstinguish our natural affections."

A.D. *147.* At the age of 25, he married Faustina: a wife no way suited to such an husband. She soon bore him a daughter; and, in the same year, the senate conferred on him all manner of honours and powers; even higher than on any of his predecessors; and he ever employed them for the good of the state; always promoting men solely on account of their merit; and seemed to pay still greater deference to Antoninus the Emperor, perpetually attending him, and doing him all manner of kind offices; so that their mutual friendship was inaccessible to all the attempts of designing men, to raise any distrusts or suspicions between them.

A.D. *161.* Upon the death of Antoninus Pius, the senate obliged Marcus Aurelius to take upon him the government; and he assumed L. Verus as partner in it. They both took the name of Antoninus; and Marcus betrothed his daughter Lucilla to Verus. After this, they celebrated, with the greatest magnificence, the funeral, or, apotheosis of Antoninus; the ceremonies of which are told by all antiquaries; and each of the <9> new Emperors made a funeral oration upon him.

As soon as he was settled in the supreme power, application was made from all quarters, by the heathen priests, philosophers, and governors of provinces, for leave to persecute the Christians. But, whatever persecution there might be in the remoter provinces, we have no assurance that it was authorised by the Emperor; as indeed it was intirely contrary to his principles and inclination. 'Tis even denyed by Valesius, in his notes upon Eusebius, that the apology of Justin Martyr called the first, tho' truly the second, was addressed to this Emperor, or to the senate, during his reign. He brings several reasons to prove that both these apologies were wrote and presented to Antoninus Pius.[14] 'Tis, however, probable, that there have been some considerable persecutions, in several parts of the empire, during his reign. Eusebius preserves to us a letter of this Emperor's, upon applications made by some of the heathens, for leave to persecute the Christians, when they had been terrified by some pretended prodigies and earthquakes. It was directed to some general council of Asia, and <10> carries along with it many characters of this author, tho' some ascribe it to his predecessor.[15]

> Marcus Aurelius Antoninus, &c. To the assembly of Asia, greeting. I am sure the gods will take care that such men as you describe, should not be hid; and it suits themselves much better to punish such as refuse them worship, than you. Your harassing them with charges of Atheism, only confirms them more in their sentiments. To them it must be eligible, rather to die for their own God, under such accusations, than to live. Thus they always defeat you; throwing away their lives rather than do what you require of them. As to those earthquakes, for some time past, which yet continue, 'tis proper to admonish you, to compare your conduct with theirs. They, on such occasions, confide more in their God; but you, all this time, through your ignorance, neglect the Gods, as well as other things, and all the worship due to that immortal Being, whose worshippers, the Christians, you are harassing and persecuting to death. Many of the go-<11>vernors of provinces wrote about these matters, to my divine father; and he prohibited their giving the Christians any disturbance; unless they were found making some attempts against the Roman state. Many have applied to me about the same matter. I wrote to them in the same sentiments with my father. If any shall still persist in prosecuting them, merely as Christians, let the person prosecuted be acquitted, tho' it should appear he were a Christian; and let the prosecutor be punished.

This letter, and that extraordinary character which the Christian writers, as well as the heathen, give to this Emperor, for justice, and lenity of temper, must easily convince us that he never could authorise such persecution of men, merely for christianity.

In this first year of his reign, his son Commodus was born; whose horrid vices were, they say, fore-boded by several dismal prodigies; such as inundations, earthquakes, and the burning of several cities. The Emperor was immediately engaged in wars on all sides; by the invasions of the Parthians, all the way to Syria; and of the Catti, into Ger-<12>many, as far as to the country of the Grisons: the Britons too revolted. Calphurnius[16] Agricola was sent to command in Britain; Aufidius Victorinus to oppose the Catti;[17] and Verus went against the Parthians.

But as soon as Verus left Rome, and was no longer overawed by the authority and virtue of Antoninus, he gave himself up to all debauchery, and fell sick at Canusium. M. Antoninus went thither to see him, and gave him his best advice as to his future conduct. Verus, upon his recovery, continued his march; but was not reformed by his sickness. He plunged again into all sort of debauchery at Daphne, one of the suburbs of Antioch, and committed the war to his lieutenants; which they managed successfully. Antoninus, pleased with the success, and, either unapprised of his returning to his vices, or, hoping to reclaim him by all the ties of affection, offered him in marriage his daughter Lucilla, a princess of singular beauty; and sent her to him, while he was in Syria. He declined going with her himself; lest any should imagine he aimed to share the glory of these conquests. He wrote to <13> the several * proconsuls and governors in her way, to be at no vain expence in her reception, as she passed through their provinces; but to let her perform her journey in a private manner. This princess shewed as little regard to virtue, or her character, as her husband. Upon the success † of this war, the two Emperors had a triumph.

About this time, upon an insurrection of the Germans, Antoninus marched against them in person; and from his own judgment of the abilities of Pertinax,[18] who afterwards was raised to the empire, made him one of his lieutenants; and never had reason to repent of his choice. This war was also successful. The Germans were defeated, after their many vigorous efforts, by the bravery of the Emperor and his army. Antoninus shewed his wisdom and steddiness on this occasion, when the victorious army, after their great and dangerous services, demanded an augmentation of their pay: he refused it; telling them that "he could not do it but at the expence of their brethren and kinsmen; for whom he was accountable to God."[19] <14>

* A.D. 167.

† A.D. 168.

A.D. *169.* The year following, a more dangerous war arose from the Quadi and Marcomanni; while the plague also raged in Italy. The Emperor used great variety of sacrifices and religious rites, to appease the Gods; and then went against the enemy, taking Verus along with him, who rather inclined to have continued in his debaucheries at Rome. Antoninus soon conquered the enemy; and, in his return, Verus died of an apoplexy at Altinum, or, as some suspect, by poison, given him by his wife Lucilla, upon finding an incestuous intrigue of his with his own sister.

About this time, the governors of some remote provinces renewed the persecution against the Christians. There is no other evidence of the Emperor's authority interposed, or countenance given, for this purpose, except, that, in answer to a letter of the governor of Gaul, asking what the Emperor inclined should be done with some Christian prisoners, he ordered, "that such only as confessed, should be put to death, and the rest released."[20] Now, Christians were ordinarily accused for other crimes than any religious tenets; such <15> as treason and sedition, the murdering of infants, and eating them, and incestuous debaucheries in their assemblies. 'Tis very credible the Emperor intended by this order, that only such should die, as confessed these crimes, and not all such as confessed that they were of the Christian religion; for, at that rate, scarce any would have been released; and yet, upon this ambiguity, there was, in some provinces, a violent persecution. 'Tis thought that Antoninus was not at Rome in the year 166, but abroad, when Justin Martyr is said to have suffered.[21] It was probably on this occasion, that Athenagoras composed, and sent to the Emperor, his beautiful and just defence of the Christians yet extant;[22] insisting for less ambiguous orders, that none should be punished for the name of Christian; but only upon a fair trial, whether they were guilty of the crimes laid to their charge; and vindicating the Christians from them: This, probably, procured them peace, during the rest of this reign.

The Marcomanni and Quadi, assisted by the Sarmatians, Vandals, and other nations, made more terrible efforts than ever, attacked Antoninus's army, <16> and put the Romans to flight, with a great slaughter of near 20000. But the Emperor rallied them at Aquileia, and defeated the enemy, and drove them out of all Pannonia.[23]

About this time, the Moors ravaged Spain, and the shepherds in Egypt took arms, and gave the greatest disturbance to the Romans in that province; but both were quelled by the vigilance of the Emperor, and the bravery of his lieutenants who commanded there;[24] while he was heading the armies in the north; where he forced at last the barbarous nations to submit to his own terms.

When peace was restored, the Emperor was continually employed for the good of his people; making wise laws, for prevention of frauds, and the speedy administration of justice, and reforming all abuses; sharing his power with the Senate. He discovered the greatest penetration, as well as fidelity, toward the public, in searching out and promoting men of ability and integrity, to all the great offices; and the greatest patience and constancy, in the administration of justice, and consulting in the Senate about public affairs; scarce ever losing one moment of his time. His assidui-<17>ty was the more surprizing, that his health had, for some years, been exceedingly impaired by the great fatigues he had endured. He was particularly inquisitive about the censures past upon his conduct; which he bore with the greatest meekness; his aim being only that he might reform whatever was amiss in it. He would admit of no lofty titles, nor that impious flattery of building altars and temples to himself.

The old enemies of the Romans, the Marcomanni, watching their opportunity; when the Roman troops were diminished by a plague, and the treasury much exhausted, which the Emperor's compassion for his people kept very low, perfidiously renewed their hostilities. He supplied his treasury, by selling, under a clause of redemption, the most valuable moveables of his palace; and his army, even by employing the gladiators.

Before he marched against the enemy, he lost his second son Verus, then seven years old; and bore it with such fortitude, that he omitted no public business on that account. This expedition proved more tedious and dangerous <18> than any of the former. He at first gave them a defeat; having exposed himself to the utmost hazard; from which, the grateful love of his soldiers protected him. After the battle, the Emperor himself went to the field, weeping over the slain among the enemies, and endeavouring to preserve all that could be cured or relieved.

The enemy, soon after, by skirmishing parties, feigning a flight, led the Emperor and his army into such straits amidst mountains, that they were inclosed on all sides, and could not escape; all the passes being possessed by the enemy. Here they were like to perish with heat and thirst, deprived of all water. They made some vigourous efforts to force their way; but without other effect, than to convince them that they were reserved sacrifices to the fury of the Barbarians. All the Emperor's efforts to rouse the spirits of the fainting soldiers, were vain. He is said to have committed himself and them to God, with the most ardent prayers; appealing to God for the innocence of his conduct in life. There were also many Christians in the army; employed no doubt, in like supplications to God. <19> In the event, clouds suddenly arose, and thunder, with a most plentiful shower; while all the lightning fell among the Barbarians: With this, the Romans take courage, and the enemy are dismayed. The Romans attack them in this confusion, and put them to flight, with great slaughter, enraged with the fresh remembrance of their late danger.

The heathens ascribe this deliverance to the Emperor's piety;[25] and the Christians universally to the prayers of the legion of Mitilene,[26] which some ignorantly averred had on this occasion got the name of the Thundering Legion. That name was given to this legion, in the days of Augustus, for a quite different reason, because they had thunderbolts engraved or painted on their shields.[27] 'Tis told indeed confidently, by Christian writers near those times, that the Emperor was advised by the captain of his guards, to employ the Christians of his army in prayer to their God, who, he said, refused nothing to their prayers; and that he did so, and found the surprizing event immediately answering upon their prayers; and that, in consequence of this, he wrote to the Senate, to stop all prosecutions against them, and give them full <20> liberty for the exercise of their religion. 'Tis not improbable, from these bold affirmations of Christians, so near the time of that event, that there has been such a letter; tho' the one now bearing that stile, is reputed by many to be a forgery.[28] No doubt, such a letter would be suppressed by an heathen Senate.

Antoninus pursued this war, with the greatest bravery, conduct, and clemency; sometimes, in the pursuits, going himself into the woods and marshes, where the poor Barbarians were lurking, and protecting them from the fury of his own soldiers. At last, he defeated them intirely, by many perilous encounters; and possessed himself of all their fortresses. He had added all these countries as provinces to the Roman empire, had he not been interrupted by the revolt of Cassius; and even forced to accept of less advantageous terms of peace from these Barbarians, than they had formerly agreed to.

The Emperor's conduct in the whole affair, of this revolt, deserves to be more particularly related; as by it his temper, and the greatness of his soul, is more shown than by his glorious military atchievements. <21>

Cassius had been endeared to the army, by his early atchievements in Armenia, Egypt, and Arabia. He was a man of great art, courage, and patience, but prodigal, and dissolute; tho' he could well conceal his vices. He revived the antient strict military discipline, with great rigour, and kept the army sober, and constantly employed. On the account of these good qualities, Cassius was employed by the Emperor to recover the army quartered in Syria from their luxury, contracted under Verus; and he was much recommended by the Emperor to the governors of these eastern provinces. When he was thus promoted, he formed high designs, pretended to draw his pedigree from the old Cassius,[29] and talked much of restoring the old common-wealth. Verus, before his death, had suspicion of his ambitious designs, from his conduct, and his jests upon Antoninus's studious disposition; and wrote his suspicions to Antoninus, warning him to prevent his designs against him and his children, by putting him to death. To which, this was Antoninus's answer.[30]

> I have read your letter; which shews more of an anxious and timor<22>ous spirit, than of that becoming an Emperor, and suits not my government. If the Gods have decreed him the empire, we cannot dispatch him, tho' we would. You know your great grandfather's proverb, "no prince ever killed his successor." But if 'tis not decreed him, he will perish without any cruelty of ours. There is no condemning a man whom no body accuses, and whom the army loves. And, then, in cases of treason, we are deemed to have injured even those persons who are fully convicted. You know what your grandfather Adrian used to say, "The lot of sovereigns is hard, they are never credited about conspiracies formed against them, till they fall by them." I cite him to you, rather than Domitian, the author of the observation; because the best sayings of Tyrants have not the weight they may deserve. Let Cassius take his own way; especially, since he is a good general, keeps strict discipline, is brave, and necessary to the state.

As for caution about my children, by dispatching him, let my children perish, if Cassius better deserves the love of <23> the Romans than they, and it be more the interest of our country, that Cassius should live, than the children of Marcus.

A.D. *175*. Cassius, when he had formed the ambitious design, either raised a report of Antoninus's death, and that the army in Pannonia had elected himself for Emperor, or took occasion, from this report, to assume the sovereign power. He gave all places in the army to his friends, and caused all to submit to him, from Syria to mount Taurus. He sends a letter to his son at Alexandria, as a manifesto, inveighing against the corruptions in the administration, the extortions of the proconsuls and governors, and the decay of antient rigour and severity of manners, under a bookish Emperor, who neglected public affairs; and concludes, "Let the Gods favour the Cassii, and the common-wealth shall regain its antient dignity."[31]

Martius Verus, sent accounts of all these things to Antoninus; and he endeavoured to conceal them from the army; but, the matter was soon divulged: Upon this, he addressed the army, (as Dion Cassius relates),[32] to this effect. He <24> first expressed the deepest regret for the impending misery of a civil war, the corruption of men, the ingratitude and perfidy, discovered by those to whom he had done the kindest offices, and in whom he had confided: But he exhorted his soldiers, not to imagine that all faith and integrity were gone out of the earth. He had still many faithful and brave friends: He had no fear of success; supported both by his own innocence, his knowledge of the dastardly disposition of these dissolute troops and nations who had revolted, and his experience of the fidelity and bravery of these he addressed. He subjoined the tenderest expressions of clemency and pity, even toward Cassius, and that preserving his life, and pardoning him, would be to him more joyful than any triumph.

He wrote also to the same purpose to the Senate, which immediately declared Cassius a traitor, and confiscated his estate to the city, since the Emperor would not take it to himself. He wrote also to Faustina this letter.

"Verus's account of Cassius was true, that he designed to usurp. You have heard what the fortune-tellers <25> have told him. Come, therefore, to Alba, that we may consult about these affairs, without fear, under the protection of the Gods." She returned this answer. "I will go to Alba to morrow, as you order; but must advise you, if you love your children, to extirpate these rebels. Both the officers and soldiers, are grown very seditious. They will cut you off, unless you prevent them."

Faustina being detained, contrary to her expectation, the Emperor wrote to her to meet him at Formiae, where he was to embark, but she was detained at Rome, by the sickness of her daughter, and wrote him this Letter.

> In a like revolt of Celsus, my mother advised Antoninus Pius, first, to shew his tenderness and goodness to his own, and then to others. A prince cannot be deemed to have the just fatherly affection to his people, who neglects his wife and children. You see the tender years of Commodus. Our son-in-law Pompeianus is old, and a stranger. Consider, then, how you ought to treat Cassius and his associates. Don't spare <26> those, who would not, if they were victorious, spare you, nor me, nor our children. I shall speedily follow you. Fadilla's sickness hindered me from meeting you at Formiae.—I shall send you accounts, if I don't overtake you, what Cassius's wife and children, and son-in-law, are talking about you.[33]

Cassius made all efforts to strengthen his party. He wrote a long letter to Herod,[34] a man of good abilities, who commanded in Greece, and had fallen under Antoninus's displeasure for some maladministration, to engage him to join against Antoninus. But Herod had such veneration for the Emperor, that before he had read out all Cassius's letter, he returned him this short answer; "Herod to Cassius. You are mad."[35]

Cassius succeeded no better in soliciting some other provinces to revolt; and began to lose his credit with the army; and, at last, was dispatched by some of them, about three months after his revolt; and his head was sent to Antoninus, before he left Formiae, or had returned an answer to Faustina's last letter. On this occasion, he wrote to her thus.

> My dear Faustina, <27> You shew a most dutiful concern for me, and our children. I have read your Letters to me at Formiae twice over; pressing me to be severe toward the conspirators with Cassius; but I am resolved to spare his children, his son-in-law, and his wife, and shall write to the Senate, that they make no rigid proscription, nor any cruel punishments. Nothing can more recommend a Roman Emperor to the love of all nations, than clemency. 'Twas for this virtue that Cesar and Augustus were

> reputed Divinities. This obtained your father the title of Pius. Had the war ended as I would have wished, Cassius himself had not died. Don't be afraid. The Gods protect me. My fatherly affection to mankind must be acceptable to them. I have made Pompeianus our son-in-law consul for next year.[36]

Some thought this clemency too great. One used the freedom to ask him, how he thought Cassius would have treated him and his family, had he been victorious? He replied, "I have not served the Gods so ill, or lived in such a manner, that I had reason to fear <28> the Gods would allow Cassius to conquer me": And counted over most of the Emperors who had been dethroned and assassinated; shewing, that their own tyranny or folly occasioned their fate.[37]

Of his letter to the Senate, this part is yet preserved:

> In gratitude, therefore, for my victory, you have made my son-in-law consul; whose years seemed long ago to have claimed it; had not some brave worthy persons intervened, to whom that debt was first to be paid by the state. As to the revolt of Cassius, I beseech and obtest you, Fathers, that, laying aside your rigour, you would act suitably to my clemency, and your own. Let no Senator be put to death, or punished; nor the blood of any eminent person be shed. Let the banished return; and restore the estates of the proscribed. Would to God I could recall to life many of the dead. I never can like an Emperor's resentment of any injury aimed at himself. It appears too severe, even when very just. You must, therefore, pardon the sons of Cassius, his son-in-law, and his wife. But, why say I par-<29>don? they have committed no crime. Let them live secure; and feel they live under Antoninus. Let them live on the fortune of the family given up amongst them: Let them enjoy their gold and silver plate, and furniture: Let them live in wealth, and security; and at their full liberty to stay or go as they please; and carry with them, among all nations, the marks of my clemency, and of your's. This clemency to the wives and children of the proscribed, Conscript fathers, is but a small matter. I must request you further: defend all the conspirators of the Senatorian or Equestrian order, from death, proscription, fear, infamy, popular odium, and all manner of vexation. Allow it, for the honour of my government; that, in this case of usurpation, those who were killed in the suppressing of the tumult, may be deemed justly slain.[38]

This letter was read with innumerable acclamations and blessings. The Emperor buried Cassius's head decently, expressing no small grief for the loss of such a man. He marched immediately to the East: soon appeas-<30>ed the revolt, with the greatest clemency; and reformed many abuses. When he came to Syria, he burned all the papers of Cassius without reading them, to prevent entertaining suspicions or hatred against any. Some say, this had been done by his faithful friend Martius Verus, before his arrival; justly presuming, it would be pleasing to the good Emperor; and saying, if it was not, he could willingly die, to save the lives of so many of his fellow-citizens.

A.D. *176.* Faustina died in this expedition, near mount Taurus. The Senate, out of mean flattery, renewed their severity against the late conspirators; thinking it would be some alleviation of the Emperor's sorrow, to shew their zeal for him. But, upon the first notice of it, he wrote the most pressing letter to the Senate, to stop these proceedings, concluding, "If I cannot obtain from you the lives of all the conspirators, I shall wish to die."[39]

Cassius's eldest son Mecianus was killed in his government at Alexandria, on the very day in which Cassius was killed: His other children were only banished to an island; retaining all <31> their estates. His daughter, indeed, and son-in-law, continued in Rome; and were treated in a friendly manner by Antoninus. The Senate paid extravagant honours to Faustina. Antoninus, having settled the East, returned to Rome, after eight years absence; having extended his liberality to Athens, the old seat of learning, heard Aristides the orator[40] at Smyrna, and having been initiated in the Eleusinian mysteries:[41] On this occasion he gratified the Romans * with magnificent shews, and great liberality to the distressed.

The peace of the empire was soon disturbed by new commotions in the North. The Scythians took arms again, and attacked the Emperor's lieutenants. And he, tho' old and infirm, resolved upon another expedition: Nor could his friends of the Senate, who were exceedingly solicitous about his life, dissuade him from it. He spent three days in discoursing with them, and advising them about state affairs; and about the great principles of

* A.D. 177.

philosophy; and then set out for the army. In this expedition, his prudence and valour appeared invariably the same, and were always suc-<32>cessful; tho' the particulars of the wars are not preserved. But, at Vienna in Austria, or at Sirmium, he was seized with a distemper; which, in a few days, put an end to his glorious life. When he apprehended there was no hope of his recovery, his strength of mind and resignation to the divine will, made him easy, as to his own death; but his affection to his country gave him considerable anxiety. Tho' his son had not disclosed his vicious dispositions during his life, yet the examples of Nero and Domitian made him dread that any good instructions he had received, or any dispositions of his to virtue, would not be able to withstand the temptations he would be exposed to in that dangerous elevation. He saw his northern conquest very unsettled; and other provinces not sufficiently established. With all these cares oppressing him, his sickness and pains recurred more violently the last day of his life, and made him aware of his approaching end: Upon this, he called for his principal officers, who stood around his bed: He presented to them his son; and, exerting all his strength, he sate up, and spoke to this effect. <33>

> I am not surprized that you are troubled to see me in this condition. It is natural to mankind, to be moved with any sufferings of their fellow-creatures; and, when they are before our eyes, they excite a deeper compassion. But, you are under more peculiar tyes to me. From my consciousness of the most sincere affection to you, I presume you have the like to me. Now is the opportunity, for me to discern that the honours I have conferred on you, and the long series of kind offices done, were not employed in vain; and for you, to make grateful returns, and to shew you have not forgot the favours you received. You see there my son, who was educated by your selves, just entring into manhood, like a ship in a stormy sea, needing prudent pilots; lest, being carried aside, through want of experience, he be intirely shipwrecked among vices. Be you to him, therefore, so many fathers in my stead; always watching over him, and giving him good counsels: For, no treasures can satisfy the luxury of tyrants; nor any guards protect them, when they have lost the affections of <34> their people. These princes only have had safe and long reigns, who have infused into the minds of their people, not any dread by their cruelty, but an hearty love by their goodness. Such alone, as obey with good-will, and not from

> necessity, are to be confided in, and will obey their prince, or suffer for him, without flattery and dissimulation; nor will such ever rebel, or prove refractory; except when they are forced into it by insolent oppression. In unlimited power, 'tis hard to set proper measures or bounds to men's passions. If you suggest such thoughts to him, and keep him in mind of what he now hears, you will make him an excellent prince to yourselves, and to all the state, and do the most grateful office to my memory; as by this alone you can make it immortal.[42]

As he was thus speaking, his voice failed, he fell down on the bed, and died next day, in the 59th year of his age. Never was there a more universal undissembled sorrow, than what ensued among all ranks; who loudly bewailed his death, with all possible encomiums of his virtues: All which <35> were no more than his due; and with the dearest appellations of their good Emperor, their general, their protector, their father, or their brother.

The only prejudices which can obstruct the most favourable reception of these divine meditations, from the author's character, are these two: First, his continuing in the Pagan religion; even zealously sacrifising to false Gods, deifying his predecessor, and admitting the like honours to be paid to Verus and Faustina: and, secondly, his suffering the Christians to be persecuted, during his reign.

As to the first, tho' no man of sense can vindicate the heathen worship; as it was full of ridiculous superstitions; without any proper evidence; yet, let us not imagine it worse in the wiser heathens, than it truly was. Maximus Tyrius,[43] and many others, assure us, that all Wise men in the heathen world, believed only one supreme God, or, original cause, of all.[44] We see that Antoninus, and all the Stoics, agreed in this. But, they also believed there were many inferior created spirits, to whom, the government of certain parts of na-<36>ture was delegated by the supreme God; that the souls of some good men were advanced to this dignity; and that honours were to be paid to these presiding spirits; according to old traditions and custom. Now, this very doctrine generally prevailed, both in the eastern and western christian churches, for many centuries; even from the 5th to the reformation; without any other difference than that of sound; the heathens using the words God, or, Daemon, for what christians called Angels and

Saints; and both often raised to this dignity, the souls of persons, who had very little real virtue. The persons denoted by these names in the heathen and christian religions, were, indeed, different. The heathens worshiped the old heathen heroes and princes, and the christians their own heroes and martyrs. Nay the protestants allow that created beings may have delegated powers from God, and be employed as ministering spirits to the heirs of salvation, in their several nations; and superintend the civil affairs of them. But, having no particular knowledge who these Angels or Saints are, nor how they are employed; nor any evidence that they can know our devotions, our <37> prayers, or expressions of gratitude to them; and, seeing all such worship prohibited in the holy scriptures, as it generally has a bad tendency; they universally abstain from it, and condemn it. But, the moral evil of such practices, in those who have had no prohibitions by revelation, is not so great as we commonly apprehend it. Some men of little constancy in their conduct, who have been guilty of some very bad actions, have had also some eminent virtues not universally known. Nay 'tis probable the vices of Faustina were never known to Antoninus; (See B. I. 14). Verus too had his virtues; and many of his vices have been hid from our author. 'Tis a small fault to err on the charitable side, about the dead. Let us shew an impartial candour in this matter; remembring what mixed characters are recorded of some Jewish and Christian authors whose works we read with veneration.

As to the second charge, of persecuting the Christians:[45] Let us remember, that we have no proof of his giving orders for it: We can only charge him with the omission of his duty, in not making a strict inquiry into the cause of the Christians: This, tho' a great fault, is less than that of the apostle Paul, who himself persecuted with <38> great fury; and yet could afterwards truly say, he had served God with all good conscience; that is, sincerely, according to what he then thought his duty. To extenuate this fault in the Emperor, not to mention his perpetual avocations, by almost continual wars, beside the multitude of civil affairs in so vast an empire, let us remember, that, whatever better knowledge the inferior magistrates might have of the matter of fact, the princes must, generally, have had only such views of the Christians as the zealot pagan priests and magistrates presented to them. Now, they were represented as a confederacy for the most monstrous wickedness; such as, the murdering of infants, and feeding on them, all incestuous impurities, avowed atheism, the blaspheming all the Gods; and rebellion against the state. This last is the common charge, made by all persecutors, against such as differ from the established orthodoxy: As we see in all the defences of the R. catholic persecutions in France, and the protestant persecutions in England and Scotland; when the clergy have once persuaded the legislator, impiously to invade the prerogatives of God, over the consciences of <39> men, by penal laws about such religious opinions, and forms of worship as are no way hurtful in society.

Under these impressions of the Christians; a prince of great goodness might even directly order a persecution against them; not, indeed, without the guilt of a great omission of his duty; since he ought to have made a more thorough inquiry into the matter; and his ignorance could scarce be wholly invincible. But, his intention might be only the suppression of the most odious crimes, which he thought chargeable on the Christians.

But, grant he had persecuted the Christians upon their religious opinions, their rejecting and reviling the heathen Gods, and their rites of worship: Let such as make this objection to his character, consider, that any persecution is the more odious, the smaller the difference is, between the religious tenets of the persecutor, and those of the persecuted; as it shews a greater insolence of pride and ill-nature, to be so much provoked for such small differences; And it shews also the baser sentiments about the Deity, to conceive him so furious and captious, that the smaller mistakes in opinion or wor-<40>ship, can exclude his creatures intirely from his favour, and from all compassion or mercy, notwithstanding their hearty intention and desire to please him, as far as they know what is acceptable to him.

Now, the christian religion was intirely opposite, in every thing almost, to the Pagan. It rejected all their popular Gods: Nay, the early Christians averred them all to be impure devils, and that their worship was instituted by such devils; and refused any sort of joint worship with them. A devout heathen, deeply prejudiced by education, in favour of these popular Gods, and confirmed by a philosophy which espoused a good deal of the popular superstitions, would be under strong temptations from his very devotion, while under these mistakes, to suppress Christianity: This is a great extenuation of the Emperor's guilt.

But, what shall we say of Christians persecuting each other, who yet believe in the same God, and the same Saviour, and own the same grand practical rules of life, of loving God with all our heart, and our neighbour as ourselves! Let none make this objection to Antoninus, but those, who, from their hearts, abhor <41> all Christian persecutions, who cannot hate their neighbours, or deem them excluded from the divine favour, either for neglecting certain ceremonies, and pieces of outward pageantry, or for exceeding in them; for different opinions, or forms of words, about some metaphysical attributes or modes of existence, which all sides own to be quite incomprehensible by us; for the different opinions about human liberty; about which the best men who ever lived have had opposite sentiments: for different opinions about the manner in which the Deity may think fit to exercise his mercy to a guilty world, either in pardoning of their sins, or renewing them in piety and virtue. As for these who are conscious of such sincere undissembled good-will to all, even those whom they think mistaken in such points; who have no partial attachments to their own parties, from prejudices of education, and their uniting in the same cause; no vanity or pride exciting any anger at the different opinions of others, opposite to what they in their own wisdom have pronounced sound and orthodox, and so detracting from their superior penetration, and diminishing their glory <42> and popularity; Those who find the simple, peaceful, meek, and humble love of truth alone, influencing their sentiments, and a perpetual love to God, and a calm uniform charity operating in their hearts toward all men, even those who despise and affront their religious sentiments; persons of this character, may with some shew of decency, reject these noble devout sentiments, on account of the author's having persecuted, or suffered others to persecute during his reign. But such men will easily see, that these pious and charitable meditations and suggestions must be valuable for their own sakes, and useful to every attentive reader; whatever were the sins or failings of the author.

'Tis needless, I hope, to prevent another silly prejudice; as if because the author was not a Christian, he could have no real piety or virtue acceptable to God, none of these divine influences, which we are taught are necessary to every good work. No doubt, he is not to be defended in his neglecting to examine the evidences of christianity, or, in not embracing it. But, let men consider the power of education, and how much he was employed from his <43> very youth, in a constant course of public business, which allowed little leisure. How little probability could there occur to him, that, in a sect at that time universally despised, and represented, not only as weak and illiterate, but most horridly impious, immoral, and flagitious, he should find any better instructions in theories of religion, or any better motives to virtuous actions, than what were among the philosophers? We see with what a just contempt of ease, pleasure, and luxury, he keenly embraced the scheme of philosophy most remarkable for piety, austerity, and disinterested goodness; and how long christian magistrates, spirited up by the pretended embassadors of the meek Jesus, have been persecuting their fellow-christians with fire and sword; and that for very honourable tenets; often much better than those of the persecutors. Let this be a warning to all men, against rashly entertaining ill-natured representations of whole sects or bodies of men. Christians may be ashamed to censure our author on this account; considering how rashly, arrogantly, and presumptuously, they are cursing one another in their synodical anathemas; and in their creeds, <44> pronouncing eternal damnation on all who are not within the pale, or hold not the same mysterious tenets or forms of words.

'Tis but a late doctrine in the christian church, that the grace of God, and all divine influences purifying the heart, were confined to such as knew the christian history, and were by profession in the christian church. The earliest Christians and martyrs were of a very different opinion. However, they maintained that it is by the merits of our Saviour alone, men can either be justified or sanctified; yet they never denyed these blessings could be conferred on any who knew not the meritorious or efficient cause of them. To maintain they could not, is as absurd as to assert, that a physician cannot cure a disease, unless the patient be first instructed in the whole art of medicine, and know particularly the physical principles by which the several medicines operate. Nay, the early Christians believed the spirit of Christ operated in Socrates, Plato, and other virtuous heathens; and that they were Christians in heart, without the historical knowledge: And, sure, we may charitably judge the same of this <45> Emperor, who plainly depended on God for such sanctifying influences; and recommends them as the matter of our most earnest prayers; and often, with the deepest humility and simplicity of heart, * acknowledges that he owes to God's preventing grace, in his providence about him, all those virtuous dispositions, in which he had any delight or complacence. <46>

* B. I. 14. B. IX. 40. B. IV. 26. and in many other places.

THE MEDITATIONS OF THE EMPEROR MARCUS AURELIUS ANTONINUS

BOOK I

1. From[1] my grandfather * Verus I learned to relish the beauty of manners, and to restrain all anger. From the fame and character my † father obtain'd, modesty, and a manly deportment. ‡ Of my mother; I learned to be religious, and liberal; <47> and to guard, not only against evil actions, but even against any evil intention's entering my thoughts; to content myself with a spare diet, far different from the softness and luxury so common among the wealthy. Of my great- § grandfather; ** not to frequent public schools and auditories; but to have good and able teachers at home; and for things of this nature, to account no expence too great.

2. He who had the charge of my education, taught me not to be fondly attached to any of the contending parties †† in the chariot-races, or in the combats of the gladiators.[2] He taught me also to endure labour; not to need

* Annius Verus, who had been thrice Consul, and was made a Senator under Vespasian.

† Annius Verus, who died when Antoninus was a child.

‡ Domitia Calvilla Lucilla, daughter of Calvisius Tullus, who had been twice Consul.

§ Probably by the mother, *viz.* Catilius Severus.

** 'Tis not certain whether the negative particle should be here or not.[3]

†† The keenness of these contentions among the Romans in that age, is abundantly known.

many things; to serve myself, without troubling others; not to intermeddle with the affairs of others, and not easily to admit of accusations against them.

3. Of Diognetus;[4] not to busy myself about vain things, not to credit the great professions of such as pretend to work wonders, or of sorcerers, about their <48> charms, and their expelling Demons; and the like. Not to keep * Quails, nor to be keen of such things; to allow others all freedom in conversation; and to apply myself heartily to philosophy. Him also I must thank, for my hearing first Bacchius, then Tandasis, and Marcianus;[5] that I wrote dialogues in my youth, and took a liking to the philosopher's little couch and skins, and such other things, which by the Grecian discipline belong to that profession.

4. To Rusticus[6] I owe my first apprehensions, that my temper needed redress and cure, and that I did not fall into the ambition of the common Sophists, either in writing upon the sciences, or exhorting men to philosophy by public harangues; as also, that I never affected to be admired by ostentation of great patience in an ascetic life, or of activity and application; and that I gave over the study of rhetoric, poetry, and the elegance of language; that I did not affect any airs of grandeur, by walking at home in my senatorial robe, or by any such things. I observed also the simplicity of style in his letters, parti-<49>cularly in that, which he wrote to my mother from Sinuessa. I learned also from him an easiness and proneness to be reconciled and well pleased again with those who had offended me, as soon as any of them inclined to be reconciled; to read with diligence; not to rest satisfied with a light and superficial knowledge; nor quickly to assent to great talkers: Him also I must thank, that I met with the discourses of Epictetus[7] which he gave me.

5. From Apollonius[8] I learned true liberty, and invariable stedfastness; and to regard nothing else, not even in the smallest degree, but right and reason; and always to remain the same man, whether in the sharpest pains, or after the loss of a child, or in long diseases. To him I owe my seeing in a living example, that it was possible for the same man to be both vehement and remiss, as occasion requir'd. I learn'd of him, not to fret when my reasonings were not apprehended. In him I saw an instance of a man, who esteem'd his excellent skill and ability in teaching others the principles of

* For fighting, or incantations.

philosophy, the least of all his endowments. Of him also I learned how to receive from friends, what are thought <50> favours, so as neither to be on that account subjected to them, nor yet seem insensible and ungrateful.

6. From Sextus[9] a pattern of a benign temper, and of a family, governed with true paternal affection and a stedfast purpose of living according to nature; to be grave and venerable, without affectation; to observe sagaciously the several dispositions and inclinations of my friends; not to be offended with the ignorant, or with those who follow the vulgar opinions without examination: His conversation was an example, how a man may accomodate himself to all men and companies; for tho' his company was sweeter, and more pleasing than any sort of flattery, yet he was at the same time highly respected and reverenced. No man was ever more happy than he in comprehending, finding out, and arranging in exact order, the great maxims necessary for the conduct of life. He taught me by his example, to suppress even the least appearance of anger, or any other passion; but still, not withstanding this perfect tranquillity, to possess the tenderest and most affectionate heart; and to be apt to approve and applaud others, and yet with-<51>out noise: to desire much literature, without ostentation.

7. From Alexander the critic,[10] to avoid censuring others, or flouting at them for a barbarism, solecism, or any false pronounciation; but dextrously to pronounce the words as they ought, in my answering, approving, or arguing the matter, without taking direct notice of the mistake; or by some other such courteous insinuation.

8. From Fronto;[11] to be sensible, how much envy, deceit, and hypocrisy, surrounds princes; and that generally those we account nobly born, have somehow less natural affection.

9. Of Alexander the platonist;[12] not often, nor without great necessity, to say, or write to any man in a letter, that I am not at leisure, nor thus under pretext of urgent affairs, to decline or defer the duties, which, according to our various ties, we owe to those among whom we live.

10. Of Catulus;[13] not to contemn any friend's expostulation, tho' injust; but to strive to reduce him to his former disposition: freely and heartily to speak well of all my masters, upon any oc-<52>casion, as it is reported of * Domitius, and Athenodotus; and to love my children with true affection.

* There are no other memorials of these two persons.[14]

11. From my brother * Severus, to love my kinsmen, and to love truth and justice. To him I owe my acquaintance with † Thraseas, Helvidius, Cato, Dion, and Brutus. He gave me also the first conception of a republic, founded upon equitable laws, and administred with equality of right; and of a monarchic government, which chiefly regards the liberty of the subjects. Of him I learned likewise, to maintain a constant, disengaged, and uninterrupted study and esteem of philosophy; to be bountiful and liberal in the largest measure; always to hope the best; and to be unsuspicious about the affections of my friends. I observed in him a candid openness in declaring what he disliked in the conduct of others; and that his friends might easily see, without the trouble of conjectures, what he liked or <53> disliked; so open and plain was his behaviour.

12. From Claudius Maximus;[15] in all things to have power over myself, and in nothing to be hurried away by any passion: to be chearful and couragious in all sudden accidents, as in sicknesses to have an easy command of my own temper; to maintain a kind, sweet, and yet grave deportment; to execute my designs vigorously without freting. Whatever he said, all men believed, he spake, as he thought; and that whatever he did, it was with a good intent. He taught me, not to be easily astonished or confounded with any thing, never to seem in a hurry, nor yet to be dilatory, or perplexed, without presence of mind, or dejected, fretful, angry, or suspicious; and to be ready to do good to others, to forgive, and to speak truth; and in all this, to appear rather like one who had always been straight and right, than ever rectified or redressed; nor was there any, who thought himself undervalued by him, or who could find in his heart to think himself a better man than him: Nor did he ever affect the praise of being witty. <54>

13. ‡ From my father I learned meekness, and constancy, without wavering in those things, which after a due examination and deliberation were determined; to be little solicitous about the common honours; patience of labour, and assiduity, and readiness to hear any man, who offered any thing tending to the common good; an inflexible justice toward all men; a just

* This either the philosopher Claudius Severus, whom he calls his brother from his strong love to him, or some cousin whose memory is not otherways preserved to us.[16]

† These were eminent characters, in the two preceeding ages.[17]

‡ Antoninus Pius, his father by adoption.

apprehension when rigour and extremity, or when remissness and moderation were in season; abstinence from all impure lusts: and a sense of humanity toward others. Thus he left his friends at liberty, to sup with him or not, to go abroad with him or not, as they inclined; and they still found him the same, after their affairs had hindered them to attend him. I learned of him accuracy and patience of inquiry in all deliberations and counsel. He never quitted the search, satisfied with the first appearances. I observed his zeal to retain his friends, without cloying them, or shewing any foolish fondness; his contentment in every condition; his chearfulness; his forethought about very distant events; <55> his exact care even about small matters, without noise. How he restrained all acclamations and flattery: How vigilantly he observed all things necessary to the government, and managed accurately the public revenue, and bore patiently the censures of others about these things: How he was neither a superstitious worshipper of the Gods, nor an ambitious pleaser of men, nor studious of popularity; but sober in all things, stedfast, well-skilled in what was honourable, never affecting novelties. As to these things which are subservient to ease and conveniency, of which his fortune supplied him with great affluence; he used them without pride, and yet with all freedom; enjoyed them without affectation when they were present; and when absent, he found no want of them. He was not celebrated, either as a learned acute man, or one of a sharp wit, or as a great declaimer; but a wise, experienced, complete man; one who could not bear to be flattered; able to govern both himself and others; I further observed the great honour he paid to all true philosophers, without upbraiding those who were not so; his sociableness, his gracious and delightful conversation, <56> without cloying. His regular moderate care of his body, neither like one desirous of long life, or over studious of neatness, and elegancy; and yet not as one who despised it: Thus, through his own care, he seldom needed any internal medicines, or outward applications: But especially how ingenuously he would yield without envy, to any who had obtained any peculiar faculty, as either eloquence, or the knowledge of the laws, or of ancient customs, or the like; and how he concurred with them strenuously, that every one of them might be regarded and esteemed, for that in which he excelled; and altho' he observed carefully the ancient customs of his fore-fathers, yet it was without ostentation.

Again, how he was not fickle and capricious, but loved to continue both in the same places and businesses; and how after his violent fits of the head-ach, he returned fresh and vigorous to his wonted affairs. Again, that he neither had many secrets, nor often; and such only as concerned public matters: His discretion and moderation, in exhibiting of shows for the entertainment of the people, in public buildings, largesses, and the like. In all these things he acted <57> like one who regarded only what was right and becoming in the things themselves, and not the applauses which might follow. He never bathed at unseasonable hours; had no vanity in building; was never solicitous, either about his meat, or about the nice workmanship or colour of his cloaths, or about the beauty of his servants. His apparel was plain and homely, such as that he chose to wear at Lorium, cloath made at Lunuvium;[18] and at Tusculum, he wore a short cloak, sometimes making apologies for the plainness of his dress. His conversation was far from any inhumanity; or incivility, or impetuosity; never doing any thing with such keenness that one could say * he was sweating about it; but on the contrary, in all things, he acted distinctly, as at leisure, without confusion, regularly, resolutely, and gracefully. A man might have applied that to him which is recorded of Socrates, that he knew both how to abstain from or enjoy those things, in want whereof most men shew themselves weak; and in the fruition, intemperate: He remained firm and constant in both events, <58> with a just self-government, and shewed a perfect and invincible soul; such as appeared in him during the sickness of Maximus.

14. To the Gods I owe my having good grand-fathers, and parents, a good sister, good masters, good domesticks, affectionate kinsmen, and friends, and almost all things good: and that I never thro' haste and rashness offended any of them; tho' I had such a temper as might have led me to it, had occasion offer'd; but by the goodness of the Gods, no such concurrence of circumstances happen'd as could discover my weakness: that I was not long brought up with my father's concubine; that I retained my modesty, and refrained from all venereal enjoyments, even longer than was necessary; that I lived under the government of such a prince and father, who took away from me all pride and vain-glory, and convinced me, that it was not

* This was a proverbial expression.

impossible for a prince to live in a court, without guards, extraordinary apparel, torches, statues, or such pieces of state and magnificence; but that he may reduce himself almost to the state of a private man, and yet not become more <59> mean or remiss in those publick affairs, wherein power and authority are requisite. That I have had such a brother, * as by his disposition might stir me up to take care of myself; and yet by his respect and love delighted me; that my children wanted not good natural dispositions, nor were distorted or deformed in body; that I was no great proficient in the studies of rhetoric and poetry, and in other faculties, which might have engrossed my mind, had I found myself successful in them; that I prevented the expectations of those, by whom I was brought up, in promoting them to the places and dignities, they seem'd most to desire; that I did not put them off, in the common way, with hopes and excuses that since they were but young I would do it hereafter. I owe to the Gods that ever I knew Apollonius, Rusticus and Maximus; that I have had occasion often and effectually to meditate with myself and inquire <60> what is truly the life according to nature; so that, as for the Gods, and such suggestions, helps and inspirations, as might be expected from them, I might have already attained to that life which is according to nature; and it was my own fault that I did not sooner, by not observing the inward motions and suggestions, yea, and almost plain and apparent instructions of the Gods; that my body, in such a life, hath been able to hold out so long; that I never had to do with † Benedicta and Theodotus, yea, and afterwards, when I fell into some foolish passions, that I was soon cured; that, having been often displeased with Rusticus, I never did any thing to him, for which afterwards I had occasion to repent: that since it was my mother's fate to die young, she lived with me all her latter years: that as often as I inclined to succour any who were either poor, or fallen into some distress, I was never answered by the managers of my revenues that there was not ready mo-<61>ney enough to do it; and that I myself never had occasion for the like

* Probably Verus, whose vicious passions might rouse this excellent man's attention to himself, or perhaps Antoninus did not know his vices for a great part of his life, and 'tis certain Verus had a great esteem for Antoninus, and was a man of ability.

† These two persons are unknown, 'tis possible they have been remarkably dangerous to the youth at court.

succour from any other; that I have such a wife, so obedient, so loving, so ingenuous; that I had choice of fit and able men, to whom I might commit the education of my children; that by dreams I have received divine aids, as, for other things, so, in particular, how I might stay my spitting of blood, and cure my vertigo, which happen'd successfully to me at Cajeta; and, that, when I first applied myself to philosophy, I did not fall into the hands of some sophist, nor spent my time in reading many volumes, nor embarrassed myself in the solution of sophisms, nor dwelt upon the study of the meteors. All these things could not have thus concurred, without the assistance of the Gods and * fortune.

These things in the country of the Quadi near Granua.[19] <62>

* See, B. II. art. 3.

BOOK II

1. Say thus to thyself every morning: to day I may have to do with some intermeddler in other mens affairs, with an ungrateful man; an insolent, or a crafty, or an envious, or an unsociable selfish man. These bad qualities have befallen them through their ignorance of what things are truly good or evil. But I have fully comprehended the nature of good, as * only what is beautiful and honourable; and of evil, that it is always deformed and shameful; and the nature of those persons too † who mistake their aim; that they are my kinsmen, by partaking, not of the same blood or seed, but of the same ‡ intelligent divine part; and that I cannot be <63> hurt by any of them, since none of them can involve me in any thing dishonourable or deformed. I cannot be angry at my kinsmen, or hate them. We were formed by nature for mutual assistance, as the two feet, the hands, the eyelids, the upper and lower rows of teeth. Opposition to each other is contrary to nature: All anger and aversion is an opposition.

2. Whatsoever I am, is either this § poor flesh, or the animal spirit, or the governing part. Quit your books: Be no longer distracted with different views. You have it in your own power. As one who is shortly to die, despise

* This, according to the high style of the Stoics, that virtuous affections and actions are the sole good, and the contrary the sole evil.[1]

† This is the meek sentiment of Socrates, that as all error is involuntary, so no man is willingly unjust or wicked in his actions: Since all desire truth and goodness.

‡ The Stoics spoke of the rational soul, as a part of the divinity, taken from that infinite intelligent aetherial nature, which pervades and surrounds all things.[2]

§ The apostle Paul alludes to this notion in praying that we may be sanctified in soul, spirit, and body: many ancients conceived in men two principles distinct from the body, one the animal soul or life, like that in beasts, the other the rational, like the divinities or angels. In the former which they supposed to be air, they placed all the sensations and passions. See B. III. art. 16.

this fleshly part, this putrifying blood, and bones, and the net-work texture of nerves, veins, arteries. Consider the nature of mere animal spirit or life, air, and that always changing, breathed forth and drawn in again. The third part is that which go-<64>verns. Think thus: you are now old; suffer not that noble part to be enslaved, or moved about by * unsociable passions, without its own approbation. Repine no more at what now befalls you according to fate, nor dread what may befall you hereafter.

3. Whatever the Gods ordain, is full of wise providence. What we ascribe to fortune, happens not without a presiding nature, nor without a connexion and intertexture with the things ordered by providence. Thence all things flow. Consider, too, the necessity of these events; and their utility to that whole universe of which you are a part. In every regular structure, that must always be good to a part, which the nature of the whole requires, and which tends to preserve it. Now, the universe is preserved, as, by the † changes of the <65> Elements, so, by the changes of the complex forms. Let these thoughts suffise; let them be your maxims, laying aside that thirst after multitudes of books; that you may die without repining, meek, and well satisfied, and sincerely grateful to the Gods.

4. Remember how long you have put off these things; and how often you have neglected to use the opportunities offered you by the Gods. It is high time to understand what sort of whole you are a part of; and who that President in the universe is, from whom you flowed, as a small stream from a great fountain. There is a certain time appointed for you, which, if you don't employ in making all calm and serene within you, it will pass away, and you along with it; and never more return.

5. Let this be your stedfast purpose to act continually, in all affairs, as becomes a Roman, and a man, with true unaffected dignity, kindness of heart, freedom, and justice; and disentangle your soul from other solicitudes. You shall thus disentangle yourself, if you perform each action as if

* A metaphor from puppets, mov'd by others. Such are men when led by their passions against what their higher faculties incline to and recommend.[3]

† The Stoics supposed that aether condensed, produced air, air condensed became water, and water thus too became earth: That earth was rarified into water; water into air, and air into aether, and these changes were always going on in the universe.[4]

it were your last: without temerity, or any passionate aversion to what reason approves; with-<66>out hypocrisy or selfishness, or freting at what providence appoints. You see how few these maxims are, to which, whoever adheres, may live a prosperous and divine life. If a man observe these things, the Gods require no more of him.

6. Go on, go on, o my soul! to affront and dishonour thy self! yet a little while, and the time to honour thyself shall be gone. Each man's life is flying away, and thine is almost gone, before thou hast paid * just honour to thyself; having hitherto made thy happiness dependent on the minds and opinions of others.

7. Let nothing which befalls thee from without distract thee; and take leisure <67> to thy self, to learn something truly good. Wander no more to and fro; and guard also against this other wandering. For there are some too who trifle away their activity, by wearying themselves in life, without having a settled scope or mark, to which they may direct all their desires and all their projects.

8. Seldom are any found unhappy for not observing the motions and intentions in the souls of others. But such as observe not well the motions of their own souls, or their affections, must necessarily be unhappy.

9. Remember these things always: what the nature of the universe is: what thine own nature: and how related to the universe: What sort of part thou art, and of what sort of whole: and that no man can hinder thee to act and speak what is agreeable to that whole, of which thou art a part.

10. Theophrastus,[5] as becomes a philosopher, says justly, that in comparing crimes together, † (for in a popular style they may be compared)

* 'Tis one of the most ancient maxims or precepts, "Reverence or stand in awe of thyself" which is the most remote from any encouraging of pride or vanity. It means, that men, conscious of the dignity of their nature, and of that temper of soul, and course of action which they must approve, should continually endeavour to behave suitably to their dignity, in preserving that temper, and practising such actions, with a sincere simple view to answer the end for which God created them, with such dignity and such endowments; and be ashamed to act unsuitably to them. Now, to be influenced by views of glory from men, is what Antoninus here reckons among the dishonours or affronts done to ourselves. See, art. 16 of this book. And B. III. art. 6. and others.[6]

† It was one of the paradoxes of the Stoics, that all crimes were equal, and so no occasion for comparisons.

these are greater, which men are incited to, by <68> lust, or desire of pleasure, than those which flow from anger. For the angry man seems to be turned from right reason, by a sort of pain and contraction seizing him unawares. But he who sins from lust, conquer'd by pleasure, seems more dissolute, weak, and effeminate in his vices. He says justly, and as becomes the dignity of a philosopher, that the crime committed for pleasure, deserves an higher censure, than that committed from the impulse of pain. One in the latter case seems like a person who is forced into anger by injuries first received; but one in the former, like him who first injures another, at the instigation of some lust of pleasure.

11. Undertake each action as one aware he may next moment depart out of life. To depart from men, if there be really Gods, can have nothing terrible in it. The Gods will involve you in no evil. If there are no Gods, or, if they have no regard to human affairs, why should I desire to live in a world without Gods, and without providence? But Gods there are, undoubtedly, and they regard human affairs; and have put it wholly in our power, that <69> we should not fall into what is * truly evil. Were there any real evil in other things, they would have also put it in the power of man to have avoided them altogether. But how can that which makes not one a worse man, be said to make a man's life worse? And it could neither be from any ignorance, or want of power, to prevent or rectify them, when it knew them, that the nature presiding in the whole has overlooked such things. We cannot ascribe such gross misconduct to it, either from want of power, or want of skill, as that good and evil should happen confusedly and promiscuously, both to good and bad men. Now, death and life, glory and reproach, pain and pleasure, riches and poverty, all these happen promiscuously to the good and bad. But as they are neither honourable nor shameful, they are therefore neither good nor evil.

12. 'Tis the office of our rational power, to apprehend how swiftly all things vanish. How the corporeal forms, are swallowed up in the material World, and the memory of them in the tide of ages. Such are all sensible things, especially <70> those which ensnare us by pleasure, or terrify us by

* That is, moral evil, or, vice.

pain, or are celebrated with such vanity. How mean, how despicable, how sordid, how perishable, how dead are they! What sort of creatures are they, whose voices bestow renown? What is it to die? Would one consider it alone, and by close thought strip it of those horrible masks with which it is dressed, would he not see it to be a work of nature, and nothing else? He must be a child, who dreads what is natural. Nay, it is not only a work of nature, but useful to nature. Our rational power should apprehend, too, how a man is related to God, and by what part; and in what state this part shall be, when it returns to him again.

13. Nothing is more miserable, says one, than he who ranges over all things, and dives even into things below the earth, and strives by conjectures to discover what is in the souls of others around him, and yet is not sensible of this, that 'tis sufficient for a man to dwell and converse with that * divinity which is within him, and pay it the genuine worship. <71> It is then worshipped and honoured, when it is kept pure from every passion, and folly, and from repining at any thing done by Gods or men. Whatever is done by the Gods, is venerable for its excellence. What flows from men, we should entertain with love, since they are our kinsmen; or, sometimes, with pity, as proceeding from their ignorance of good and evil. They are not less pityably maimed by this defect, this blindness, than by that which hinders them to distinguish between black and white.

14. † If thou shouldst live three thousand years, or as many myriads, yet remember this, that no man loses any other life than that he now lives; and that he now lives no other life than what he is parting with, every instant. The longest life, and the shortest, come to one effect: since the present time is equal to all, what is lost or parted with is equal to all. And for the same reason, what is parted with, is only a moment. No man at death parts with, or, is deprived of, what is either past or future. For how can one take from a man what <72> he hath not? We should also remember these things, first, That all things which have happened in the continued revolutions from

* Thus the Stoics call the rational soul, the seat of knowledge and virtue: deeming it a part of the divinity, ever pervaded, attracted, and inspired by it to all moral good, when the lower passions are restrained.

† The first sentiment in this paragraph, is too subtile and frigid.

eternity, are of the same kind with what we behold: And 'tis of little consequence, whether a man beholds the same things for an hundred years, or an infinite duration. Again that the longest and the shortest lives have an equal loss at Death. The present moment is all which either is deprived of, since that is all he has. A man cannot part with what he has not.

15. All depends upon opinion; as the sayings of Monimus[7] make evident. The usefulness of his sayings appear, if one attend to his pleasantries, as far as truth confirms them.

16. The soul affronts itself, when it becomes, as far as it can, an abscess or wen in the universe. Freting at what happens, is making itself an abscess from that nature, which contains all other parts. Again, when it has aversion to any man, and opposes him with intention to hurt him, as wrathful men do. And thirdly, it affronts itself, when conquered by pleasure or pain. Fourthly, when it does or says any thing hypocritically, feignedly, or falsly. Fifthly, when it does not <73> direct to some proper end all its desires and actions, but exerts them inconsiderately, without understanding. Whereas, even the smallest things should be refered to the end. Now, the end of rational beings should be this, to follow the * reason and law of their most antient and venerable city or country.

17. The duration of human life is a point; its substance perpetually flowing; the senses obscure; and the compound body tending to putrefaction: The soul is restless, fortune uncertain, and fame injudicious. To sum up all, the body, and all things related to it, are like a river; what belongs to the animal life, is a dream, and smoak; life a warfare, and a journey in a strange land; surviving fame is but oblivion. What is it then, which can conduct us honourably out of life, and accompany us in our future progress? philosophy alone. And this consists in preserving the divinity within us free from all affronts and injuries, superior to pleasure and pain, doing nothing either inconsiderately, or insincerely and hypo-<74>critically; independent on what others may do or not do: embracing chearfully whatever befalls or is appointed, as coming from him, from whom itself was derived; and,

* By this country or state is understood the universe governed by God. The end therefore is acting the part God has appointed to us by the constitution of our nature.

above all, expecting death with calm satisfaction, as conceiving it to be only a dissolution of these elements, of which every animal is compounded. And if no harm befalls the elements when each is * changed into the other, why should one suspect any harm in the changes and † dissolution of them all? It is natural, and nothing natural can be evil. This at Carnuntum.[8] <75>

* Earth to water, water to air, air to fire, and so backwards.

† Perhaps he intends the universal destruction of this world. See X. 7.

BOOK III

1. One ought to consider, not only that, each day, a part of his life is spent, and the remainder grown less, but that it is very uncertain, tho' he should live longer, whether his understanding shall continue equally sufficient for his business, and for those theories which make one skilled in things divine and human. For if one begin to dote in these things, he may, perhaps, continue to breathe, to receive nourishment, to have vain imaginations, and exert the low appetites; but the true power of governing himself, of performing completely the duties of life, of considering distinctly all appearances which strike the imagination, and of judging well this very point, whether he should depart from life or not, and all other powers which require a well exercised vigorous understanding, must be intirely extinguished in him. We should, therefore, make haste, not only because death is every day so much nearer, but because the power of considering well and under-<76>standing things, often leaves us before death.

2. This also should be observed, that such things as ensue upon what is well constituted by nature, have also something graceful and attractive. Thus, some parts of a well baked loaf will crack and become rugged. What is thus cleft beyond the design of the baker, looks well, and invites the appetite. So when figs are at the ripest, they begin to crack. Thus in full ripe olives, their approach to putrefaction gives the proper beauty to the fruit. Thus, the laden'd ear of corn hanging down, the stern brow of the lyon, and the foam flowing from the mouth of the wild boar, and many other things, considered apart, have nothing comely; yet because of their connexion with things natural, they adorn them, and delight the spectator. Thus, to one who has a deep affection of soul, and penetration into the constitution of the whole, scarce any thing connected with nature will fail to recommend itself agreeably to him. Thus, the real vast jaws of savage

beasts will please him, no less than the imitations of them by painters or statuaries. With like pleasure will his chaste eyes behold <77> the maturity and grace of old age in man or woman, and the inviting charms of youth. Many such things will he experience, not credible to all, but only to those who have the genuine affection of soul toward nature and its works.[1]

3. Hippocrates[2] after conquering many diseases, yielded to a disease at last. The Chaldeans foretold the fatal hours of multitudes, and fate afterwards carried themselves away.[3] Alexander, Pompey, and Caius Caesar,[4] who so often razed whole cities, and cut off in battle so many myriads of horse and foot, at last departed from this life themselves. Heraclitus,[5] who wrote so much about the conflagration of the universe, died swollen with water, and bedaubed with ox-dung. Vermin destroyed Democritus,[6] [the inventor of the atomical philosophy:] and another sort of vermin destroyed Socrates.[7] To what purpose all this? You have gone aboard, made your voyage, arrived to your port, go ashore. If into another life and world, the Gods are also there: if into a state of insensibility; at least you shall be no longer disturbed by sensual pleasure or pain, or be in slavery to this mean cor-<78>poreal vessel. Is not the soul, which is often enslaved to it, much more excellent than the body? The soul is intelligence and deity. The body, earth, and putrifying blood.

4. Spend not the remainder of your life in conjectures about others, except where it is subservient to some public interest: conjecturing what such a one is doing, and with what view, what he is saying, what he is thinking, what he is projecting, and such like; this attention to the affairs of others, makes one wander from his own business, the guarding of his own soul. We ought, therefore, to exclude from the series of our thoughts, whatever is superfluous or vain; and much more every thing intermeddling and ill-natured; and enure ourselves to think on such things, as, if we were of a sudden examined, what are we now musing upon, we could freely answer, such or such matters: so that all within might appear simple and good-natured, such as becomes a social being, who despises pleasure, and all sensual enjoyment, and is free from emulation, envy, suspicion, or any other passion that we would blush to own we were now indulging in our minds. A man <79> thus disposed wants nothing to entitle him to the highest dignity, of a priest and fellow-worker with the Gods, who rightly employs

the divinity within him; which can make the man undefiled by pleasure, invincible by pain, inaccessable to reproach, or any injuries from others: A victorious champion in the noblest contention, that against the passions: deeply tinctured with justice; embracing with all his heart whatever befalls, or is appointed by providence. Seldom solicitous, and that not without some generous public view, what another says, does, or intends: Solely intent on his own conduct, and thinking continually on what is appointed to him by the governor of the universe. Making his own conduct beautiful and honourable; and persuaded that what providence orders is good. For, each one's lot is brought upon him by providence, and is advantageous to him. Remember, that, whatever is rational, is a-kin to thee, and that it suits human nature to take care of every thing human. Nor ought we to desire glory from all, but only from those who live agreeably to nature. For others; still remember, how they live at home, how abroad, how in the <80> dark, how in the light, and with what a wretched mass they are blended. Thus, one won't value the praise of such men, for they cannot please or applaud themselves.

5. Do nothing with reluctance, or forgetting the * kind social bond, or without full inquiry, or hurried into it by any passion. Seek not to set off your thoughts with studied elegance. Be neither a great talker, nor undertaker of many things. And let the God within thee find he rules a man of courage, an aged man, a good citizen, a Roman, who regulates his life, as waiting for the signal to retreat out of it, without reluctance at his dissolution; who needs not for a bond of obedience, either the tie of an oath, or the observation of others. Join also a chearful countenance, an independence on the services of others, a mind which needs not retirement from the world, to obtain tranquillity; but can maintain it without the assistance of others. One should rather ap-<81>pear to have been always straight and right, and not as amended or rectified.

6. If you can find any thing in human life better than justice, truth, temperance, fortitude; or, to sum up all, than to have your mind perfectly

* The Stoics always maintained, that by the very constitution of our nature, all men are recommended to the affectionate good-will of all: which would always appear, were it not for the interfering of falsely imagined interests.[8]

satisfied with what actions you are engaged in by right reason, and what providence orders independently of your choice: if you find any thing better, I say, turn to it with all your soul, and enjoy the noble discovery. But if nothing appears more excellent than the divinity seated within you, when it hath subjected to its self all its passions, examined all appearances which may excite them, and, as Socrates expresses it, has torn itself off from the attachments to sense; has subjected it self to the Gods, and has an affectionate care of mankind: If you find all things mean and despicable in comparison with this, give place to nothing else: for, if you once give way, and lean towards any thing else, you will not be able, without distraction of mind, to preserve the preference of esteem and honour to your own proper and true good. For it is against the law of justice, that any thing of a different kind withstand the proper good of the rational and <82> social nature; such as the views of popular applause, power, riches, or sensual enjoyments. All these things, if we allow them even for a little to appear suitable to our nature, immediately become our masters and hurry us away. But do you I say, with liberty, and simplicity of heart, chuse what is most excellent, and hold to it resolutely. What is most excellent is most advantageous. If so to the rational nature, retain it; but if only to the animal, renounce it. And preserve the judging power unbyassed by external appearances, that it may make a just and impartial inquiry.

7. Never value that as advantageous, which may force you to break your faith; to quit your modesty, or sense of honour; to hate, suspect, or imprecate evil on any one; to dissemble; or to desire any of these things which need walls or curtains to conceal them. He who to all things prefers the soul, the divinity within him, and the sacred mysteries of its virtues, makes no tragical exclamations, complaints, or groans. He needs neither solitude nor a croud; and, what is greatest of all, he lives without either desires or fears of death. And whether the soul shall use this surrounding <83> body, for a longer or shorter space, gives him no solicitude. Were he to depart this moment, he is as ready for it, as for any other work, which can be gracefully, and with honour, accomplished; guarding in the whole of life against this alone, that his soul should ever decline, or be averse to any thing which becomes the rational and social nature.

8. In the well-disciplined and purified mind you will find nothing putrid, impure, or unsound. Fate can never surprise his life unfinished, as one says of a tragedian who goes off before he ends his part: You will find nothing servile or ostentatious, or subjected to others by any partial bond; nor yet broken off from them, by any hatred; nothing which needs correction or concealment.

9. Cultivate with all care that power which forms opinions: All depends on this, that no opinion thy soul entertains, be inconsistent with the nature and constitution of the rational animals. Our natural constitution and furniture is intended to secure us from false and rash assent, to engage us in kindness to all men, and in obedience to the Gods. <84>

10. Quit, therefore, other things, and retain these few. Remember also that each man lives only the present moment: The rest of time is either spent and gone, or is quite unknown. It is a very little time which each man lives, and in a small corner of the earth; and the longest surviving fame is but short, and this conveyed through a succession of poor mortals, each presently a-dying; men who neither knew themselves, nor the persons long since dead.

11. To the former subjoin this further rule: To make an accurate definition or description of every thing which strikes the imagination, so as to view what sort of thing it is in its own nature, and in all its parts considered distinctly; and give it, with thy self, its proper name, and to all the parts in its composition, into which also it must be resolved. Nothing is more effectual for giving magnanimity, than a methodical true examination of every thing which may happen in life, and while you consider them, to revolve at the same time, in what sort of regular universe they happen, for what use they are fit, of what importance they are to the whole, of what to man, the citizen of that higher city, of <85> which the other cities and states are but as families. To examine what that is which affects the mind, of what compounded, how long it can endure, and what virtue it is fit to exercise; such as meekness, fortitude, truth, fidelity, simplicity, contentment, or the rest? We should therefore say of each event, this comes from God; this happens according to that destined contexture and connexion of events, or by conjunction with them in fortune; this comes from one of my own tribe, my kinsman, my friend, ignorant, perhaps, of what is agreeable to nature:

but I am not ignorant of what is so; and, therefore, I must behave toward him with good-will and justice, according to the natural and social law. As to things * indifferent, I pursue them according to their real estimation or value.

12. If, in consequence of right reasoning upon natural principles you discharge your present duty with diligence, resolution, and benignity, without any <86> bye views, and keep unviolated and pure the divinity within you as if just now about to restore it to the Gods who gave it: If you adhere to this without further desires or aversions, completely satisfied in discharging your present offices according to nature, and in the heroic sincerity of all your professions, you will live happily. Now your doing this none can hinder.

13. As † physicians have always their machines and instruments at hand for sudden occasions, so have you always at hand the grand maxims requisite for understanding things divine and human, and for doing every thing, even the most minute, as aware of the connexion between these two. For, neither will you rightly discharge any duty to men, nor any duty to God, if, at the same time, you regard not the connexion between things human and divine.

14. Quit your wandering: for you are neither like to read over again your own commentaries and meditations, or the actions of the ancient Greeks and Romans, or the collections you have made <87> out of the writings of others, which you have been storing up for your old age. Make haste, then, to your proper end: cast away vain hopes and speedily succour yourself if you have that care of yourself; you may at present.

15. Men don't understand how many things are signified by these words, ‡ to steal, to sow, to purchase, to be in tranquillity, to discern what's to be

* Thus the Stoics call all the goods or evils of fortune, relating to our bodies or estates: Which they allowed to have some value, or estimation, or importance, but would not call them absolutely good or evil.[9]

† The same person was physician, chirurgeon, and apothecary among the antient Greeks and Romans.

‡ The Stoics made frequent use of these words metaphorically in their moral reasonings about the virtues and vices of their conduct, and the natural events in the universe. See, B. IV. 36. for one Instance.

done. The bodily eye sees not these things: another sort of sight must discern them.

16. The body, the * animal soul, the intellectual. To the body belong the senses: to the animal soul, the appetites and passions: to the intellectual, the maxims of life. To have sensible impressions exciting imaginations, is common to us with the cattle. To be moved, like puppets, by appetites and passions, is common to us with the wild beasts, with the most effeminate wretches, Phalaris,[10] and Nero, with atheists, and with traitors to their country.[11] If these things, then, are common to the lowest and most odious <88> characters, this must remain as peculiar to the good man; to have the intellectual part governing and directing him in all the occurring offices of life; to love and embrace all which happens to him by order of providence; to preserve the divinity placed in his breast, pure, undisturbed by a croud of imaginations, and ever calm and well-pleased, and to follow with a graceful reverence the dictates of it as of a God; never speaking against truth, or acting against justice. And, tho' no man believe he thus lived, with simplicity, modesty, and tranquillity; he neither takes this amiss from any one; nor quits the road which leads to the true end of life; at which he ought to arrive pure, calm, ready to part with life, and accommodated to his lot without reluctance. <89>

* See above, B. II. art. 2.

BOOK IV

1. When the governing part is in its natural state, it can easily change and adapt itself to whatever occurs as the matter of its exercise. It is not fondly set upon any one sort of action. It goes about what seems preferable, with a proper * reservation.[1] And if any thing contrary be cast in, makes this also the matter of its proper exercise. As a fire, when it masters the things which fall on it, tho' they would have extinguished a small lamp: the bright fire quickly assimilates to itself and consumes what is thrown into it, and even thence increases its own strength. <90>

2. Let nothing be done at random, but according to the complete rules of art.

3. They seek retirements in the country, on the sea-coasts, or mountains: you too used to be fond of such things. But this is all from ignorance. A man may any hour he pleases retire into himself; and no where will he find a place of more quiet and leisure than in his own soul: especially if he has that furniture within, the view of which immediately gives him the fullest tranquillity. By tranquillity, I mean the most graceful order. Allow yourself continually this retirement, and refresh and renew your self. Have also at hand some short elementary maxims, which may readily occur, and suffise to wash away all trouble, and send you back without freting at any of the

* The word here translated reservation, is a noted one among the Stoics, often used in Epictetus, Arrian, and Simplicius.[2] It means this, that we be still aware that all external things depend on fortune, and are not in our power; and that our sole good is in our own affections, purposes, and actions: If therefore we meet with external obstacles to our outward actions, we may still retain our own proper good; and can exert proper affections and actions upon these very obstacles; by resignation to God, patience under injury; good-will toward even such as oppose us, and by persisting in any good offices, which remain in our power.

affairs to which you return. What vice of mankind can you be chagrined with, when you recollect the maxim, that "all rational beings were formed for each other"; and that, "bearing with them is a branch of justice," and that, "all mistakes and errors are involuntary," and "how many of those who lived in enmity, suspicion, hatred, and quarrels, have <91> been stretched on their funeral piles, and turned to ashes?" Cease, then, from such passions. Will you fret at that distribution which comes from the whole, when you renew in your remembrance that disjunctive maxim: "either it is providence which disposes of all things, or atoms"; or recollect how many have proved the universe to be a regular state, under one polity. Or will you be touched with what regards your body, when you consider, that the intellectual or governing part, when it once recovers itself, and knows its own power, is not concerned in the impressions made on the animal soul, whether grateful or harsh. Recall, too, all you have heard and assented to, about pleasure and pain. Or shall the little affair of character and glory disturb you, when you reflect how all things shall be involved in oblivion; and the vast immensity of eternal duration on both sides; how empty the noisy echo of applauses; how fickle and injudicious the applauders; how narrow the bounds within which our praise is confined: the earth itself but as a point in the universe: and how small a corner of it the part inhabited: and, even there, how few are they, and of how little worth, who <92> are to praise us! For the future, then, remember to retire into this little part of yourself: Above all things, keep yourself from distraction, and intense desires. Retain your freedom, consider every thing as a man of courage, as a man, as a citizen, as a mortal. Have these two thoughts ever the readiest in all emergencies: one, that "the things themselves reach not to the soul, but stand without, still and motionless. All your perturbation comes from inward opinions about them." The other, that "all these things presently change, and shall be no more." Frequently recollect what changes thou hast observed. The world is a continual change; life is opinion.

4. The intellectual part is the same to all rationals, and therefore that reason also, whence we are called rational, is common to all. If so, then that commanding power, which shews what should be done or not done, is common. If so, we have all a common law. If so, we are all fellow-citizens:

and if so, we have a common city. The universe, then, must be that city; for of what other common city are all men citizens?[3] Hence, therefore, even from this com-<93>mon city, we derive our intellectual power, our reason, our law; as my earthly part is derived to me from some common earth, my moisture from some common element of that kind, my aerial part from its proper fountain, and the warm or fiery part from its proper fountain too. For, nothing can arise from nothing, or return into it. Our intellectual part hath also come from some common fountain of its own nature.

5. Death is, like our birth, a mystery of nature; the one a commixture of elements, the other a resolution into them: In neither is there any thing shameful, or unsuitable to the intellectual nature, or contrary to the intention of its structure.

6. From such men such actions must naturally and necessarily proceed. He who would have it otherwise, may as reasonably expect figs should be without juice. This, too, you should always remember, that in a very short time both you and he must die; and, a little after, not even the name of either shall remain.

7. Take away opinion, and you have removed the complaint, "I am <94> hurt." Remove "I am hurt," and you remove the harm.

8. What makes not a man worse than he was, makes not his life worse; nor hurts him either without or within.

9. 'Tis for some advantage in the whole, that nature acts in this manner.

10. If you attend well, you will find that whatever happens, happens justly. I don't mean only in an exact order and destined connexion, but also according to justice, and from one who distributes according to merit. Go on in observing this, as you have begun: and whatever you do, do it so as you may still remain good, according to the intellectual and true notion of goodness. Observe this in all your actions.

11. Don't entertain such opinions as the man who affronts you has, or wishes you to entertain: but look into these things as they truly are.

12. You should always have these two rules in readiness; one, to act only that which the reason of the royal and legislative faculty suggests for the interests of mankind; the other, to be ready to change your conduct, when any one present can rectify you, and make you quit any of your opinions.

But let this <95> change be always made upon some probable species of justice, or public utility, or such like; and not any view of pleasure, or glory to yourself.

13. Have you reason? I have. Why don't you use it? When it performs its proper office, what more do you require?

14. You have arisen as a part in the universe, you shall disappear again, returning into your source; or, rather, by a change shall be resumed again, into that productive intelligence from whence you came.

15. Many pieces of frankincense are laid on the altar: One falls, then another. And there's no difference, whether sooner or later.

16. Within ten days you'll appear a God to them, who now repute you a wild beast or an ape, if you turn to observe the moral maxims, and to reverence your intellectual part.

17. Don't form designs, as if you were to live a thousand years. Death hangs over you. While you live, while you may, become good.

18. What agreeable leisure does he procure to himself, who takes no notice what others say, do, or intend; but at-<96>tends to this only, that his own actions be just and holy; and, according to Agathon,[4] that there be nothing black or ill-natured in his temper? He ought not to be looking around, but running on the straight line, without turning aside.

19. The man who is solicitous about a surviving fame, considers not that each one of those who remember him, must soon die himself, and so must his successor a little after him, till at last this remembrance be extinguished, which is handed down through a series of stupid perishing admirers. Grant your memory were immortal, and these immortal, who retain it; yet what is that to thee? Not to say, what is that to the dead? but what is it to the living, except * for some further view? In the mean time, you unseasonably quit what nature hath put in your power, by grasping at something else dependent on another.

20. Whatever is beautiful or honourable, is so from itself, and its excellence rests in itself: its being praised is no part of its excellence. It is neither <97> made better nor worse by being praised. This holds too in lower beau-

* The Stoics denyed fame to be desirable, except as it gave opportunities of more extensive good offices.[5]

ties, called so by the vulgar; in material forms, and works of art. What is truly beautiful and honourable, needs not any thing further than its own nature to make it so. Thus, the law, truth, benevolence, a sense of honour. Are any of these made good by being praised? Or, would they become bad, if they were censured? Is an emerauld made worse than it was, if it is not praised? Or, is gold, ivory, purple, a dagger, a flower, a shrub, made worse on this account?

21. If the animal souls remain after death, how hath the aether contained them from eternity? How doth the earth contain so many bodies buried, during so long a time? As in this case the bodies, after remaining a while in the earth, are dissipated and changed, to make room for other bodies, so the animal souls removed to the air, after they have remained some time, are changed, diffused, rekindled, and resumed into the original productive spirit, and give place to others in like manner to cohabit with them. This may be answered, upon supposition that the souls survive their bodies. We may consider, beside <98> the human bodies which are buried, the bodies of so many beasts, which we and other animals feed on. What a multitude of them is thus consumed, and buried in the bodies of those who feed on them, and yet the same places still afford room, by the changes into blood, air and fire. The true account of all these things is by * distinguishing between the material, and the active or efficient principle.

22. Don't suffer the mind to wander. Keep justice in view in every design. And in all imaginations which may arise, preserve the judging faculty safe.

23. Whatever is agreeable to thee, shall be agreeable to me, O graceful universe! Nothing shall be to me too early, or too late, which is seasonable to thee; whatever thy seasons bear, shall be joyful fruits to me, O nature! From thee are all things; in thee they subsist; to thee they return. Could one say, "thou dearly beloved city of Cecrops!" And wilt thou not say, "thou dearly beloved city of God!"[6] <99>

24. "Mind few things," said one, "if you would preserve tranquillity." He might rather have said, mind only what is necessary, and what the reason of the creature formed for social life and public good recommends,

* The author's sentiment here is not well known by the critics. Some make the active principle to be meerly the form.[7]

and in the way it directs. And this will not only secure the tranquillity arising from virtuous action, but that also which arises from having few things to mind. Would we cut off the most part of what we say and do, as unnecessary, we should have much leisure and freedom from trouble. We should suggest to ourselves on every occasion this question; is this necessary? But we ought to quit, not only unnecessary actions, but even imaginations; and, thus, superfluous actions, diverting us from our purpose, would not ensue.

25. Make trial how the life of a good man would succeed with you, of one who is pleased with the lot appointed him by providence, and satisfied with the justice of his own actions, and the benevolence of his dispositions.

26. You have seen the other state, try also this. Don't perplex yourself. Has any man sinned or offended? The hurt is to himself. Hath any thing succeeded <100> with you honourably? Whatever befalls you was ordained for you, by the providence of the whole, and spun out to you by the destinies. To sum up all, life is short. You must make the best use of the present time, by a true estimation of things, and by justice: and retain sobriety in all relaxations.

27. Either there is an orderly well disposed universe, or a mixture of parts cast together, without design, which, yet, make an orderly composition. Or, can there subsist in thee a regular structure, and yet no regular constitution be in the universe? and that when we see such very different natures blended together, with conspiring harmony?[8]

28. Consider the deformity of these characters, the black or malicious, the effeminate, the savage, the beastly, the childish, the foolish, the crafty, the buffoonish, the faithless, the tyrannical.

29. He is a foreigner, and not a citizen of the world, who knows not what is in it; and he too, who knows not what ordinarily happens in it. He is a deserter, who flies from the governing reason in this polity. He is blind, whose intellectual eye is closed. He is the beggar, who always needs something from <101> others, and has not from himself all that is necessary for life. He is an abscess of the world, who withdraws or separates himself from the reason which presides in the whole, by repining at what befalls: That same nature produces this event which produced thee. He is the seditious

citizen, who * separates his private soul from that one common soul of which all rational natures are parts.

30. One acts the philosopher without a coat, and another without any books; and a third half-naked. Says one, I have not bread, and yet I adhere to reason. Says another, I have not even the spiritual food of instruction, and yet I adhere to it.

31. Delight yourself in the little art you have learned, and acquiesce in <102> it. And spend the remainder of your life, as one who with all his heart commits all his concerns to the Gods; and neither acts the tyrant or the slave, toward any of mankind.

32. Recollect, for example, the times of Vespasian;[9] you will see all the same things you see now. Men marrying, bringing up children, sickening, dying, fighting, feasting, trading, farming, flattering, obstinate in their own will, suspicious, undermining their neighbours, wishing the death of others, repining at their present circumstances, courting mistresses, hoarding up, pursuing consulships and kingdoms: This life of theirs is past, and is no more. Come down to Trajan's days;[10] you'll see the same things again: That life too is past. Consider other periods of time, and other nations, and see how many, after their keen pursuits of such kinds, presently fell, and were dissolved into their elements. But chiefly represent to your mind those whom you yourself knew vainly distracted with such pursuits, and quitting that course which suited the structure of their nature, not adhering to it, nor contented with it. But you must also remember, that, in each action, there is a <103> care suited and proportioned to the importance of the affair: And thus you'll not be disgusted, that you are not allowed to be employed longer than is proper, about matters of less value.

* All vice is such a separation, as the Stoics define virtue to be an agreement or harmony with "nature" in our affections and actions. They tell us this nature is two-fold, the common nature presiding in the universe, or the deity, and the individual or proper nature in each one. We conform to the common nature, by acquiescence in all events of providence, and by acting the part which the structure of our proper nature requires and recommends, especially the governing part of it, we at once conform to both the common nature and the proper; since our constitution was framed by God, the common nature.

33. Words formerly the most familiar are now grown obscure, and in like manner, the names of such as were once much celebrated, are now become obscure, and need explication; such as, Camillus, Caeso, Volesus, Leonnatus; soon after them, Scipio, Cato; and then Augustus; after him, Hadrian, and Antonine.[11] All things hasten to an end, shall speedily seem old fables, and then be buried in oblivion. This I say of those who have shone in high admiration. The rest of men, as soon as they expire, are unknown and forgotten. And then, what is this eternal memory? 'Tis wholly vain and empty. About what then should we employ our diligence and solicitude? This alone, that our souls be just, our actions social, our speech entirely sincere, and our disposition such as may chearfully embrace whatever happens; as being necessary; as well known; and as flowing from such springs and causes. <104>

34. Resign yourself willingly to your destiny, allowing it to involve you in what matters it pleases.

35. All things are transitory, and, as it were, but for a day; both those who remember; and the things, and persons remembred.

36. Observe continually, that all things exist in consequence of changes. Enure yourself to consider that the nature of the universe delights in nothing more than in changing the things now existing, and in producing others like them. The things now existing are a sort of seed to those which shall arise out of them. You may conceive that there are no other seeds than those that are cast into the earth or the womb; but such a mistake shews great ignorance.

37. You must die presently, and yet you have not attained to the * true simplicity and tranquillity; nor to that freedom from all suspicion of hurt by external things; nor have you that kind affection toward all; nor do you place your <105> true wisdom solely in a constant practice of justice.

38. † Look well into their governing part, and their cares, what things they study to avoid, and what they pursue.

* This simplicity is one constant stable purpose, or acting according to the will of God, that part he has pointed out to be good and suited to the dignity of our nature.[12]

† This is designed to abate our desire of esteem from weak injudicious men; not, to recommend a prying into the business or characters of others.

39. Thy evil cannot have its subsistence in the soul of another; nor in any change or alteration of the body which surrounds thee. Where, then? In that part of thee, which forms opinions concerning evils. Let this part form no such opinions, and all is well. Tho' this poor body, which is nearest to thee, be cut, or burned, or suppurated, or mortify, let the opinionative power be quiet; that is, let it judge that, what may equally befall a good man or a bad, can be neither good or evil. For what equally befalls one who lives according to nature, and one who lives against it, can neither be * according to nature, nor against it.[13] <106>

40. Consider always this universe as one living being or animal; with one material substance, and one spirit; and how all things are referred to the sense of this spirit; and how it's will accomplishes all things, and how the whole concurs to the production of every thing; and what a connexion and contexture there is among all things.

41. "Thou art a poor spirit, carrying a dead carcase about with thee," says Epictetus.[14]

42. There is no evil befalls the things which suffer a change; nor any good in arising into being from a change.

43. Time is a river, or violent torrent of things coming into being; each one, as soon as it has appeared, is swept off and disappears, and is succeeded by another, which is swept away in its turn.

44. Whatever happens, is as natural, and customary, and known, as a rose in the spring, or fruit in summer. Such are diseases, deaths, calumnies, treache-<107>ries, and all which gives fools either joy or sorrow.

45. Things subsequent are naturally connected with those which preceeded: They are not as numbers of things independent of each other, yet necessarily succeeding; but they are in a regular connexion. And as things now existing are joined together in the most apposite contexture; so, those which ensue, have not barely a necessary succession, but a wonderful suitableness and affinity to what preceeded.

* That is, such things are neither agreeable nor contrary to the nature of the rational soul, or the divine part: nor are they either its good or its evil. But when one speaks of the whole animal, made up also of an animal soul and a body, these things are agreeable or contrary to this compound, and this the Stoics strongly assert against the Pyrrhonists. See, Cicero de finib. l. 3. c. 5. 6. but they would not call them good or evil.[15]

46. Remember always the doctrine of Heraclitus, that "the * death of the earth, is its becoming water; that of water its becoming air; that of air, its becoming fire. And so back again."[16] Think of † him who forgot whither the road led him: And that men are frequently at variance with that reason or intelligence, with which they have always to do, and which governs the universe: and are surprised at those things <108> as strange, which they meet with every day. That we ought not to speak or act like men asleep; (for even in sleep we seem to speak and act); nor like children; merely because we have been so instructed by our parents.

47. If any God would assure you, you must die either to morrow, or the next day at farthest, you would little matter whether it were to morrow or the day after; unless you were exceedingly mean-spirited: for how trifling is the difference? Just so, you should repute it of small consequence, whether you are to die in extreme old age, or to morrow.

48. Consider frequently how many physicians, who had often knit their brows on discovering the prognostics of death in their patients, have at last yielded to death themselves: And how many astrologers, after foretelling the deaths of others, with great ostentation of their art; and how many philosophers, after they had made many long dissertations upon death and immortality; how many warriors, after they had slaughtered multitudes; how many tyrants, after they had exercised their power of life and death with horrid pride, as if they had <109> been immortal; nay, how many whole cities, if I may so speak, are dead: Helice, Pompeij, Herculanum,[17] and others innumerable. Then run over those whom, in a series, you have known, one taking care of the funeral of another, and then buried by a third, and all this in a short time. And, in general, all human affairs are mean, and but for a day. What yesterday was a trifling embryo, to morrow shall be an embalmed carcase, or ashes. Pass this short moment of time according to nature, and depart contentedly; as the full ripe olive falls of its own accord, applauding the earth whence it sprung, and thankful to the tree that bore it.

* See above, B. II. 4.

† This person or proverbial expression, is unknown. 'Tis applicable to such as either live extempore, without any fixed view or end in life: or to such as in pursuit of apparent goods, are involved in great miseries, by their want of consideration.

49. Stand firm like a promontory, upon which the waves are always breaking. It not only keeps its place, but stills the fury of the waves. [Wretched am I, says one, that this has befallen me. Nay, say you, happy I, who, tho' this has befallen me, can still remain without sorrow, neither broken by the present, nor dreading the future. The like might have befallen any one; but every one could not have remained thus undejected. Why should the event be called a misfortune, rather than this strength of mind <110> a felicity? But, can you call that a misfortune, to a man, which does not frustrate the intention of his nature? Can that frustrate the intention of it, or hinder it to attain its end, which is not contrary to the will or purpose of his nature; What is this will or purpose? Sure you have learned it. Doth this event hinder you to be just, magnanimous, temperate, prudent, cautious of rash assent, free from error, possessed of a sense of honour and modesty, and of true liberty; or from meriting those other characters, which whoever enjoys, hath all his nature requires, as its proper perfection? And then, upon every occasion of sorrow, remember the maxim, that this event is not a misfortune, but the bearing it courageously is a great felicity.][18]

50. 'Tis a vulgar meditation, and yet a very effectual one, for enabling us to despise death; to consider the fate of those who have been most earnestly tenacious of life, and enjoyed it longest. What have they obtained more than those who died early? They are all lying dead some where or other. Caedicianus, Fabius, Julian, Lepidus,[19] and such like, who carried out the corpses of multitudes, have been carried out <111> themselves. In sum, how small is the difference of time! and that spent amidst how many troubles! among what worthless men! and in what a mean carcase! Don't think it of consequence. Look backward on the immense antecedent eternity, and forward into another immensity. How small is the difference between a life of three days, and of three ages like Nestor's?[20]

51. Haste on in the shortest way. The shortest way is that according to nature. Ever speak and act what is most sound and upright. This resolution will free you from much toil, and warring, and artful management, and dissimulation, and ostentation. <112>

BOOK V

1. When you find yourself, in a morning, averse to rise, have this thought at hand: I arise to the proper business of a man: And shall I be averse to set about that work for which I was born, and for which I was brought into the universe? Have I this constitution and furniture of soul granted me by nature, that I may lye among bed-cloaths and keep my self warm? But, say you, This state is the pleasanter. Were you then formed for pleasure, and not at all for action, and exercising your powers? Don't you behold the vegetables, the little sparrows, the ants, the spiders, the bees, each of them adorning, on their part, this comely world, as far as their powers can go? And will you decline to act your part as a man for this purpose? Won't you run to that which suits your nature? But, say you, must we not take rest? You must: but nature appoints a measure to it, as it has to eating and drinking. In rest you are going beyond these measures; beyond what is sufficient: but in action, you have <113> not come up to the measure; you are far within the bounds of your power: you don't then love yourself; otherwise, you would have loved your own nature, and its proper will or purpose. Other artificers, who love their respective arts, can even emaciate themselves by their several labours, without due refreshments of bathing or food: but you honour your nature and its purpose much less than the Turner does his art of turning, or the dancer does his art, the covetous man his wealth, or the vain man his applause. All these when struck with their several objects, don't more desire to eat or sleep, than to improve in what they are fond of. And do social affectionate actions appear to you meaner, and deserving less diligence and application?

2. How easy is it to thrust away and blot out every disturbing imagination, not suited to nature; and forthwith to enjoy perfect tranquillity?

3. Judge no speech or action unsuitable to you, which is according to nature; and be not dissuaded from it, by any ensuing censure or reproach of others. But if the speaking or acting thus be honourable, don't undervalue yourself so much as to think you <114> are unworthy to speak or act thus. These censurers have their own governing parts, and their own inclinations, which you are not to regard, or be diverted by. But go on straight in the way pointed out by your own nature, and the common nature of the whole. They both direct you to the same road.

4. I walk on in the path which is according to nature, till I fall down to rest, breathing out my last breath into that air I daily drew in, falling into that earth whence my father derived his seed, my mother her blood, my nurse her milk for my nourishment; that earth which supplied me for so many years with meat and drink, and bears me walking on it, and so many ways abusing it.

5. You cannot readily gain admiration for acuteness: be it so. But there are many other qualities, of which you can't pretend you are naturally incapable. Approve yourself in those which are in your power, sincerity, gravity, patient diligence, contempt of pleasure, an heart never repining at providence, contentment with a little, good-nature, freedom, a temper unsolicitous about superfluities, shunning even superfluous talk; and in true grandeur of mind. Don't <115> you observe what a number of virtues you might display; for which you have no pretence of natural incapacity? And yet you voluntarily come short of them. Does any natural defect force you to be querulous at providence? to be tenacious and narrow-hearted? to flatter? to complain of the body, and charge your own faults on it? to fawn on others? to be ostentatious? to be so unsettled in your purposes and projects? No, by the Gods! you might have escaped those vices long ago. One charge, perhaps, of a slow and tardy understanding, you could not well avoid; but in this, diligence and exercise, might have helped the defect; if you had not neglected it, * nor taken a mean pleasure in it.

6. There are some, who, when they have done you a good office, are apt to charge it to your account, as a great obligation. Others are not apt thus

* The reading of the text here is uncertain.

to charge it to you, yet secretly look upon you as much indebted to them, and know sufficiently the value of what they have done. A third sort seem not to know what they have done; but are like the vine, which produces its bunches of grapes, and seeks no more when it hath yielded its proper <116> fruit. The horse, when he hath run his course, the hound, when he has followed the track, the bee, when it has made its honey, and the Man, when he hath done good to others, don't make a noisy boast of it, but go on to repeat the like actions, as the vine in its season produces its new clusters again. We ought to be among those, who, in a manner, seem not to understand what they have done. Well, but ought we not, say you, to understand this point? Is it not the property of the social being, to understand that it acts the social part? nay, by Jove! to desire too, that its partners and fellows should be sensible it acts thus? What you say is true. Yet if you misapprehend what I said above, you shall remain in one of the former classes, who are led aside from the highest perfection, by some probable specious reasons. But if you desire fully to comprehend what I said, don't be afraid that it will ever retard you in any social action.

7. This is a prayer of the Athenians, "rain, rain, kind Jupiter! upon the tilled grounds and pastures of the Athenians." We should either not pray at all, or pray with such simplicity, and <117> such kind affections of free citizens toward our fellows.

8. As, when 'tis said, that, Aesculapius[1] hath prescribed to one a course of riding, or the cold bath, or walking bare-footed; so it may be said, that the nature presiding in the whole, hath prescribed to one a disease, a maim, a loss of a child, or such like. The word "prescribed," in the former case, imports that he enjoined it as conducing to health; and in the latter too, whatever befalls any one, is appointed as conducive to the purposes of fate or providence. Our very word for * happening to one, is, to go together appositely, as the squared stones in walls or pyramids, are said by the workmen, to fall or join together, and suit each other in a certain position. Now, there is one grand harmonious composition of all things; and as the regular universe is formed such a complete whole of all the particular bodies, so the universal destiny or fate of the whole, is made a complete cause out of

* *συμβαίνειν*.[2]

all the particular causes. The very vulgar understand what I say. They tell you, "fate ordered this event for <118> such a one, and this was prescribed or appointed for him." Let us understand this even as when we say, "the physician has ordered such things for the patient": for, he prescribes many harsh disagreeable things; which, yet, we embrace willingly, for the sake of health. Conceive, then, the accomplishing and completing the purposes of the universal nature, to be in the universe, what your health is to you, and thus embrace whatever happens, altho' it should appear harsh and disagreeable: because it tends to the health of the universe, to the prosperity and felicity of Jupiter in his administration. He never had permitted this event, had it not conduced to good. We see not any particular nature aiming at or admitting what does not suit the little private system, in which it presides. Should you not on these two accounts embrace and delight in what ever befalls you; one is, that it was formed, and prescribed, and adapted for you, and destined originally by the most venerable causes; the other, that it is subservient to the prosperity, and complete administration of that mind, which governs the whole; nay, by Jupiter! to the stability and permanence of <119> the whole. For, the whole would be maimed and imperfect, if you broke off any part of this continued connexion, either of parts or causes. Now, you break this off, and destroy it, as far as you can, when you repine at any thing which happens.

9. Don't fret, despond, or murmur, if you have not always opportunities as you desire, of acting according to the right maxims. If you are beat off from them, return to them again; and content yourself that your actions are generally such as become a man; and rejoice in these good offices to which you return. Don't return to philosophy with reluctance, as to a severe tutor, but as to your medicine; as one who has tender eyes, flies to the * sponge and the egg; as another flies to plaisters, a third to fomentation. You should require no more than being conscious that you have obeyed reason, and rest yourself in this. Remember that philosophy requires no other things than what your nature requires. But you are often wanting something different. What can be easier and sweeter than these things, which are agreeable to <120> nature? Sensual enjoyments by their pleasure insnare

* A common medicine for tender eyes.

us. But consider, can there be any thing sweeter than magnanimity, liberty, or self-command, simplicity of heart, meekness, purity? What is sweeter than wisdom, when you are conscious of success and security from error in what belongs to the intellectual and scientific powers?

10. The natures of things are so covered up from us, that, to many philosophers, and these no mean ones, all things seem uncertain and incomprehensible. The Stoics themselves own it to be very difficult to comprehend any thing certainly. All our Judgments are fallible. Where is the infallible man, who never changes his opinion? Consider the objects of our knowledge; how transitory are they, and how mean! how often are they in the possession of the most effeminately flagitious, or of a whore, or a robber! Review again the manners of your contemporaries, they are scarce tolerable to the most courteous and meek disposition; not to mention that few can well comport with their own manners, but are often angry with themselves. Amidst such darkness and filth, and this perpetual flux of substance, of time, of <121> motions, and of the things moved, I see nothing worthy of our esteem or solicitude. On the contrary, the hopes of our natural dissolution should be our consolation, and make us bear with patience the time of our sojourning among them: refreshing ourselves with these thoughts; first, that nothing can befall us but what is according to the nature of the whole: and then, that it is always in our power, never to counteract the Deity or Genius within us: to this no force can compell us.

11. To what purposes am I now using my animal powers? This should be matter of frequent self-examination: As also, what are the views and purposes of that governing part, as we call it? What sort of soul have I? of what character? Is it that of a trifling child? of a passionate youth? of a timorous woman? of a tyrant? of a tame beast, or a savage one?

12. Of what value the things are, which many repute as good, you may judge from this; If one previously conceives the true goods, prudence, temperance, justice, fortitude, he cannot bear any thing attributed to them which does not naturally agree to the true <122> kinds of good. But one thinking of what the vulgar repute as good, can patiently hear, and will with pleasure entertain as proper to the subject, that known raillery of the comic poet.[3] And thus even the vulgar conceive the preeminence of the former; otherwise, they would not be offended with the application of that

jest to them, and reject it as unworthy of the subject. But we all relish that jest, when 'tis applied to riches, and all the possessions subservient to luxury, as being suitable to the subject, and humourously expressed. Go on, then, and ask yourself, are these things to be honoured and reputed as good, which, when we consider, we can yet deem it proper raillery to apply to the possessor, the jest, "that he has such abundance of finery around him on all sides, he can find no place where he can ease himself."

13. I consist of an active and a material principle. Neither of these shall return to nothing; as they were not made out of nothing. Shall not, then, every part of me be disposed, upon its dissolution, into the correspondent part of the universe; and that, again, be changed into some other part of the uni-<123>verse; and thus to eternity? By such changes I came into being, and my parents too, and their progenitors, from another eternity. We may assert this, * tho' the world be governed by certain grand determined periods of dissolution and renovation.[4]

14. Reason, and the art of the rational agent, are powers which are satisfied with themselves and their own proper action, (without the aid of what is external or foreign to them). They act from their internal principle, and go straight forward to the end set before them. The actions are called right, or straight, from their straight road to their end. †

15. None of these things should be deemed belonging to a man as his perfection, which don't belong to him as he is a man; which can't be demanded <124> of him as a man; which the structure of his nature does not undertake for; and which do not perfect his nature. The supreme end or happiness of man, cannot, therefore, consist in such things, nor be completed by them. Did any such things belong to man as his perfection, it would never be a suitable perfection in him to despise and oppose them; nor would he be commendable for making himself independent of them,

* The Stoics seem to have believed a series of great periodical conflagrations, from all eternity, by which the material world and the grosser elements, were rarified and absorbed again into the pure aether, which they deemed to be the Deity; and recreated again out of this eternal original substance: and that these alternate creations and conflagrations, were from eternity: and from the one to the other, was the great philosophic year.

† Viz. acting according to our nature, be the external event what it will. See, B. IV. 37.

and not needing them. Were they truly good, it would never be the part of a good man to quit or abate his share of them. But the more one remits of his share of certain things reputed good, the more patiently he bears being deprived of them by others, the better we must esteem the man to be.

16. Such as the imaginations are which you frequently dwell upon, such will be the disposition of your soul. The soul receives a tincture from the imagination. Tincture thy soul deeply by such thoughts as these continually present that, wherever one may live, he may live well: one may live in a court, and, therefore, one may live well in it. Again, whatever one's natural structure and powers are fitted for, 'tis for this purpose he is designed; and by <125> a natural impulse is carried to it; and his supreme end is placed in that to which he is thus carried. In this end consists his advantage, and his good. The good of a rational creature is in society; for, we have long ago demonstrated, that we were formed for society. Nay, was it not manifest, that the inferior kinds were formed for the superior, and the superior for each other? Now, the inanimate are inferior to the animated; and the merely animated are inferior to the rational.[5]

17. 'Tis the part of a mad-man to pursue impossibilities. Now, 'tis * im-<126>possible the vicious should act another part than that we see them act.

18. Nothing can befall any man, which he is not capable by nature to bear. The like events have befallen others; and they, either through ignorance that the event hath happened, or through ostentation of magnanim-

* That is, during these their present opinions, dispositions, habits, and confused imaginations: all which they have fallen into according to that plan, which infinite wisdom originally concerted for the most excellent purposes; seeing it to be necessary, that there should be very different orders of being, some more, some less perfect; that many particular evils must be connected with the necessary means of incomparably superior good; that these imperfections and evils are prerequisite to the exercise of the most divine virtues, in the more perfect orders of beings; which must be the ground of their eternal joy: and that many evils are even requisite means of reclaiming the less perfect beings from their vices, and setting them upon the pursuit of their truest happiness. Such thoughts must repress ill-will and all anger against the vicious; but don't hinder our discerning the misery and deformity of vice. And a Stoic allows the vicious could refrain from their vices, if they heartily inclined to do so.

ity, stand firm and unhurt by them. Strange! then, that ignorance or ostentation should have more power than wisdom!

19. The things themselves * cannot in the least touch the soul; nor have any access to it; nor can they turn or move it. The soul alone can turn or move itself; and such judgments or opinions, <127> as she condescends to entertain, such she will make all occurrences become to her self.[6]

20. In one respect, men are the most dearly attached to us, as we are ever obliged to do good to them: but in another respect, as they sometimes obstruct us in our proper offices, they are to be reputed among things indifferent, no less than the sun, the wind, or a savage beast; for, any of these may obstruct us in the discharge of our proper external offices; but, none of them can obstruct our purpose, or our dispositions, because of that † reservation and power of turning our course. For the soul can convert and change every impediment of its first intended action, into a more excellent object of action; and thus 'tis for its advantage to be obstructed in action; and it advances in its road, by being stopped in it.

21. Reverence that which is most excellent in the universe; which employs all parts of it as it pleases, and governs all. In like manner, reverence that which is most excellent in yourself. Now, this is of a like nature with the former, as it <128> is what employs and directs all other powers in your nature; and your whole life is governed by it.

22. What is not hurtful to the ‡ state or city, cannot hurt the citizen. Make use of this rule upon every conception of any thing as hurting you.

* The Stoics, after Plato, seem to conceive the rational soul, in which, our judgments, opinions, and calm purposes of action subsist, to be a being or substance distinct both from the gross body, and the animal soul, in which are the sensations, lower appetites and passions. The rational soul, say they, is the man; the seat of true perfection and happiness; or, of misery; and of a durable nature, capable of subsisting separated from the other two parts; and of commanding all their motions, during this union with them, or imprisonment in them; capable of performing its proper, natural, lovely, beatific offices, independent of these lower parts; nay, of making the adverse accidents, which befall them, the occasion, or matter, of its most excellent beatific exercises.

† See, B. IV. 1. As also the note upon the preceeding section in this book.

‡ This city is the universe. A mind entirely conformed and resigned to God, the great governour of this city, and persuaded of his wisdom, power, and goodness, cannot imagine any event to be hurtful to the universe; and when it is united in will with God, it

If the city is not hurt by it, I cannot be hurt. If the city should receive hurt by it, yet we should not be angry at him who hurt it, but * shew him what he has neglected, or how he has done wrong.[7]

23. Consider frequently, how swiftly all things which exist, or arise, are swept away, and carried off. Their substance is as a river in a perpetual course. Their actions are in perpetual changes, and the causes subject to ten thousand <129> alterations. Scarce any thing is stable. And the vast eternities, past and ensuing, are close upon it on both hands; in which all things are swallowed up. Must he not, then, be a fool, who is either puffed up with success in such things; or is distracted, and full of complaints about the contrary; as if it could give disturbance of any duration?

24. Remember how small a part you are of the universal nature; how small a moment of the whole duration is appointed for you; and how † small a part you are of the object of universal fate, or providence.

25. Does any one injure me? Let him look to it. He hath his own disposition, and his own work. I have that disposition, which the common president nature wills me to have, and act that part, which my own nature recommends to me.

26. Keep the governing part of the soul ‡ unmoved by the grateful or painfull commotions of the flesh; and let it <130> not blend itself with the body; but circumscribe and seperate itself; and confine these passions to those bodily parts. When they ascend into the soul, by means of that sympathy constituted by its union with the body, there is no withstanding of the sensation which is natural. But let not the governing part add also its opinion concerning them, as if they were good or evil.

27. We should live a divine life with the Gods. He lives with the Gods, who displays before them his soul, pleased with all they appoint for him,

---

must acquiesce in all that happens, and can make all events good to itself, as they are occasions of exerting the noblest virtues, which are its supreme good.

* This is an impossible supposition, but the sentiment just, according to the Stoic opinion; see the note on art. 17. of this book.

† And thence you'll see how just and merciful it may be, to subject your little transitory interests, to those of the great universe, and to that plan of providence, which is fittest for the whole.

‡ See, art. 19. of this book.

and doing whatever is recommended by that divinity within, which Jupiter hath * taken <131> from himself, and given each one as the conductor, and leader of his life. And this is the intellectual principle and reason in each man.

28. Can you be angry at one, whose arm-pits or whose breath are disagreeable? How can the man help it, who has such a mouth or such armpits? They must have a smell. But, says one, man has reason: he could by attention, discern what is injurious in his actions; [these may justly raise anger.] Well, God bless you, you have this reason too. Rouse then his rational dispositions, by your rational dispositions; instruct, suggest to him, what is right. If he listens to you, you have cured him, and then there is no occasion for anger. Let us have no tragical exclamations against the vices and injuries of others; nor a base concurrence with them, like that of harlots.

29. You may live at present in the same way you would chuse to be living, when you knew your death was approaching. If you are hindered to do so, then you may quit life; and yet without conceiving the quiting it as evil. If my house be smoaky, I go out of it; and where is the great matter? While no such thing forces me out, I stay as <132> free; and who can hinder me to act as I please? But my pleasure is, to act as the rational and social nature requires.

30. The soul of the universe is kind and social. It has, therefore, made the inferior orders for the sake of the superior; and has suited the superior beings for each other. You see how it hath subordinated, and co-ordinated,

* The Stoics conceived the divine substance, to be an infinitely diffused and all-pervading aether, the seat of all wisdom, power and goodness: and that our souls were small particles of this aether: and that even those of brutes were particles of the same, more immersed and entangled in the grosser elements. *Divinae particulam aurae.* HORACE.[8]

Esse apibus partem divinae mentis, & haustus
Aetherios, dixere. Deum namque ire per omnes
Terrasque tractusque maris, coelumque profundum:
Hinc pecudes, armenta, viros, genus omne ferarum;
Quemque sibi tenues nascentem arcessere vitas:
Scilicet huc reddi, deinde, & resoluta referri
Omnia ———

Virg. Geor. IV. 220.[9] See also,
Aeneid. VI. 724. to 746.[10]

and distributed to each according to its merit, and engaged the nobler beings into a mutual agreement and unanimity.

31. [Examine yourself thus:] how have you behaved toward the Gods, toward your parents, your brothers, your wife, your children, your teachers, those who educated you, your friends, your intimates, your domestics? Have you never said or done any thing unbecoming, toward any of them?[11] Recollect through how many affairs of life you have past, and what offices you have been able to sustain and discharge. The history of your life, and of your * publick service to the Gods, is not completed. What beautiful and honourable things are seen in your life? What pleasures and what <133> pains have you despised? What occasions of vain ostentation have you designedly omitted? Toward how many perverse unreasonable creatures, have you † exercised discretion and lenity?

32. Why should the instructed, the intelligent, and skilful soul be disturbed by the rude and illiterate? What soul is truly skilful and intelligent? ‡ That which knows the cause and the end of all things, and that reason which pervades all substances in all ages, and governs the whole universe by § certain determined periods.

33. Presently you shall be only ashes and dry bones, and a name; or, perhaps, not even a name. A name is but a certain noise or sound, or echo. The things most honoured in life are but vain, rotten, mean; little dogs snapping at each other; children squabling and vying with each other; laughing, and presently weeping again. But integrity, modesty, justice, and truth, ** "From the wide range of earth have soar'd to heaven." What, then, should detain thee here? Since all things sensible are <134> in perpetual change, without any stability: The senses themselves but dull, and apt to admit false appearances: The animal life, but an exhalation from blood: To have reputation among such animals, is a poor empty thing. Why, then, should you not wait patiently for either your extinction, or translation into

* Observe here the same divine sentiment with the Apostle; that whatever we do in word or deed, we should do it as to God.

† Here he is recommending not only forgiveness, but the returning good for evil.

‡ The knowledge of God and his providence, is the true wisdom.

§ See above, B. V. 13.

** Hesiod. I. 195.[12]

another state? And, till the proper season for it comes, what should suffise thee? To reverence and praise the Gods, and to do good to men, bearing with their weakness, abstaining from injuries,[13] and considering external things subservient to thy poor body and life, as what are not thine, nor in thy power.

34. You may always be prosperous, if you go on in the right way, in right opinions and actions. These two advantages are common to Gods, to men, and every rational soul; one, that they can * be hindered by nothing external; the other, that they have their † proper good or happiness in their just disposi-<135>tions, and actions, and can make their desires terminate and cease here, without extending further.

35. If this event be neither any vice of mine, nor any action from any vitious disposition of mine, nor be hurtful to the whole, why am I disturbed by it. Nay, who can hurt the whole?

36. Don't let your imagination hurry you away incautiously in any seeming distress of your friend. Assist him to the utmost of your power, as far as he deserves in these ‡ indifferent sorts of things; but, don't imagine that he has sustained any evil. There is no evil in such things. But, as in the § comedy,[14] the old foster-father asks from the child, with great earnestness, his top, as a token of his love, tho' he knew well it was a childish toy; just so, you must act in life about the toys which others value. When you are vehemently declaiming from the rostrum, should one say to <136> you, "What, man, have you forgot the nature of these things you are so keen

* See above, B. V. 19. and B. IV. 1.

† *Quae vobis, quae digna, viri, pro talibus ausis,*
Praemia posse rear solvi? pulcherrima primum
Di, moresque dabunt vestri.
Aeneid. IX. 253.[15]

Di tibi, &c.
Et mens sibi conscia recti,
Praemia digna ferent. Aeneid. I. 607.[16]

‡ The Stoics called all external advantages or disadvantages, respecting the body or fortune, things indifferent, neither good, nor evil; but they allowed this difference among them, that some were according to nature, and preferable; others contrary to nature, and to be rejected.

§ This comedy is not known.

about." Nay, say you, "tho' I have not forgot it, yet I know these are matters of serious concern to others"; and, therefore, you do well to act thus. But take care you don't in your own sentiments become a fool, because others are fools. You may so manage, that, in whatever place or time one comes upon you, you may be found a man of an happy lot. He has the happy lot, who distributes one to himself. The happy lots are good dispositions of soul, good desires and purposes, and good actions. <137>

BOOK VI

1. The matter of the universe is obedient, and easily changed: the intelligence, which governs it, has no cause in itself, of doing evil to any. It has no malice; nor can it do any thing maliciously; nor is any one hurt by it. It is the cause of all that happens, as it executes all things.

2. Provided you act the part that becomes you, let it be of no account with you, whether you do it shivering with cold, or agreeably warm; whether drousy through long watching, or refreshed with sleep; whether in good report, or bad report; whether by dying, or by any other action. For, dying is one piece of the natural business of every living creature. 'Tis sufficient, then, if it be well performed.

3. Look narrowly into things. Let not the proper quality, or dignity, of any thing, escape your observation.

4. All things now existing shall speedily be changed, either * by exhaling <138> and rarifying, if all be one substance; or be dissolved and dispersed into the several elements.

5. The governing mind in the universe, knows its own dispositions and actions, and the nature of that matter it is acting upon.

6. The best sort of revenge, is, not to become like the injurious.

7. Delight thy self in this one thing, and rest in it; to be going from one kind social action to another, with remembrance of God.[1]

8. The governing part is that which rouses, and turns, and forms itself, such as it chuses to be; and makes every event appear such to itself, as it inclines.

* See above, B. V. 13. Others of the antients believed, there were four original immutable elements, out of which all compound bodies were formed, and into which they were resolved.

9. All things are accomplished by the nature presiding in the whole; nor can they be influenced by any other, either surrounding it without, or contained as distinct within it, or externally annexed to it.

10. Either the universe is a confused mass and intertexture, soon to be dispersed; or one orderly whole, under a providence. If the former; why should I wish to stay longer in this confused mix-<139>ture; or be solicitous about any thing, further than "* how to become earth again"? Or, why should I be disturbed about any thing? The dispersion will overtake me, do what I please. But, if the latter be the case; then I adore the governour of the whole, I stand firm, and trust in him.

11. When you find yourself forced, as it were into some confusion or disturbance, by surrounding objects, return into yourself as speedily as you can; and depart no more from the true harmony of the soul, than what is absolutely unavoidable. You shall acquire greater power of retaining this harmony, by having frequent recourse to it.

12. Had you, at once, a step-mother, and a mother; tho' you respected the former, yet your constant resort and refuge, would be the latter: Such to you is the court and philosophy. Return often to your true mother, philosophy; and refresh yourself: She will make the affairs of the court tolerable to you, and make you tolerable to those about it.

13. You may revolve such thoughts as these, about the nicest delicacies of sense: about food, this is the dead car-<140>case of a fish, a fowl, a hog: about wine, this is the juice of a little grape: about your purple robes, this is the wool of a sheep, steeped in the blood of a little shell-fish: about venereal enjoyments, they are the attrition of a base part of our body, and a convulsive sort of excretion of a mucus. These conceptions, touching so nearly, and explaining the nature of these subjects, how powerful are they to display to us their despicable value? Thus[2] we should employ the mind, in all parts of life: when things occur, which, at first, seem worthy of high estimation: we should strip them naked, and view their meanness; and cast aside these pompous descriptions of them, by which they seem so glorious. External pomp and high language, are great sophisters; and most impose upon us, when we are employed in matters commonly reputed of

* Homer Iliad. 7. 91.[3]

great dignity. Remember * what Crates said, about the solemn gravity of Xenocrates.

14. The objects of vulgar admiration, may be reduced to some general classes. First, such as are preserved by mere cohesion, or, regular, but inanimate structure, or organisation; such as stones, timber, fig-trees, vines, olive-trees. Men, <141> a rank higher, admire things preserved by an animal soul; such as flocks and herds. The admiration of a third and higher class of men, with a more elegant taste, turns upon what is accomplished by a rational soul; not as it is akin to the universal spirit; but as artificial, and otherwise ingenious, and acute; and merely on this account. Thus, numbers of † slaves are valued. But he who honours and admires the rational soul, as universal, and social, or public-spirited, in this universal city, he will despise these other objects of admiration; and, above all things, he will study to preserve his own rational soul, in these social dispositions and affections; and co-operate with those souls which are akin to it, in the same purpose.

15. Some things hasten into being: Some hasten to be no more: Some parts of things in being, are already extinct. These fluxes and changes renew the world; as the constant flux of particular periods of time, ever present to us new parts of the infinite eternity. In this vast <142> river, what is there, among the things swept away with it, that one can value; since it can never be stopped or retained? As if one should grow fond of one of the sparrows, as it flies by us, when it shall be immediately out of sight. Such is the life of each man; an exhalation from blood, ‡ or a breathing in of air: and such as it is to draw in that air, which you are presently to breath out again every minute, such also is this whole power of breathing, which you received, as it were, yesterday, or the day before, when you were born; and must presently restore again to the source whence you derived it.

16. There is little valuable, either in perspiring, like vegetables; or breathing, as cattle, and wild beasts do; or in having sensible impressions made upon the imagination; or in being moved like puppets,[4] by our several passions and appetites; or in mere herding together; or in being nourished.

* This saying is not known.

† Slaves were chiefly valued, according as they had Genius for, and were instructed in the more elegant arts, painting, statuary, sculpture, music, acting, and even medicine.

‡ See, B. II. 2. and the note upon it.

There is nothing in this superior to the discharging again what is superfluous of the food we have taken in. What, then, is valuable? To be received with claps of applause? Not at all. Nor is the applause of tongues <143> more valuable. The praises of the vulgar are nothing but the noise of tongues. If you have, then, quit the pursuit of this trifling sort of glory, what remains as valuable? This one thing, I imagine, * to move, or stop yourself, in all desires or pursuits, according to the proper fabric or structure of your nature: For, this is what all design and art is tending to; this is all its aim, that the thing formed by art, should be adapted to the work it is designed for. This, the planter, and the vine-dresser, the horse-rider, and the breeder of the hound, are in quest of. At what does all education and instruction aim? In this, therefore, is placed all that is valuable. If you succeed well in this, you need not be solicitous to acquire any thing further. Won't you, then, cease to value other things? If you don't, you'll never attain to freedom, self-contentment, independency, or tranquillity: for, you must be enviously and suspiciously vying with those who can deprive you of such things as you highly value; laying snares for those who possesss them; and pining with vexation, when you want them; and even accusing the Gods. But, <144> the † reverencing and honouring your own intellectual part, will make you agreeable to yourself, harmonious with your fellows, and in a perfect concord with the Gods; praising whatsoever they distribute or appoint to men.

17. The elements are tossed upwards, downwards, and all around. The motions of virtue are like none of these; but are of a more divine sort; going on in a way not easily discerned, and ‡ ever prosperous.

18. What strange conduct is this! Some men cannot speak a good word of their contemporaries, with whom they live; [and, one would thence imagine, they could not value being praised by them;] and yet are very solicitous, about gaining the praises of posterity, whom they never saw, nor shall see. This seems as foolish, as to be concerned that we cannot obtain the praises of the ages which preceeded our existence.

* See, IX. 12.

† B. II. 6. and the note upon it.

‡ B. IV. 37. and B. V. 14. and 19. and the notes.

19. If any thing seems exceedingly difficult for you to accomplish, don't conclude it to be impossible to all men: but rather, if you see any thing possible to <145> man, and a part of his proper work, conclude that you also may attain to it.

20. If, in the exercises, one has torn us with his nails, or bruised us accidentally with his head, we express no resentment; we are not offended; nor do we suspect him for the future, as a person secretly designing our destruction: and yet we are on our guard against him; not as an enemy, or a person suspected; but with a good-natured caution, for our own safety. Let us thus behave in all parts of life, and conceive many things thus done, as in the exercises. Let us, as I said, be upon our guard; but without suspicion or enmity.

21. If any one can convince me, or shew me, that my sentiments, or conduct, has been wrong; I will joyfully alter them. 'Tis truth I am searching for, which never hurts any man. But men are often hurt, by remaining in error and ignorance.

22. I endeavour, to do my duty, and what becomes me. Other things don't give me solicitude: They are either inanimate, or irrational; or wandering from the right way, and ignorant of it.

23. I endeavour, as one possessed of reason, to use the brute animals, and <146> all other irrational objects, with magnanimity and freedom; and to act the kind and social part, toward my fellow-men; who enjoy reason as I do. In all things, implore the assistance of the Gods; and repute it of no consequence, for what space of time you shall continue thus employed. Three hours of such a life is sufficient. [As well as the three ages of Nestor.][5]

24. Alexander of Macedon, and his muleteer, when they died, were in a like condition. They were either * resumed into the original productive causes of all things, or † dispersed into the atoms. <147>

* The Stoics spoke doubtfully about a future state,[6] whether the rational souls subsisted as separate intelligences, or were absorbed in the divinity. Many believed a separate existence of good souls for a thousand years, and of the eminently virtuous, for eternity, in the dignity of Gods, which we would call that of angels, with delegated powers of governing certain parts of the universe.

† This later branch, is the Epicurean doctrine, which the Stoics opposed. But they, and the Platonists too, imitating Socrates's manner, generally propose this alternative,

25. Consider, how many different things are done, in each one of our bodies; and in our souls too, in the very same moment; and you will the less wonder, that far more, nay, that all things which now happen, at once exist in this one universal system, we call the world.

26. Should one desire you to spell the name Antoninus, would you not distinctly pronounce to him each one of the letters? Should he turn into any angry dispute about it, would you also turn angry, and not rather mildly count over the several letters to him? Thus, in our present business, our duty consists of a great many numbers, or elements: [according to the many different relations and obligations of each person:] ought we not to observe all these calmly; and, without anger at those who are angry with us, go straight on in executing what is our present business?

27. Is it not cruel, to restrain men from desiring, or pursuing, what appears to them as their proper good or advantage? And yet you seem chargeable in a certain manner with this conduct, when you are angry at the mistakes, and wrong actions of men: for, all are carried toward what appears to them their proper <148> good. But, say you, it is not their proper good. Well: instruct them, then, and teach them better, and don't be angry with them.

28. Death is the cessation of the sensual impressions, of the impulses of the appetites and passions, of the toilsome reasonings, and of the servitude to the flesh.

29. 'Tis very dishonourable in life, that the soul should fail and desert its duty; while the body can hold out, and sustain its part.

30. Take care you don't degenerate into the manners of the Cesars, or be tinctured by them. Preserve your simplicity of manners, goodness, integrity, gravity, freedom from ostentation, love of justice, piety, good nature, kind affection, stedfast firmness in your duty. Endeavour earnestly to continue such as philosophy requires you to be. Reverence the Gods, support the interests of mankind. Life is short. The sole enjoyment of this terrestrial life, is in the purity and holiness of our dispositions, and in kind

---

to shew that, at the very worst, there is no evil in death; that all external things are but mean, since they are of short duration, and are no preservatives against death. And they endeavoured to make virtue eligible, from the very feelings of the heart, abstracting from these their incertain tenets about futurity.[7]

actions. Act as it becomes the scholar of Antoninus Pius.[8] Imitate his constant resolute tenor of rational actions; his equability on all occasions; his sanctity; his serenity of countenance; <149> his sweetness of temper; his contempt of vain glory; and his close attention in examining every thing. Remember how he never quitted any subject, till he had thoroughly examined it, and understood it; and how he bore those who accused him unjustly, without making any angry returns; how he was ever calm without hurry; how he discouraged all accusations; how accurately he inquired into the manners and actions of men; how cautious he was of reproaching any; how free from fear, suspicion, or sophistry; how he was contented with a little, as to his habitation, furniture, dress, table, attendants; how patient he was of labour; how hard to be provoked; he could persist in business till the evening, without easing himself, through his great abstemiousness; how stedfast and evenly he was in his conduct to his friends; and patient of their opposition to his sentiments; and how joyfully he received any better informations from them; how religious he was, without superstitious dread: that thus the hour of death may come upon you, well aware of it, and prepared to meet it; as it came on him.

31. Awake, and call yourself up; and, as you see, when you are fully <150> roused, that these were but dreams which disturbed you; so, when you are awake in the business of life, consider the things which may disturb you, as of a like nature with those which disturbed you in sleep.

32. I consist of a mean body, and a soul. To the body all things are indifferent; for, it cannot distinguish them; and, to the intellectual part, all things are indifferent, which are not its own operations; and all its own operations are in its power; and of these, it is only affected by what are present. Its past and future operations are to it now indifferent.

33. Labour is not contrary to the nature of the hand, or the foot; while the hand is doing the proper work of an hand, and the foot what is proper to the foot. No more is labour contrary to the nature of man, as he is man; while he is doing what suits the nature of a man; and if it be not contrary to his nature, it cannot be evil to him.

34. What great sensual enjoyments may be obtained by robbers, by the most infamously dissolute, by parricides, by tyrants? [Can the happiness of man consist in them?] <151>

35. Don't you see, how common artificers, tho' they may comply to a certain length with the unskilful, yet still adhere to the rules of their art, and can't endure to depart from them? Is it not grievous, that the architect, or the physician, should shew a greater reverence to the rules of their peculiar arts, than the man [as he is rational] shews to the rules of human life; rules which are common to him with the Gods?

36. Asia, Europe, are but little corners of the universe: The whole ocean is but a drop of it: Athos[9] but a little clod. All the time of this present age is but a point of eternity. All things are but little, changeable, and presently to vanish. All things proceed from the universal governing mind, either by direct and primary intention, or by necessary consequence and connexion with things primarily intended. Thus, the horrid jaws of the lion, poisons, and whatever is pernicious, as thorns, as mire, are the consequences of those venerable and lovely things you admire. Don't, therefore, imagine them foreign to that constitution of nature which you reverence; but consider well the fountain of all things. <152>

37. He who sees things present, has seen all things which either have been from eternity, or shall be to eternity; for, all are of the like nature, and similar.

38. Consider frequently the connexion of all things in the universe, and the relation they bear to each other. All things are, as it were, entangled with each other, and are, therefore, mutually friendly. This is a natural consequence, or, in a natural series, with the other; either by connexion of place, or mutual conspiring to the same end, or by continuity of substance.

39. Adapt thy self to those things which are destined for you by providence, and love those men, with whom it is your lot to live, and that with a sincere affection.

40. An instrument, a tool, an utensil, is then right, when it is fit for its work; even tho' the artificer who formed it be gone. But, in the artful works of nature, the artificial power which formed them, remains and resides within them. You ought, therefore, to reverence them the more; and to judge, that, if you are disposed, and conduct yourself according to the intention of this artificial power which formed you, all things are as you <153> should wish. Thus, all things are to the whole, according to its inclination.

41. Whenever you imagine, any of these things which are not in your power, are good or evil to you; if you fall into such imagined evils, or are disappointed of such goods, * you must necessarily accuse the Gods, and hate those men, who, you deem, were the causes, or suspect will be causes of such misfortunes. Our solicitude about such things leads to a great deal of injustice. But, if we judge only the things in our power, to be good or evil, there remains no further cause of accusing the Gods, or of any hostile disposition against men.

42. We are all co-operating to one great work, [The intention of the universal mind in the world;] some, with knowledge and understanding, others, ignorantly, and undesignedly. Thus, I fancy, Heraclitus says, that "men asleep are also then labouring,"[10] accomplishing, on their part, the events of the universe. One contributes to this one way, and another, another way. Nay, what's beyond expectation, even the querulous and the murmurers, who attempt to oppose the course of nature, and to <154> obstruct what happens, contribute also to this purpose: for, † the world must needs have within it such persons also. Think, then, in what class you would wish to rank yourself. The presiding mind will certainly make a right use of you, one way or other; and will inlist you among his labourers and fellow-workers. Don't chuse to be such a part, as, Chrysippus says, a silly ridiculous sentiment expressed by a fool in a comedy makes, which, "of its self is very silly and vitious, but yet is an agreeable part in the play."[11]

43. Does the sun affect to perform the work of the rain, or Aesculapius that of Ceres?[12] The several stars, too, have they not different courses, but all jointly contributing to the same end?

44. If the Gods have taken counsel about me, and the things to befall me, the result of their counsel is certainly good. A God without counsel and providence is inconceivable; and, what could move them to do me any mischief? What advantage could thence accrue, either to themselves, or to the universe, about which they are chiefly concerned? If they have not taken counsel about me in particular, they certainly have about the <155> common interest of the universe. I ought, therefore, to love, and chearfully

* IX. 1.

† IX. 42.[13]

embrace, that which happens in consequence of what is well ordered for the universe. If, indeed, they take no counsel about any thing; which it would be impious to believe; for, then, we might quit sacrifising, prayers, and swearing by them, and all acts of devotion; which we now perform, from a persuasion of their presence, and concern in the affairs of human life: but, grant they took no thought about our affairs; yet, certainly, I may deliberate about myself. My deliberation must be about my true interest. Now, that is the true interest of every one, which is agreeable to the structure of his nature. My natural constitution is that of a rational being, fitted for civil society. My city and country, as I am Antoninus, is Rome; but, as I am a man, 'tis the universe. That alone, therefore, which is profitable to those cities, can be good to me.

45. Whatever happens to any one, is profitable to the whole. This is enough. But, if you attend, you will see this also holds universally; that, what happens to any one man, is profitable also to others. Let the word profitable be * taken, here, <156> in a more popular sense, to relate to things indifferent.

46. As it happens in the theatre and such places of the shows, that the same and like things, always presented, at last cloy us; the same happens in the whole of life: for, all things, earlier or later, are just the same, and from the same causes. How long, then, can we desire to stay gazing on them.

47. Consider frequently, that all men, of all sorts, of all kinds of studies or pursuits, of all nations, have died. Return back to Philistio, Phoebus, and Origanio.[14] Go to other tribes, we must all remove to that place, whither so many great orators, so many venerable philosophers, Heraclitus, Pythagoras, Socrates, and so many heroes, have gone before; and so many generals and princes have followed. Add to these, Eudoxus, Hipparchus, Archimedes,[15] and other acute, sublime, laborious, artful, and arrogant genii; yea, such as have wittily derided this fading mortal life, which is but for a day; such as Menippus,[16] and his brethren. Consider that all these are long since in their graves. And, what is there calamitous in this to them; or

* See, B. II. 1.

<157> even to such obscure men, whose names don't remain? The one thing valuable in this life, is, to spend it in a steddy course of truth, justice, and * humanity, toward even the false and unjust.

48. When you would chear your heart, consider the several excellencies and abilities of your acquaintances; such as, the activity of one, the high sense of honour and modesty in another, the liberality of a third, and other virtues, in others. Nothing rejoyces the heart so much as the appearances or resemblances of the virtues, in the manners of those we converse with, frequently occurring to our view. Let us, therefore, have them ready to reflect upon.

49. Are you grieved that you are only of such or such a small weight, and not three hundred weight? No more reason have you to be grieved that you live to such an age, and not to a greater. Be content, as with the quantity of matter, so, with the space of time appointed for you.

50. Let us study to convince others of what is just; but, let us ourselves act what is just, whether they will or not. <158> Should one oppose you with superior force, then rouse your resignation to providence, and your tranquillity; and improve this obstruction for the exercise of some other virtue; and remember, your former purpose was taken up with this † reservation, that you were never to aim at impossibilities. What, then, did you chiefly propose? To make a good attempt. In this you succeed; altho' you don't obtain what you first aimed at.

51. The vain-glorious man places his good in the action of another; but the sensual, in his own suffering or passive feeling: The wise man places it in his own action.

52. You have it in your power, to have no such opinion, and thus to keep your soul undisturbed. The external things themselves have no power of causing opinions in us.

53. Enure yourself to attend exactly to what is said by others, and to enter into the soul of the speaker.

54. What is not the interest of the hive, is not the interest of the bee.

* Here again the divine sentiment of returning good for evil.[17]

† See above, B. IV. 1.

55. If the sailors revile the pilot, and the patients the physician, whom will they attend to, and obey? And, how will <159> the one procure safety to the sailors, or the other to the patients?

56. How many of those who entered the world along with me, are gone off before me?

57. To men in the jaundice, honey seems bitter; and water is formidable to those who are bitten with a mad-dog. To boys the ball seems beautiful and honourable. Why am I angry? Has error in the mind less power than a little bile in the man who is in the jaundice, or a little poison in the man who was bit?

58. No man can hinder you to live according to the plan of your nature. And nothing can befall you, contrary to the plan of the universe.

59. Examine well, what sort of men they are; whom they study to please; and with what views; and by what actions they expect to please them. How speedily eternity will sweep them away into obscurity! and how many it hath already swept away! <160>

BOOK VII

1. What is vice? 'Tis what you have often seen. Have this thought ready on all emergences that they are such things as you have often seen: you'll find all things, earlier or later, just the same. Such matters as fill all histories of the antient, or middle, or present ages: of such things, all cities and families are full. Nothing is new. Every thing is ordinary, and of short duration.

2. How can the grand maxims of life ever become dead in the soul, unless the opinions suitable to them be extinguished? And it is still in your power to revive and kindle again these true opinions. I can always have the sentiments I ought to have about such things; why, then, am I disturbed? What is external to my soul, is of no consequence to it. Be thus persuaded, and you stand upright and firm. You may revive when you please. Consider things again, as you have done formerly. This is reviving again.

3. The vain solicitude about shows, scenical representations, flocks and herds, <161> skirmishing, little bones cast in for contention among little dogs, baits cast into a fish-pond, the toiling of Ants, and their carrying of burdens, the fluttering of affrighted flies, the involuntary agitations of puppets by wires! We ought to persist amidst such things with good-nature, without storming at them; and be persuaded that such is the worth of each person, as is the value of the things he pursues.

4. In Conversation, we should give good heed to what is said; and in business, to what is done: in the former, that we may understand what is signified; and, in the latter, to what end it is refered.

5. Is my understanding sufficient for this subject or not? If it is sufficient, I use it as an Instrument given me by the universal nature for this work: If it is not, I either give place in this work to those who can better execute it; unless it be some way incumbent as duty upon me; and, in that case, I execute it as well as I can, taking the aid of those, who, by directing my

mind, can accomplish something seasonable and useful to the public. For whatever I do, whether by my self, or with the assistance of others, <162> ought to be directed to that, alone, which is useful and suitable to the public.

6. How many of those, who were once much celebrated, are now delivered up to oblivion? and how many of those who sung the praises of others, are now entirely gone?

7. Don't be ashamed to take assistance. Your design should be to discharge your duty, as it is a soldier's to storm a breach in a wall. What if, because of your lameness, you cannot mount the works alone? you may do it with the assistance of others.

8. Be not disturbed about futurity: You shall come to encounter with future events, possessed of the same reason you now employ in your present affairs.

9. All things are linked with each other, and bound together with a sacred bond: Scarce is there one thing quite foreign to another. They are all arranged together in their proper places, and jointly adorn the same world. There is one orderly graceful disposition of the whole. There is one God in the whole. There is one substance, one law, and one reason common to all intelligent beings, and one truth; as there must be one sort of perfection to all beings, who are of <163> the same nature, and partake of the same rational power.

10. Every thing material shall soon vanish, and be swallowed up in the matter of the whole. Every active principle shall soon be resumed into the intelligence and cause of the whole. And the memory of every thing shall soon be buried in eternity.

11. In the rational being, the same conduct is agreeable to nature, and agreeable to reason.

12. Either shew yourself as one always upright, or as one well corrected and amended.

13. As the several members are in an organised body, such are all rational beings, tho' distant in place; since both are fitted for one joint operation. This thought will more deeply affect your heart, if you often speak to yourself thus, I am a member of that great rational body or system. If you merely call yourself a * part of mankind, you don't <164> yet love mankind from

* Thus a stone may be called a part of a rude heap. A member refers to a regular

your heart, nor does the doing of good yet ultimately delight you, without further views. You only do good, as matter of duty and obligation, and not as doing, at the same time, the greatest good to yourself.

14. Let external things affect, as they please, the * things which can be affected by them; let those complain of them which suffer by them. But if I can prevent any apprehension that the event is evil, I am not hurt. And it is in my power to prevent it.

15. Let any one do or say what he pleases, I must be a good man. Just as if the gold, the emerauld, or the purple were always saying, let men do or say what they please, I must continue an emerauld, and retain my lustre.

16. Is not the governing part the sole cause of its own disturbance? Does it not raise in it self its fears, its sorrows, its desires? If any other thing can raise its fears or sorrows, let it do so. 'Tis in its own power not to be moved by opinions about such incidents. Let the despicable body take thought, if it can, for it self; lest it suffer any thing, and complain when it suffers. The † soul which is ter-<165>rified or dejected, or which is struck with imaginations or opinions about such things, would suffer nothing, if you would not give it up to such imaginations. The governing part is free from all indigence or dependence, if it don't make it self indigent. In like manner, it may be free from all disturbance and obstruction, if it don't disturb and obstruct it self.

17. To have good-fortune is to have a good divinity governing our lot; or a good divinity, within, governing us. Be gone, then, imagination! Go, by the Gods! as you came: for I have no more use for you. You came, according to the old custom: I am not angry with you; only, be gone.

18. Does one dread a change? What can arise without changes? What is more acceptable or more usual to the nature of the whole? Can you warm your bagnio, unless wood undergoes a change? Can you be nourished, unless your food is changed? Or, can any thing useful be accomplished, without changes? Don't you see, then, that your undergoing a change, too, may be equally necessary to the nature of the whole?

---

whole, an organised body, in which the safety and prosperity of each member depends on that of the whole, and the happiness of the whole requires that of each member.

* See, B. V. 19. and the note upon it.

† See, B. V. 19.

19. Through the substance of the universe, as through a torrent, flow all <166> particular bodies; all, of the same nature; and fellow-workers with the whole; as the same members of our body co-operate with each other. How many a Chrysippus, and Socrates, and Epictetus,[1] hath the course of ages swallowed up? Let this thought occur to you, about every person, and event.

20. About this alone I am solicitous; that I may not do any thing unsuitable to the constitution of a man; or in another manner than it requires; or in a time not suitable.

21. The time approaches when you shall forget all things, and be forgotten by all.

22. 'Tis the part of a man to * love even those who offend him; and this one may do, if he would consider that those who offend are our kindred by nature; that they offend through ignorance, † and unwillingly; and that, in a little, both we and they must die: and especially, that they have done thee no dammage; for, they cannot make thy soul worse than it was before.

23. The presiding nature forms out of the universal substance, as out of wax, <167> sometimes a colt; and then, changing that again, out of its matter forms a tree; and afterwards, a man; and then, something different; and each of these forms subsisted a little while. There can be nothing dismal in a chest's being taken asunder, as there was nothing dismal in it's being at first joined together.

24. A wrathful countenance is exceedingly against nature. When the countenance is often thus deformed, its beauty dies, and cannot be revived again. By this very thing you may ‡ apprehend that it is against reason.

If the sense of moral evil is gone, what reason could one have for desiring to live?

25. All things you behold, shall the nature presiding in the universe change; and out of their substance make other things; and others, again, out of theirs; that the universe may be always new.

* Here the divine precept of loving our enemies, or such as injure us.

† Luke, XXIII. 34.[2]

‡ See the like sentiment in Cicero de offic. L. I. c. 29. Licet ora ipsa cernere iratorum, aut eorum qui libidine aliqua, aut metu commoti sunt; aut voluptate nimia gestiunt, &c.[3]

26. When one has offended, or done any thing wrong; consider what opinion of his, about some good, or evil, hath led him into this misconduct. When you <168> discover this, you will pity him; and neither be surprised, nor angry. Perhaps, you yourself may imagine the same thing, or some such like thing, to be good. If you don't at all look upon such things as good or evil, you can easily be indulgent and gentle to those who are in a mistake.

27. Don't let your thoughts dwell upon what you want, so much, as, upon what you have. And consider the things you enjoy, which are dearest to you; how earnestly and anxiously you would desire them, if you wanted them: And yet be on your guard; lest, by your delighting in the enjoyment of such things, you enure yourself to value them too much; so that if you should lose them, you would be much disturbed.

28. Wind thyself up within thy self. The rational governing part has this natural power, that it * can fully satisfy itself, in acting justly; and, by doing so, enjoying tranquillity.

29. Blot out all imaginations. Stop the brutal impulses of the passions. Circumscribe the present time; and apprehend well the nature of every thing which happens, either, to yourself, or, to others. Distinguish between the mate-<169>rial and the active principle. Consider well the last hour. The fault another commits there let it rest where the guilt resides.

30. Apply your mind attentively to what is said in conversation; and enter deeply into what is done, and into those who do it.

31. Rejoice yourself with simplicity, modesty, and the thoughts of the indifference of all things between virtue and vice; love mankind; and be obedient to the Gods. Says one.—"all things by certain laws." † But what if all be elements and no more? 'Tis sufficient that even in that case, all happens by an inevitable law; except ‡ a very few things.

32. Concerning death. 'Tis either a dispersion, or atoms, a vanishing, an extinction, or a translation to another state.

33. Concerning pain. What is intolerable must soon carry us off. What is lasting is tolerable. The understanding can preserve a calm, by its opin-

* See, B. V. 19.

† The intention here is very doubtful.[4]

‡ He means probably these which the Stoics say, are in our own power.

ions; and the governing part becomes no worse. The * parts which suffer by pain, let them determine about it if they can. <170>

34. Concerning Glory. Consider the understandings of those who confer praises, what they shun? and what they pursue? And, as heaps of sand are driven upon one another, the latter bury and hide the former: Just so, in life, the former ages are presently buried by the ensuing.

35. This from † Plato. To the man who has a true grandeur of soul, and a view of the whole of time, and of all substance; can human life appear a great matter? 'Tis impossible, says he. Can then such a one conceive death to be terrible? 'Tis impossible.

36. 'Tis a saying of Antisthenes, 'tis truly royal to do good and be reproached.[5]

37. 'Tis unworthy, that our countenance should be obedient to our soul, and change and compose itself as the soul directs, while yet the soul cannot conform and adorn itself, according to its own inclination.

38. "Vain is all anger at th' external things
For they regard it nothing. —"[6]

39. "Give joy to us, and to th' immortal Gods."[7] <171>

40. "For life is, like the loaden'd ear, cut down;
And some must fall, and some unreap'd remain."[8]

41. "Me and my children, if the Gods neglect,
It is for some good reason."[9]

42. "For I keep right and justice on my side."[10]

43. Don't sorrow along with them, nor be inwardly moved.

44. 'Tis thus in Plato. "I would give him this just answer. You are much mistaken, man, to think that a man of any worth makes much account between living and dying. Ought he not to consider this alone, whether he acts justly or unjustly, the part of a good or of a bad man?"[11]

45. He says again. "In truth, O Athenians! wheresoever one has placed himself by choice, judging it the fittest for him; or ‡ wheresoever he is <172>

* B. V. 19. and B. II. 2.

† Republic, B. 6.[12]

‡ Of the same kind, is the following divine sentiment of Epictetus; Arrian, II. 16.[13] "For the future, O God! Use me as thou pleasest, thy will is my will. I am equally ready

placed by his commander; there, I think, he ought to stay at all hazards; making no account of death; or any other evil, but vice."[14]

46. Again. "But, pray, consider, whether what is truly noble and good, be not placed in something else than preserving life; or, in being preserved. Nor is it so very desirable to one of a truly manly disposition to continue in life a long time; nor ought he to love it much. But, he should rather commit this to the will of God; assenting to the maxim of even our old women, that 'no man can avoid his destiny,' and study how he shall pass, as virtuously as he can, the time destined for him."[15]

47. Consider the course of the stars; as thinking that you revolve along with them; consider, also, continually, the changes of the elements into each other. Such extensive thoughts purge off the filth of this terrestrial life.

48. This is beautiful in Plato. "When we consider human life, we should view, as from an high tower, all <173> things terrestrial; such as herds, armies, men employed in agriculture, in marriages, divorces; births, deaths, the tumults of courts of justice, desolate lands, various barbarous nations, feasts, wailings, markets; a medley of all things, in a system adorned by contrarieties."[16]

49. Consider things past; the revolutions of so many empires; and thence you may foresee what shall happen hereafter; for they shall be just of the same nature; nor can they break off the harmony or concert now begun. Hence, 'tis much the same to view human life for forty or for a myriad of years; for, what further can you see?

50. To earth returns whatever sprung from earth.
    But what's of heav'nly seed remounts to heaven.[17]

Euripides intends by this, either the disentangling again of the entangled atoms, or some such dispersion of immutable elements.

51. By meats and drinks and charms and magic-arts,
    Death's course they would divert, and thus escape, <174>
    The gale that blows from God we must indure.
    Toiling, but not repining ———.[18]

---

for whatever thou orderest. I plead not against any thing which thou thinkest proper. Lead me whithersoever thou willest. Cloath me in what dress thou willest. Is it thy will I should be a magistrate, or a private man; remain in my own country, or in exile; be poor, or rich? In all these will I vindicate thee before men."

52. He is a better wrestler than thou art; be it so. He is not more social and kind, nor more modest; nor better prepared to meet the accidents of life; nor more gentle toward the offences of his neighbours.

53. Wherever one can act according to that reason which is common to Gods and men, there, there's nothing terrible. Where we can have the advantage or enjoyment of acting prosperously, according to the structure of our nature, there we should suspect no hurt.

54. In all places and times, you may devoutly acquiesce and be satisfied with what befalls you, and have just dispositions toward your neighbours, and * skill-<175>fully examine all arising imaginations; that none may insinuate themselves, till you thoroughly comprehend them.

55. Don't be prying into the souls of those around you, but look well into this; whither it is that nature leads you: The nature of the whole, by external events; and your own nature, by suggesting what part you should act. Each one should act the part he is fitted for by his nature. Other beings are fitted to be subservient to the rational; as all inferior beings are subordinated to the superior; and the rational are formed for each other. What the structure of human nature is chiefly adapted to, is a social communication of good; and, next to this, is the command over all bodily appetites and passions. 'Tis the proper work of the rational and intelligent power, to † circumscribe itself, and to be unconquerable by the appetites and passions. For, both these are inferior faculties, common to the brutes. The intellectual part claims to itself this power over them, and not to be subjected to them; and that, very justly; as, by its own nature, fitted to command, and employ all these lower powers. The third office pointed out by the <176> constitution of the rational nature, is to guard against rash assent, and error. Let

* This examination of the images of fancy, so often mentioned by Antoninus, is one of the most excellent means for preserving purity of mind. Vice first enters the soul, under the disguise of some apparent good, nay, under some colours of virtue; but, when the will is not suffer'd to give its consent to any of the propositions of fancy, until they are stript of all disguise; and considered according to their own real value; the moral turpitude of bad actions must determine us to reject them; and thus preserve innocence and integrity.[19]

† B. V. 19.

the governing part retain these things, and go straight on in her course; and she has all her own good or perfection.

56. Consider your life as now finished and past. What little surplus there is beyond expectation, spend it according to nature. *

57. Love and desire that alone which happens to you, and is destined by providence for you; for, what can be more suitable? † <177>

58. Upon every accident, keep in view those to whom the like hath happened. They stormed at the event; thought it strange; and complained. But where are they now? They are gone for ever. Why would you act the like part? Leave these unnatural changes and commotions to those fickle men, who thus change, and are changed. Be you intent upon this; how to make good use of such events. You may make an excellent use of them; they may be matter of ‡ virtuous action. Only attend well to yourself, and resolve to be a good man in all your actions. And still remember, that the external things, about which your actions are employed, are indifferent.

59. Look inwards; § within is the fountain of good; which is ever springing up, if you be always digging in it. <178>

* It may be remembered here once for all, the life according to nature, in Antoninus, is taken in a very high sense: 'Tis living up to that standard of purity and perfection, which every good man feels in his own breast: 'Tis conforming our selves to the law of God written in the heart: 'Tis endeavouring a compleat victory over the passions, and a total conformity to the image of God. A man must read Antoninus with little attention, who confounds this with the natural man's life, condemned by St. Paul.[20]

† The practice of this great maxim, would produce the most perfect tranquillity of mind: For, a man who desires only what God destines him, can never be disappointed; since infinite power, wisdom, and goodness, must always accomplish its designs; and, as he loves all his works, every event ordered by him, must be really best for the whole, and for the individuals to which it happens: An intimate and permanent conviction of this, must be the best foundation for the practice of the maxim here recommended. See the citation from Epictet. in the note at 46.[21]

‡ Viz. of filial love, and submission to God, of manly fortitude and patience; of meekness and goodness toward these very men, who are the causes of such external misfortunes. Those who storm'd and fretted at such accidents have not, by all their efforts, escaped them.

§ The author of this advice, had the best opportunities of trying all the happiness which can arise from external things. The dissipating pursuits of external things, stupify the nobler powers. By recollection we find the dignity of our nature: the diviner powers are disentangled, and exert themselves in all worthy social affections of piety and humanity; and the soul has an inexpressible delight in them.[22]

60. We should study also a stability of body; free from loose inconstant motion. For, as the soul displays itself by the countenance, in a wise and graceful air; so, it should in the whole body. But these things are to be observed without affectation.

61. The art of life resembles more that of the wrestler, than of the dancer; since the wrestler must ever be ready on his guard, and stand firm against the sudden unforeseen efforts of his adversary.

62. Revolve often what sort of men they are, whose approbation you desire; what sort of souls they have. Thus, you will neither accuse such as unwillingly mistake, nor will you require their approbation, if you look into the springs of their sentiments and affections.

63. 'Tis against its will, says Plato, that any soul is deprived of truth.[23] You may say the same of justice, temperance, good-nature, and every virtue. 'Tis highly necessary to remember this continually: You will thence be made gentler toward all. <179>

64. Upon any pain, recollect, that there's no moral turpitude in it; nor does it make the soul the worse, or destroy it; either as it is rational, or social. As to the far greater part of those pains we are subject to, the maxim of Epicurus[24] may assist you, "that it cannot both be intolerable and lasting": especially, if you remember the narrow bounds within which it is confined; and don't add opinions to it. Recollect this, too, that many other things fret us, which we don't repute of the same nature with pain, tho' they truly are: Thus, drowsiness, when one would be lively; being too warm; and the want of a natural appetite. When you are fretted with any of these things, rouse your mind, by saying thus to yourself: What? Do you yield yourself as vanquished by pain?

65. Entertain no such affection toward the most inhuman of your fellows, as they have toward their fellows.

66. Whence do we conclude that Socrates had a bright genius,[25] and an excellent disposition? 'Tis not enough that he died gloriously; or argued acutely with the sophists; or that he kept watch patiently in the Areopagus;[26] or that when he <180> was ordered * to apprehend the innocent Salamin-

* He had received these orders from the thirty tyrants; who intended to put Leo the

ian, he gallantly disobeyed at all hazards the unjust command; or because of any stately airs or gate he assumed in public, which, too, one may justly disbelieve: [tho' charged on him by Aristophanes:] 'Tis this we should look to, what sort of soul he had: Could he satisfy himself, without further view, in being * just toward men, pious toward God, not vainly provoked by the vices of others, nor servilely flattering them in their ignorance; counting nothing strange which was appointed by the President of the universe; nor sinking under it as intolerable; nor yielding up his soul to be affected by the passions of the body?

67. Nature hath not so † blended the soul with the body, as that it cannot circumscribe itself, and execute its own office by itself. One may be a most divine man, and yet be unknown to all. Remember this always: and this also, <181> that the happiness of life consists in very few things. And tho' you despair of becoming a good logician, or naturalist, you need not therefore despair of becoming free, possessed of an high sense of honour and modesty, kind and social, and resigned to God.

68. You may live superior to all force, in the highest delight, were all men loudly to rail against you as they please; tho' wild beasts were to tear the poor members of this corporeal mixture, which has been nourished along with you. What hinders the soul to preserve itself amidst these things, in all tranquillity, in just judgments about the things which surround it, and in a proper use of what is cast in its way? So that the judgment may say, "such is thy real nature, tho' thou appearest otherwise." The ‡ faculty which directs how to use every thing, may say, "it was such an event as thou art, that I wanted. For whatever occurs, is to me § matter of rational and social virtue, and of the proper art of man or God. Whatever occurs is familiar, and suited either to the <182> purpose of God or man; and is not new nor untractable, but well known and easy."

Salaminian to death, and seize his estate. Socrates at all hazards disobeyed them, in the height of their power. This Plato mentions in the apology, and in one of his letters.[27]

* See the note at X. 11.

† See, B. V. 19.

‡ That is, the intellectual part, or the rational soul.

§ See, B. VII. 58.

69. The perfection of manners can make one spend each day as his last; and keep himself always calm, without sloth or hypocrisy.

70. The Gods, who are immortal, are not fretted, that, in a long eternity, they must always bear with such a numerous wicked world: Nay, further, they always take care of it. * Yet you who are presently to cease from being, must be fretted and tired with it, tho' you are one of these wretched creatures yourself!

71. 'Tis ridiculous that you don't endeavour to repress, and fly from all vice in yourself, which you have in your power to do; but are still striving to restrain it in others, and avoid the effects of it; which you can never do.

72. Whatever the rational and social power observes, as neither subservient to any improvement of the understanding, nor of social dispositions; it just-<183>ly deems inferior to itself, and below its regard.

73. When you have done a kind office, and another is profited by it, why do you, † like the fools, require any thing further, and thus want also the reputation of beneficence, and to get returns? ‡

74. No man is tired of what is gainful to him. Your gain consists in acting according to nature. Since the gain is yours, why should you be weary of such a course of action?

75. The presiding nature of the whole once set about the making this universe. And now either we must allow, that all things, even the worst we see, happen, § according to a necessary consequence or connexion, with those excellent things primarily intended; or must say, there was no rational intention or design, in the production of these things which are most excellent; which yet appear to be the peculiar objects of intention in the universal mind. The remembring this will make you much more serene on many occurrences. <184>

* The most powerful motive to forgiveness and to return good for evil. See, Matth. V. 45, 46, 47, 48. See, Cambray's dialogue of Socrates, Alcibiades, and Timon.[28]

† In the high language of the Stoics, the vulgar, and all who are not completely wise and virtuous, are called fools and mad-men.[29]

‡ See, IX. 42. near the end.

§ See, IX. 28.

BOOK VIII

1. This will repress the desire of vain-glory, that you cannot make the whole of your life, from your youth, appear such as became a philosopher. 'Tis known to many, as well as to your own conscience, that you were far from true wisdom. If this be your aim, you must be full of confusion: It can be no easy matter for you to gain the reputation of a philosopher. Nay, the grand purpose of your life is opposite to this view of reputation. If you know wherein true excellence consists, away with this affair of reputation, and the opinions of others. Be satisfied with this, that what remains of life, be it more or less, be spent as the constitution of your nature requires. Study this point exactly; and be solicitous about nothing else, but knowing what your nature requires, and acting accordingly. You have experienced many wanderings, without finding happiness. 'Tis not found in philosophical arguments, nor in riches, nor in fame, nor in sensuality. Not at all. Where, then, is it to be found? In acting the part which <185> human nature requires. How shall you act thus? By retaining firmly the great maxims from which our desires and actions flow. What maxims? Those concerning good and evil: "that nothing is truly good to a man, which does not make him just, temperate, courageous, and free: and that nothing can be evil to a man, which gives him not the contrary dispositions."

2. About every action, thus examine yourself; What sort of one is it? Shall I never repent of it? I shall presently be dead, and all these things gone. What further, then, should I desire, if my present action be such as becomes an intellectual and social being, subject to the same law with the Gods? *

* As, all intelligent beings are, by their nature, under the same immutable eternal law of promoting the good and perfection of the whole. This, in the supreme Being, flows essentially from his nature: in created beings, it is a gift from him.[1]

3. Alexander, Caius,[2] Pompey, what were they in comparison with Diogenes,[3] Heraclitus,[4] and Socrates? These latter knew the natures of things, and their causes, and materials: And thus their governing parts were employed. As to the former, what a multitude of <186> things were the objects of their care? To how many were they enslaved? *

4. Such men † will go on doing such actions, tho' you should burst with indignation.

5. In the first place, be not disturbed or put into confusion. All things happen according to the nature of the whole. In a little time you shall be gone, as Hadrian,[5] and Augustus.[6] And, then, attentively consider the nature of what occurs to you: Remember you must persist in the purpose of being a good man. Act, then, inflexibly what suits the nature of a man, and speak always what appears to you just, and yet with calm good-nature and modesty; and without Hypocrisy.

6. 'Tis the constant business of the universal nature, to be transferring what is now here, into another place; to be changing things, and carrying them hence, and placing them elsewhere. All are changes; all are customary; you need not fear any thing new. All are subjected to the same law.

7. Every being is satisfied while it continues prospering. The rational nature is prosperous, while it assents to no false or uncertain opinion; and has its affections directed to something social and <187> kind; and its desires and aversions turned toward these things alone which are in its power; while it embraces contentedly whatever is appointed by the universal nature. For, of that it is a part, as a leaf is a part of a tree. In these, indeed, the leaf is a part of an insensible irrational system, which can be obstructed in the intention of its nature: but the human nature is a part of that universal nature which ‡ cannot be obstructed, and is intelligent and just. This nature distributes, suitably to all, their proper portions of time, of matter, of active principle, of powers, and events. § This you will find, if you don't merely compare one circumstance of one with the corresponding circum-

* See, IX. 29.
† See, the note on B. V. 17.
‡ See, IV. 1. and the note.
§ See, IX. 3.

stance in another, but consider the whole nature and circumstances of one, and compare them with the whole of another.

8. You want, perhaps, opportunity for reading. But you never want opportunity of repressing all insolence; of keeping yourself superior to pleasure, and pain, and vain-glory; and of restraining all anger against the insensible, and the ungrateful; nay, even of retaining an affectionate concern about them. <188>

9. Let no man hear you accusing either a court-life, or your own life.

10. Repentance is a self-reproving, because we have neglected something useful. Whatever is good, must be useful in some sort, and worthy of the care of a good and honourable man. But never did such a man repent of his neglecting some opportunity of sensual pleasure: Such pleasure, therefore, is neither good nor profitable.

11. [Ask yourself thus about every thing,] What is the nature of it, according to its constitution and end? What is its substance or matter? What, as to its active principle? What is its business in the universe? How long shall it endure?

12. When you are averse to be roused from sleep, consider that it is according to your constitution, and that of human nature, to be employed in social actions. To sleep, is common to us with the brutes. What is peculiarly suited to the nature of each species, that must be most familiar, most adapted, and most delightful to it.

13. Upon each occurrence which affects the imagination, continually endeavour to apprehend its nature, and its effect upon our affections; and to reason well about it. <189>

14. When you have to do with any one, say thus to yourself: What are this man's maxims about good and evil, pleasure and pain, and the causes of them; about glory and infamy, death or life? If he have such maxims, there is nothing wondrous or strange, that he acts such a part. And then we shall recollect too, that he is under * a necessity of acting thus.

15. Remember, that, as it would be silly to be surprized that a fig-tree bears figs, so is it equally, to be surprized that the universe produces those things of which it was ever fruitful. 'Tis silly in a physician, to be surprized

* See, V. 17. VI. 27. IX. 42.

that one is fallen into a fever; or in a pilot, that the wind has turned against him.

16. Remember, it equally becomes a man truly free, to change his course, of himself, when he thinks fit, and to follow the advice of another who suggests better measures; for this is also your own action, accomplished according to your own desire, and judgment, and understanding.

17. If this matter is in your own power, Why do you act thus? If it is not, whom do you accuse? It must either be the a-<190>toms, or the Gods. To accuse either is a piece of madness. There is nothing therefore to be accused or blamed. Correct the matter, if you can. If not, to what purpose complain? Now, nothing should be done to no purpose.

18. What dies is not gone out of the verge of the universe. If that which is dissolved stays here, and is changed, it returns to those elements, of which the world and you too consist. These too are changed, and don't murmur at it.

19. Every thing is formed for some purpose: the horse, the vine. Why do you wonder at this? The sun too is formed for a certain office, and so are the * other Gods. For what end are you formed? <191> For sensual enjoyments? See if the Sentiments of your soul can bear this thought.

20. As he who throws the ball, not only intends its motion and direction, but the place where it should stop; so, the nature of the whole intends the ceasing of each being, no less than its commencing and continuance. What better is the ball while ascending or descending, than when fallen or stopt? What good is it to the bubble in water that it continues? or evil, that it is broken? The same you may say of the lamps, when extinguished.

21. Turn out the inner side of this body, and view it: What shall it become when it grows old, or sickly, or dead? The applauded and the applauder,

* Tho' one supreme original deity was acknowledged by almost all the better sects of the heathen philosophers, yet they conceived great numbers of superior natures, created indeed, but with very great natural excellencies, and invested with great powers of government, in certain parts of the universe. Many Christians believed the same general tenet. The heathens called those superior beings Gods, and Christians called them Angels. The heathens imagined these inferior Gods or Angels, residing in the sun, the stars, and planets. This the Christians justly denied, and keenly opposed; as it had occasioned much superstitious and idolatrous worship in the heathen world.[7]

are of short continuance; the rememberer and the person remembered: And all this, too, in a little corner of one climate, where, too, all don't agree in the characters they give; nay, few agree with themselves. And this whole earth is but a point.

22. Attend well to what is at present before you; whether it be a maxim, an action, or a speech. 'Tis just you should suffer, because you neglect your present business; and would rather become a good man to morrow, than to day. <192>

23. Am I in action; I refer it to some benefit thence to accrue to mankind. Does any thing befall me? I accept it, as referring it to the Gods, the fountain of all things; from whom all things are ordered in a fixed series.

24. What things occur in bathing? How do they appear? Oil, sweat, dirt, water, the filth of the skin; all nauseous. Such are all parts of animal life; all the objects before us.

25. Lucilla buried Verus, and soon after was buried herself. Secunda buried Maximus, and then Secunda herself was buried. Epitynchanus buried Diotimus, and then Epitynchanus was buried. * Antoninus buried Faustina, and then Antoninus was buried. Celer buried Hadrian, and then Celer followed.[8] All go the same way: Those artful men, who foretold the fates of others, or were swoln with pride, where are they now? Charax, Demetrius Platonicus, Eudaemon,[9] and such others? All were but for a day; and are gone long ago. Some scarce remembered for any time after their death; some gone into a fable; and of some, even the old fable itself is vanished. Remember these things; that either this corporeal mixture <193> must be dispersed: or that the spirit of life must be either extinguished; or removed, and brought into another place.

26. The joy of man is in doing the proper office of a man; and this consists in good-will toward his own tribe, or species, in contempt of sensual impressions; in distinguishing the profitable appearances; in considering the nature of the whole, and the things which happen according to it.

27. All of us stand in three relations: the first, toward the present immediate causes; the second toward the divine cause which effects all things; the third, toward our neighbours with whom we live.

* These two are Antoninus Pius[10] and his wife Annia Faustina.

28. Pain is either an evil to the body; and, then, let the body pronounce it to be evil; or, to the soul: But, the soul * can maintain her own serenity and calm; and not conceive pain to be evil. All judgment, intention, desire, and aversion, are within the soul; to which no evil can ascend.

29. Blot out the false imaginations; and say often to yourself thus; 'Tis now in my power to preserve my soul free from all wickedness, all lust, all confusion or disturbance. And yet, as I discern the natures of things, I can use them <194> all in proportion to their value. Remember this noble power granted you by nature.

30. In your speeches, whether in the senate or elsewhere, aim rather at a decent dignity, than elegance; and let your speech ever be sound and virtuous.

31. The court of Augustus, his wife, daughter, grand-children, step-sons; his sister, and Agrippa, his kinsmen, intimates and friends, Arius, Maecenas;[11] his physicians, sacrificers; all yielded to death. Go next, not merely to the death of one, but of a whole family or name; as that of the Pompeys; and what we meet sometimes inscribed on tombs: "This was the last of his family." And then think; what solicitude the ancestors of such men have had, that they might leave a succession of their own posterity; and yet it was necessary, there should be a last one of that race. Thus you see the death of a whole kindred.

32. † Make yourself regular, by regulating your several actions, one by one; so that if each action answers its end, and have what perfection belongs to it, you may be satisfied. Now, in this, nothing can hinder you. But, say you, may not <195> something external withstand me? Nothing can hinder you to act the just, the temperate, the wise part. Some external effects of your actions may be obstructed; but, then, there may arise another action of your's, equally suited to this regularity and orderly composition of life, we are speaking of; in your acquiescence under this impediment, and your calmly converting yourself to that conduct which is in your power.[12]

33. Receive the gifts of fortune, without pride; and part with them, without reluctance.

* See, B. IV. 19.[13]

† See, B. IV. 1.[14]

34. If you have ever beheld an hand, a foot, or an head, cut off from the rest of the body, and lying dead at a distance from it: Such does one make himself, as far as he can, who repines at any event which happens, and tears himself off from the whole; or who does any thing unsociable: You are broke off from the natural unity: Nature formed you for a part of the whole; but you have cut off yourself. Yet this is glorious, that you can re-unite yourself to the whole. The Gods have granted such a power of returning again, and re-uniting with the whole, to no other parts, when they are once cut off. Consider the goodness and bounty with which <196> God hath honoured mankind. He first put it in their power, not to be broken off from this unity; and then put it in their power, even when they are thus broken off, to return, and grow together again naturally, in the condition of parts.

35. The president nature of the whole, as it hath imparted to each rational being almost all its faculties and powers; so, this one in particular, that, as the nature of the whole converts into its use, and makes subservient to its purpose, whatever seems to withstand or oppose it, and makes it a regular part of that orderly fated series; thus, each rational being can make every impediment in its way the proper matter for itself to act upon; and can use it for its grand purpose, whatever it be.

36. Don't confound yourself, by considering the whole of your future life; and by dwelling upon the multitude, and greatness of the pains or troubles, to which you may probably be exposed. But ask yourself about such as are present, is there any thing intolerable and unsufferable in them? You'll be ashamed to own it. And, then, recollect, that it is neither what is past, nor what is future, which can oppress you; 'tis only what is <197> present. And this will be much diminished, if you circumscribe or consider it by itself; and chide your own mind, if it cannot bear up against this one thing thus alone.

37. Is Panthea[15] or Pergamus now sitting and wailing at the tomb of Verus? or Chabrias and Diotimus at the tomb of Hadrian? Ridiculous work this. If they were still sitting there, would their masters be sensible of it? Or if they were sensible, would it give them any pleasure? Or, if they were pleased with it, could these men be immortal, and lament for ever? Was it not destined they should grow old and die? and when they should die, what

would have become of their masters? What is all this for, but a nauseous bag of blood and corruption?

38. If you have great penetration, exercise it in what is the subject of the greatest wisdom.

39. In the constitution of the rational creature, there is no virtue or excellence, destined to withstand or restrain justice; but I see temperance destined to restrain sensual pleasures.

40. If you remove your own opinions about the things which grieve you, you may presently stand on the surest ground. What <198> is that self? 'Tis reason. I am not reason, say you. Well: let not your reason then disturb itself. But let the part which suffers form opinions concerning this matter. *

41. An obstruction of any sense is the evil of an animal; so is the obstruction of any external motion or design: There is another sort of obstruction, which is the evil of the vegetative nature. The obstruction of the understanding is, in like manner, the evil of an intelligent nature: apply all these things to yourself. Do pain or pleasure affect you? Let the sense look to it. Does any thing obstruct any external design of yours? If you have designed without the proper † reservation, this is evil to you, as you are rational: But, if you have taken in the general reservation, you are not hurt nor hindered. No other person can hinder that which is the proper work of the intelligent nature. Nor fire, nor sword, nor a tyrant, nor calumny, can reach it. When it is as a ‡ sphere complete within itself, without any <199> corners which can be struck off by external force, it remains so.

42. It would be unjust in me to vex or grieve myself, who never willingly grieved any one.

43. One rejoices in one thing, and another in another. My joy consists in having my governing part sound; without aversion to any man, or any event incident to mankind; but beholding with a serene look, and accepting, and using, every thing in proportion to its worth.

* See, B. V. 19.

† See this explained, B. IV. 1.

‡——— *in seipse totus teres atque rotundus,*
Externi ne quid valeat per leve morari.
HOR. sat. II. 7.[16]

44. Allow to yourself the little time you have. Those who rather pursue a surviving fame, don't consider that posterity will just be such as our contemporaries, whose manners we scarce can bear: and they too will be mortal. And what is it to you, what sounds they shall make with their voices, or what opinions they shall entertain about you?

45. Take me up, and cast me where you please, I shall have my own divinity within me propitious: that is, satisfied, while its affections and actions are suited to its own structure and natural furniture. Is, then, any external event of such worth, that, on its account, my soul should suffer, and become worse than it was; becoming abject, and prostrate, as a mean <200> suppliant; and bound as a slave along with the body, or terrified? Can you find any thing which can deserve all this?

46. Nothing can befall a man which is not a natural incident of mankind; nor to an ox, nor to a vine, nor to a stone, which is not a natural incident to these species. If, then, that alone can befall any thing, which is usual, and naturally incident to it, what cause is there for indignation? The presiding nature of the whole hath brought nothing upon you, which you cannot bear?

47. If you are grieved about anything external, 'tis not the thing itself that afflicts you, but your judgment about it; and it is in your power to correct this judgment and get quit of it. If you are grieved at any thing in your own disposition; who hinders you to correct your maxims of life? If you are grieved, because you have not accomplished some sound and virtuous design; set about it effectually, rather than be grieving that it is undone. "But some superior force withstands." Then you have no cause of sorrow; for, the fault of the omission lyes not in you. "But, life is not worth retaining, if this be not accomplished." Quit life, then, with the same serenity, as if you had accom-<201>plished it; and with good-will, even toward those who withstand you.

48. Remember the governing part becomes invincible, when, collected into itself, it can be satisfied with acting only as it pleases, even when it is obstinately set upon things unreasonable. What shall it be then, when, after due deliberation, it has fixed its judgment according to reason? The soul, thus free from passions, is a strong fort; nor can a man find any stronger, to which he can fly, and become invincible for the future. He

who has not discerned this, is illiterate. He who has, and does not fly to it, is miserable.

49. Pronounce no more to yourself, beyond what the appearances directly declare. 'Tis told you, that one has spoken ill of you. This alone is told you, and not that you are hurt by it. I see my child is sick; this only I see; and not also that he is in danger of dying. Dwell thus upon the first appearances, and add nothing to them, from within; and no harm befalls you: Or, rather, add what becomes one who understands the nature of all which happens in the universe.

50. Is the cucumber bitter? Throw it away. Are there thorns in the way? Walk aside. That is enough. Don't be <202> adding; "Why were such things in the universe?" A naturalist would laugh at you, as would a carpenter, too, or a shoe-maker, if you were finding fault, because shavings and parings of their Works are lying about in their work-houses. These artificers have places too without their work-shops, where they can throw these superfluities. But the nature of the whole has no external place for this purpose: And herein its art is wonderful, that, having circumscribed itself within certain bounds, all within it which seems corrupting, waxing old, or useless, it transforms into itself, and, out of them, makes other new forms; so as neither to need matter from without, nor want a place where to cast out its superfluities. 'Tis satisfied with its own substance, its own space, and its own art.

51. Neither appear languid and tired out in Action; nor troublesome in conversation; nor inconstant in your opinions; nor dragged away in your soul, nor sallying out by the impulse of passions; nor too much hurried in life. They slay you, cut you to pieces, pursue you with curses. Does this hinder your soul to continue pure, prudent, temperate, just? As if one standing by a clear sweet foun-<203>tain, should reproach it, yet it ceases not to send forth its refreshing waters. Should he throw into it clay or dung; it will soon disperse them, wash them away, and become free from all pollution. How, then, shall you get this perpetual living fountain within you, and not a dead cistern? Form yourself anew each day into liberty, with tranquillity, simplicity, and a sense of what is decent and becoming.

52. He, who knows not there is an orderly universe, knows not where he is. He, who knows not for what purpose he was formed, knows not himself,

and knows not the world. He, who is deficient in either of these parts of knowledge, cannot tell you for what purpose he is fitted by nature. What sort of person, then, must he appear, who pursues the applauses, or dreads the censures of men, who know not where they themselves are, nor what they are?

53. Want you to be praised by a man who curses himself thrice in an hour? Can you desire to please one, who is not pleased with himself? Is he pleased with himself, who repents of almost every thing he does?

54. Don't content yourself in merely corresponding with the surrounding air, <204> by breathing in it; but correspond in sentiment with that intelligence which surrounds all things. For, this * intelligence diffuses itself to all, and advances toward all those who can draw it in, no less than the air does to such as can receive it into themselves by breathing.

55. There is no universal wickedness to hurt the universe. Particular wickedness of any individual hurts not another. It hurts himself only; who, yet, has this gracious privilege, that, as soon as he heartily desires it, he may be free from it altogether.

56. To my elective power, the elective power of another is indifferent, as his animal life, or his flesh is. And how much soever we were formed for the sake of each other, yet the governing part of each one has its own proper power: otherways, the vice of another might become my proper evil or misery: God <205> thought fit, this should not be; lest it should be in the power of another to make me unhappy.

57. The sun seems to be poured forth, and is diffused all around; but not poured out, or emptied. This diffusion is a sort of extension of its rays, and hence the † Greek word for the rays is thought to be derived. The nature

* This is a very remarkable passage; not only intimating that our dispositions to piety are the effects of the diffusive and gracious power of God; but that such is the divine goodness that he is ever ready to communicate his goodness and mercy, in the renovation of the heart, and in forming in it all holy affections, and just apprehensions of himself, to all minds which by earnest desires are seeking after him.[17]

† The Stoics studied to find out such etymologys of words, as might make them memorial hints of some useful reflection, tho' very different from the true critical etymologys. We had an instance, B. V. 8. of one more natural than this. Cicero gives many ridiculous instances when he is imitating their manner. The thought in this section is very obscure.[18]

of a ray you may observe, if you see it entring through some small hole into a darkened chamber. Its direction is straight; and it is reflected around, when it falls upon any solid body, which does not admit it into itself. Upon this the light is fixed, no part of it is lost, or falls aside. Now, such ought to be the direction and diffusion of your understanding, not an effusion or emptying of itself, but an extension of it toward even any obstacle that occurs: Not violently and impetuously dashing against it, nor falling aside, but terminating directly on it, and illuminating whatever will re-<206>ceive it. Such opaque objects as will not receive and transmit the rays, deprive themselves of the splendor.

58. He who dreads death, dreads either an extinction of all sense, or dreads a different sort of sensation. If all sense is extinguished, there can be no sense of evil. If a different sort of sense is acquired, you become another sort of living creature; and don't cease to live.

59. Men were formed for each other. Teach them better, then, or bear with them.

60. The motion of the arrow is different from that of the mind. The mind, when cautiously avoiding, or, when turning to all sides, in deliberation about what to pursue, is even then carried straight forward toward its proper mark. [viz. Acting the good part.]

61. Penetrate into the governing part of others; and lay yours open to them, to enter into it. <207>

BOOK IX

1. He who does an injury is guilty of impiety. For, since the nature of the whole has formed the rational animals for one another; each for being useful to the other according to his merit, and never hurtful; he who transgresses this her will, is thus guilty of impiety against * the most ancient and venerable of the Gods. † For the nature of the whole is the nature of all things which exist; and things which exist, are a-kin to their causes. Further, she is called truth; and is the first cause of all truths: He, then, who willingly lyes, is guilty of impiety, in as far as, by deceiving, he does an injury: and he, who lyes unwillingly; in as far as his voice dissents from the nature of the whole; as he is acting ungracefully, in opposing the comely order of the universe: For he fights against its nature and design, who sets himself against truth; <208> since nature had furnished him with means for distinguishing falsehood from truth, by neglecting which he is now unable to do it. He, too, who pursues pleasure as good, and shuns pain as evil, is guilty of impiety: for such a one must needs frequently blame the common nature, as making some unworthy distributions to the bad and the good; because the bad oftimes enjoy pleasures, and possess the means of them; and the good often meet with pain, and what causes pain; besides, he who dreads pain, must sometimes dread that which must be a part of the order and beauty of the universe: this, now, is impious: and, then, he who pursues pleasures will not abstain from injury; and that is manifestly impious. But, in those things to which the common nature is indifferent, (for she had not made both, were she not indifferent to either); he who would follow nature,

* This is a clear acknowledgement of the one supreme God.

† The original is obscure here. Probably this nature of the whole, is always to be understood of God, or the mind presiding in the whole, and governing it for the universal good, with perfect benevolence toward all.[1]

ought, in this too, to agree with her in his sentiments, and be indifferently dispos'd to either. Whoever, then, is not indifferently dispos'd to pain and pleasure, life and death, glory and ignominy, all which the nature of the whole regards as indifferent, it is plain he is guilty of impiety. When I say the common nature regards <209> them as indifferent; I mean she regards their happening or not happening as indifferent events in the grand establish'd series, in which things exist, and ensue upon others, suitably to a certain ancient purpose of that providence and design, according to which, at a certain period, she set about this fair structure and arrangement of the universe; after she had conceived and fixed the plan of all that was to exist; and appointed the distinct powers which were to produce the several substances, changes, and successions.

2. It were the more desirable lot, to depart from among men, unacquainted with falsehood, hypocrisy, luxury, or vanity. The next choice were, to expire, when cloy'd with these vices, rather than continue among them: and does not even experience, yet, persuade you to fly from amidst the plague? For a corruption of the intellectual part is far more a plague than any pestilential distemper and change of this surrounding fluid which we breathe. The one is only a pestilence to animals, as they are animals; but the other to men, as they are men.

3. Don't despise death; but receive it well-pleas'd; as it is one of the things which nature wills.[2] For such as it is to be <210> young, to be old, to grow up, to be full grown; to breed teeth, and beard, and grow grey; to beget, to go with child, to be delivered; and undergo the other natural effects which the seasons of your life produce; such is it also to be dissolved. It becomes a * man of wisdom neither to be inconsiderate, impetuous, or ostentatiously contemptuous about death; but await the season of it, as of one of the operations of nature. As you are now awaiting the season when the foetus shall come out of the womb of your wife, thus await the season when your soul shall fall out of these its teguments. If you want also a popular support, here is one which goes to the heart: you will be extremely easy with

* The Greek word is a term for one who never acts, till he has examined thoroughly, and reasoned right, on what he is going to do. See, VI. 30. in the character of Antoninus Pius.

regard to death, if you consider the objects you are going to leave; and the manners of that confused croud from which you are to be disengaged: tho' at the same time, you ought not to be offended at them; but * even to have a tender care of them, and bear with <211> them mildly. Remember, however, your removal is not from among men of the same sentiments with yourself: for this alone, were it so, could pull you back, and detain you in life; were it given you to live along with men who had attained to the same maxims of life with yourself. But, at present you see how great the fatigue and toil from the jarring courses of those you are among. So that you may say, " † Haste, death! lest I, too, should forget myself."

4. He who does wrong, does a wrong to himself. He who is injurious, does evil to himself, by making himself evil.

5. Men are often unjust by omissions, as well as by actions.

6. Be satisfyed with your present sentiments of things, if certain; your present course of action, if social; and, your present temper of mind, if well-pleased with every thing which comes from the universal cause.

7. Wipe out the fancies of imagination: stop all eager impulses to action: extinguish keen desires; and keep the governing part master of itself.

8. Among the irrationals one animal-soul is distributed; the rational, again, <212> partake of ‡ one intellectual soul: just as there is one earth to all things earthy; and as all of us, who are indued with sight, and animated, see with one light and breathe one air.

9. All things, which partake of any common quality, have a strong tendency to what is of the same kind with themselves. The earthy all tend to the earth; the watery all naturally flow together; and the aerial also; so that there is need of some intercepting partitions and violence, to prevent their confluence: What contains the nature of fire tends upwards, on account of the elementary fire; along with which all our fewel is so apt to be kindled, that any matter pretty dry is easily set on fire; because there is then a less

* Here is the precept of loving our enemies, which is also in many others of these meditations.

† As a quotation probably from some poet.[3]

‡ See, II. 1.

mixture of what hinders its kindling. * Thus, now, also, whatever partakes of the common intellectual nature, hastens, in like manner, or rather more, to mingle with, and adhere to what is a-kin to it. For the more it excels other natures, the <213> stronger is its tendency to mix with and adhere to what is a-kin to it. Thus, among irrational animals, we easily observe swarms, and herds, nurture of their young, and, as it were, mutual loves: for they have animal-souls; and the mutual attraction is found stronger in the more noble nature; such as was not found in plants, nor in stones, or wood. And then among the rational animals, begun civil-societies, friendships, families, and assemblies; nay, treaties, and truces, even in war. Among beings, again, still more excellent, there subsists, tho' they are placed far asunder, a certain kind of union: as among the stars. Thus can that superior excellence produce † a sympathy among these beings so widely distant. But observe what happens [among us:] For intellectual beings, alone, have now forgot the social concern for each other, and mutual tendency to union! Here, alone, the social confluence is not seen! Yet are they invironed and held by it, tho' they fly off. For nature always prevails. You will see what I say, if you observe.—For, sooner, may one find some earthy thing which joins to nothing earthy, than a man rent off and separated from all men. <214>

10. Man, God, and the universe, all bear fruit; and each in their own seasons. Custom indeed has appropriated the expression to the vine, and the like; but that is nothing. ‡ Reason has its fruit too, both § social and ** private. And it produces just such other things as reason itself is.[4]

* In this paragraph, he at once acknowledges the original fabric of the soul to be destined for the knowledge and love of God, and an intire harmony of will with him by resignation: and also its present degenerate state, as it is often counteracting its original destination.[5]

† See, VI. 43. XI. 27. and VII. 13.[6]

‡ The law of our nature; entire resignation to the will of God in all events, and kind affections to our fellows. See Matth. XXII. 37, 39.[7]

§ Kind offices and good-nature to our fellows, and submission to the universal providence.

** Chearful tranquillity under whatever happens, and temperance. We may supply the enumeration of its fruits from the apostle. Galat. V. 22. "Now the fruits of the spirit are love, joy, peace, long-suffering, gentleness, goodness, faith, meekness, self-command."

11. If you can, teach them better. If not, remember that the virtue of meekness was given you to be exercised on such occasions. * Nay, the Gods also exercise meekness and patience toward them; and even aid them in their pursuits of some things; as of health, wealth, glory. So gracious are they! You may be so too. Or, say, who hinders you?

12. Bear toil and pain, not as if wretched under it; nor as wanting to be <215> pitied, or admired. But will only one thing; always to act, or refrain, as social wisdom requires.[8]

13. To day I have escaped from every dangerous accident: or, rather, I have thrown out from me every dangerous accident. For they were not without; but within, in my own opinions.

14. All these things are, in our experience of them, customary; in their continuance, but for a day; and, in their matter, sordid. All at present, such as they were in the times of those we have buried.

15. The things themselves stand with out-doors, by themselves; and neither know, nor declare to us any thing concerning themselves. What declares, then, and pronounces, concerning them? † The governing part.

16. It is not in passive feeling, ‡ but in action, § the good and evil of the rational animal formed for society consists: As neither does the virtue or vice of it consist in passive-feeling, but in action.

17. To the stone thrown up, it is no evil, to fall down; nor good, to have mounted up. <216>

18. Penetrate into their governing part; and you will see what kind of judges you fear: and what kind of judges, too, they are, about themselves.

19. All things are in a state of change; and you are yourself under continual transmutation; and, in some respect, corruption: and so is the whole universe.

20. The fault of another you must leave with himself.

21. The cessation of any action, the extinction of any keen desire, or of any opinion, is as it were a death to them. This is no evil. Turn, now to your different ages; such as childhood, youth, manhood, old-age; for every

* To enable you to bear mildly the imperfections of others. See, art. 42.

† IV. 3. and V. 19.

‡ Either of pleasure or pain.

§ The exertion of our active powers.

change of these is a death. * Is there any thing alarming here? Go, now, to your life; first as it was under your grand-father, then as it was under your mother; and then as it was under † your father: and, as you find there many other alterations, changes, and endings, ask yourself, was there any thing in these to alarm me? Thus, neither is there, in the ending, ceasing, and change, of your whole life.

22. Have speedy recourse to your own governing part, and to that of the <217> whole, and to that of this man [who has offended you.] To your own, that you may make it a mind disposed to justice: to that of the whole, that you may remember of what you are a part: and to that of this man, that you may know whether he has acted out of ignorance, or design; and that you may, at the same time, consider, he is your kinsman.

23. As you are a completing part of a social system, so also let every action of yours be a completing part of a social life. If, then, any action of yours has not its tendency, either immediate or distant, to the common-good as its end, this action disorders your life, and hinders it from being uniform, and it is seditious; as a man is in a common-wealth, who, by pursuing a separate interest, breaks off his own party from the general harmony and concord.[9]

24. Quarrels of children at their play! And poor spirits carrying dead carcases about with them! Hence we may be the more deeply affected with the representations of the ‡ shades.[10]

25. Go to the quality of the § active principle; abstract it from the material, and contemplate it by itself. Then deter-<218>mine the time; how long, at furthest, this thing, of this particular quality, can naturally subsist.

26. You have indured innumerable sufferings, by not being satisfied with your own governing part, when it does those things which it is formed for doing. Enough, then, [of this dissatisfaction].

27. When another reproaches or hates you, or utters any thing to that purpose; go to their souls: enter in there; and look what kind of men they are. You will see that you ought not to disturb yourself, in order to procure

* That is, the child dies in the youth; the youth in the man; and so on.

† Antoninus Pius.

‡ A spectacle so called: as Gataker takes it.[11]

§ VII. 29.[12]

any opinion of theirs concerning you. Yet you ought to have * kind dispositions toward them: for they are by nature your friends: and the Gods, too, aid them every way; by dreams, by oracles; and even in these things they are most eager after.

28. The course of things in the world is always the same; a continual rotation; up and down; from age to age. † Either <219> the mind of the whole exerts itself in every particular event: and, if so, accept of what comes immediately from it: or has exerted itself once; and in consequence of this, all things go on since in a necessary series, ‡ in which each is connected with the other, [and all together, make up one regular complete whole,] § or atoms and indivisible particles are the origin of all things; and, if so, even those have somehow made up one orderly system of the whole. In fine; if there is any ** God, all things are right and well: or, if there is only a chance, at least you need not act by chance. †† The earth will presently cover us all: and then this earth will itself change into some other forms; and those, again, into others: and so on without end. Now, when any one considers how swiftly those changes, and transmutations roll on, like one wave upon another, he will despise every thing mortal.

29. The cause of the whole is a torrent. It carries all along with it. How <220> very little worth, too, are those poor creatures who pretend to understand affairs of state, and imagine they unite in themselves the statesman and the philosopher! mere froth! Do you, O man! that which nature requires of you, whatever it be. Set about it, if you have the means: and don't look about you, to see if any be taking notice, and don't hope for Plato's common-wealth:[13] ‡‡ But be satisfied if it have the smallest success; and

* Here again the precept of loving our enemies.

† Or the words of the original may bear this meaning. "Either the mind of the whole intends and designs each particular event; and, if so, accept of what it intends: or has once primarily intended some things; and the rest are unavoidable necessary consequences of those."

‡ See, IV. 45. VI. 36. and VII. 75.

§ Part of the original is wanting, and what remains is corrupted. The turn given it in the translation is founded on, IV. 27.

** Governing mind.

†† See this more fully in VI. 44.

‡‡ V. 9. at the beginning.

consider the event of this very thing as no small matter. For who can change the opinions of those men? Now, without a change of their opinions, what is it else but a slavery they are groaning under, while they pretend a willing obedience? Come, now, and tell me of * Alexander, Phillip,[14] and Demetrius Phalereus.[15] They know best whether they understood what the common nature requir'd of them; and train'd themselves accordingly. But, if they designed only an outward shew, to gain the applause and admiration of men, no-body has condemned me to imitate them. The business of philosophy is simple, meek, and modest. Don't lead me away after [the smoak and vapour of] a vain glorious stateliness. <221>

30. † Contemplate, as from some height, the innumerable herds; and innumerable religious rites, and navigation of all kinds, in storms, and calms; ‡ the different states of those who are coming into life, those who are associating in life, those who are leaving life. Consider also the life which others have lived formerly; the life they will live after you, and the life the barbarous nations now live: And how many know not even your name; how many will quickly forget it; how many, who perhaps praise you now, will quickly blame you: And, that neither a surviving fame is a thing of value; nor present glory; nor any thing at all [of that kind.]

31. Tranquillity as to what happens by external causes: Justice in what proceeds from the active principle within you: that is, a bent of will and course of action which rests and is satisfied in its having been exerted for the good of society; as being suited to your nature.

32. You can cut off a great many superfluous things which crowd and disturb <222> you; for they lye wholly in your own opinion: and by this you will make a great deal of room and ease to yourself. § As, by comprehending, by your judgment, the whole universe; by considering the age you live in; and by considering the quick changes of each thing, in particular; how short the time from its birth to its dissolution; how immense the space of time before its birth; and the time after its dissolution, equally infinite.

* VIII. 3.

† VII. 48, 49.

‡ Gataker seems to have mistaken this:[16] See, VII. 48. where births, marriages, and deaths, are expressed.

§ This is perhaps a new meditation, and should begin thus.—Comprehend &c.

33. All things you see will quickly perish; and those, who behold them perishing, will themselves also quickly perish: and he who died in extreme old-age, will be in the same condition with him who died early.

34. What kind of governing parts have these men! And about what things are they earnestly employed! And on what accounts do they love and honour! Imagine their minds naked before you. When they fancy their censures hurt, or their praises, profit us; how great their self-conceit!

35. Loss is nothing else but change: and in this delights the nature of the <223> whole; by which all things are formed well. From the beginning of ages they have been managed in the same way: and to all eternity, such like things will be. How can you say both that all things were formed, and that all shall be always, in a bad state. Among so many Gods, it seems, there is no sufficient power found out to rectify those things? but the universe is condemned to remain involved in never ceasing evils.[17]

36. How putrid the material substance of every thing! Water, dust, little bones, and nauseous excretions. Again; marble is but the concreted humours of the earth; gold and silver its heavy dregs: Our cloaths but hairs; and the purple colour of them, * blood. All other things are of the same kind. The animal spirit too is another such thing, passing always from one change to another.

37. Enough of this wretched life, of repining, and apish trifling. Why are you disturbed? Are any of these things new? What astonishes you? Is it the † active principle? view it well. Or, is it the material? View it also well. Besides these there is nothing else. Nay, I obtest you by the Gods, come at length to ‡ <224> more simplicity of heart, and equity in your sentiments.

It is the same thing whether you have observed these things for a hundred years, or for three.

38. If he has done wrong, the evil is his: and, perhaps, too, he has not done wrong.

39. Either all events proceed from one intelligent fountain § [in the whole] as in one body: and then the part ought not to complain of what

* Of a shell-fish.

† See, XI. 1. near the end.

‡ Others thus read the text: "Nay towards the Gods, too, behave with . . ."

§ See, IV. 40.

happens on account of the whole. Or all is atoms: and nothing else but a jumble of parts, and a dissipation again. Why are you disturbed then? [Your governing part you may still preserve exempt from chance:] * need you say to it thou art dead: thou art rotten: thou art dissembling: thou art joining the herd; feeding; and turn'd savage.

40. Either the Gods have no power at all [to aid men in any thing;] or they have power. If, then, they have no power, why do you pray? But if they have power, why don't you chuse to pray to them to enable you, neither to fear any of these things, [which are not in our <225> own power] nor desire any of them, nor be grieved about any of them; rather than for the having them, or the not having them. For, most certainly, if they can aid men at all, they can also aid them in this. But, perhaps you will say; the Gods have put this in my own power. Well, then, is it not better to use the things which are in your own power, and preserve your liberty; than perplex your self about the things which are not in your own power, and become an abject slave. And who told you the Gods don't give us their assistance, too, in the things which are in our own power? Begin, therefore, to pray about these things; and you will see. One prays; how shall I enjoy this woman! Do you; how shall I have no desire to enjoy her! Another; how shall I be freed from this man! Do you; how shall I not need to be freed from him! A third; how shall I prevent the loss of my child! Do you; how shall I not be afraid to lose him! Upon the whole; turn your prayers this way, and look what will be the effect. † <226>

41. Epicurus says: "When I was sick, my conversations were not about the diseases of this poor body: nor did I speak of any such things to those who came to me. But continued to discourse of these principles of natural philosophy, I had before established: And was chiefly intent on this; how the intellectual part, tho' it partakes of such violent commotions of the

* The Greek is corrupted and manque here, and the commentators all at a loss how to restore it. As to the sense here attempted, it is the same as sect. 28 of this book.

† Of the same kind is that beautiful passage quoted by Gataker from Arrian II, 18.[18] "Stay, mortal! Be not rash. The combat is great. The attempt God-like. It is for sovereignty; for liberty; for a current of life ever gentle, clear, and unruffled. CALL TO MIND THE DEITY. INVOKE HIM TO BE YOUR ASSISTANT AND SUPPORTER: As men at sea invoke Castor and Pollux in a storm."

body, might remain undisturbed, and preserve its own proper good. Nor did I allow the physicians to make a noise, and vaunt, as if doing something of great moment. But my life continued pleasant and happy."[19] What he did, when under a disease, do you, also, if you fall into one, or are under any other uneasy circumstances: that is, never depart from your philosophy, whatever befalls you; nor run into the silly way of the vulgar, and such as are unacquainted with nature. * It is the common maxim of all sects of philosophy; to be wholly <227> intent on what they are doing, and the instrument or means by which they do it.

42. When you are disgusted with the impudence of any one, immediately ask yourself; can the universe, then, be without the shameless? It cannot. Don't demand, then, what is impossible: For this is one of those shameless men, who must needs be in the universe. Have the same question also at hand, when shock'd at the crafty, the faithless, or the faulty in any respect. For, while you remember it is impossible but such kind of men must needs be in the universe, you will at the same time have more good-nature toward each of them in particular. It is highly useful, too, to have immediately this reflection: What virtue has nature given man, enabling him to bear with this fault [in his fellow?] † For, against the unreasonable, she has given meekness, as an antidote: And so, against another, some other ability. You are also at full liberty to set right one who has wandered. Now, every one who does wrong ‡ misses his <228> aim, and has wandered. And, then, what harm, pray, have you got? for you will find, none of those, at whom you are exasperated, have done any thing by which the intellectual part of you was like to be the worse. Now, what is your [real] evil, and harm, has all its subsistence there. And what is there evil, or strange, if the uninstructed acts like one uninstructed? Look if you ought not rather to blame yourself, for not having laid your account with this man's being guilty of such faults. For you had the means from reason to have concluded with yourself, it is likely this man will be guilty of such a fault; yet have forgot, and are surprised that he is guilty of it. But, especially, when you

* The Greek is corrupted here.

† See Epictet. Enchirid. Sect. 9.[20] and the Apostle to Titus, ch. 3. v. 1, and 3.[21]

‡ As all pursue what appears to them at that time, their proper good and happiness. See, VI. 27. VIII. 14. and especially V. 17. and the note.

blame any one as faithless, or ungrateful, turn to yourself: For the fault was, already, manifestly on your side; if, either you trusted, that one of such a disposition would keep his faith; or, if when you gave a favour, you did not give it ultimately [without further view] so as to reap all the fruit of it by your very doing it. For, what wou'd you more, when you have done a kind office to a man? Is it not enough to you, that you have acted in this according to your nature? Do you ask a reward for it? This <229> is as if the eye were to ask a reward for seeing; or the feet for walking. For, as these are form'd for a certain purpose, which when they fulfill according to their proper structure, they have their proper perfection; so, also, man, formed by nature for kind offices [to his fellows,] when he does any kind office to another, or any thing otherways conducive to the good of society, has done what he is form'd for; and has his proper good and perfection. <230>

BOOK X

1. Wilt thou, ever, O my soul! be good, and simple, and one, and naked, more apparent than the body that surrounds thee? Wilt thou ever taste of the loving and affectionate temper? wilt thou ever be full, and without wants; without longings after any thing, without desires after any thing, either animate or inanimate, for the enjoyment of pleasure? Or time, for lengthening the enjoyment? Or of place, or country, or fine climate? Or of the * social concord of men? But † satisfied with thy present state, and well-<231>pleased with every present circumstance? persuade ‡ thyself thou hast all things: all is § right and well with thee: and comes to thee from the Gods. And all shall be right and well for thee which they please to give, and which they are about to give for the safety of ** the perfect animal; the good; the just; the fair; the parent of all things; the supporter, the container, the surrounder of all things; which are [all] dissolving for the birth of such others as themselves. Wilt thou ever be able, so to live

* His leisure was perpetually broke by wars.

† Philippians, IV. 11. "I have learned, in whatever state I am, therewith to be content."[1]

Epictetus, in the Enchirid. 15.[2] "Remember, you ought to behave yourself in life, as if at an entertainment. Does any thing come, in course, to you? stretch out your hand, and take it gracefully. Does it go by you? Don't stop it. Is it not come yet? Don't long after it; but wait till it come to you. Do thus in the case of your children, of your wife, of power, of riches; and you shall be at length a worthy companion of the Gods. And if, even when set before you, you don't take, but overlook them; you shall then be not only a companion of the Gods, but a fellow-governor with them.

‡ II. Corinth. VI. 10. "Having nothing, yet possessing all things." But the whole passage from verse 3 to 11, is of the same kind, and extremely beautiful.[3]

§ Rom. VIII. 28. "All things work together for good to them who love God."

** The universe: See, IV. 23.

a fellow-citizen of * Gods and men, as, neither, in any respect, † to complain of them, nor be disapproved by them.

2. ‡ Observe what your nature demands as far as you are under the government of mere vegetative nature. Then do that, and approve it, if your nature, <232> as an animal, won't be thence rendered the worse. Next you must observe what your nature, as an animal, demands. And take to yourself every thing of this kind, if your nature, as a rational-animal, won't be thence rendered the worse. Now 'tis plain the rational nature is also social. So, use these rules, and trouble yourself for none further.

3. Whatever happens, happens such as you are either formed by nature able to bear it, or not able to bear it. If such as you are by nature form'd able to bear, bear it and fret not: But if such as you are not naturally able to bear, don't fret; for when it has consum'd you, itself will perish. Remember, however, you are by nature form'd able to bear whatever it is in the power of your own opinion to make supportable or tolerable, according as you conceive it advantageous, or your duty, to do so.

4. If he is going wrong, teach him humanely, and show him his mistake. If this be impossible for you, blame yourself; or not even yourself.

5. Whatever happens to you, it was before preparing for you from eternity; and the concatenation of causes had, <233> from eternity, interwoven your subsistence with this contingency.

6. Whether all be atoms, or there be [presiding] natures, let this be laid down as indisputable; that I am a part of the whole; and the whole must be conducted by its own nature, be that what it will: and that I am in some manner socially connected with the parts which are of the same kind with myself. For while I remember this, I shall, as I am a part, be dissatisfied with nothing appointed me by the whole. For nothing advantageous to the whole is hurtful to the part. For the whole has nothing in it but what is advantageous to itself; that being common to all natures; and the nature of the whole has this further, that it can't be forc'd by any external cause, to produce any thing hurtful to itself. By remembering, then, I am a part of

* Philip. III. 20. "Our conversation, (or as it may be rather translated, the city we belong to), is in heaven."

† Rom. XIV. 18. "Acceptable to God and approved of men." See XII. 12. and 24.

‡ See the note at V. 36.

such a whole, I shall be well-pleased with every thing which comes from it. And as far as I am in some manner one of the same family with the parts of the same kind with me, I will be guilty of nothing unsocial; nay, I will rather aim at the good of my kind; turn the whole bent of my will to the public advantage, and withdraw it from the contrary.[4] When I accomplish these things <234> in this manner, my life must needs run smooth and clear: Just so, as you would judge a citizen in a happy flow of life, who was going on in a course of action profitable for his fellow citizens, and gladly embracing whatever is appointed him by the city.

7. The parts of the whole, all the parts, I mean, which the universe contains, must needs be in a state of corruption. Let this expression be used for denoting a state of change. If then, I say, this be both evil and necessary to them, the whole cannot possibly be in a right state; since the parts are prone to change, and remarkably form'd for corrupting.—For, whether did nature herself take in hand to do evil to the parts of herself, and to make them both subject to fall into evil, and such as of necessity have fallen into evil? Or has this happened without her knowledge?—Both these are equally incredible.—And if one, quitting the notion of a [presiding] nature, mean only that things are so constituted; how ridiculous! to say, the parts of the whole, by their very constitution, tend to change; and yet be surpris'd, or fretted, at any thing, as happening contrary to the nature of things: especially, too, as the dissolution <235> of every thing is into those very elements of which it is compos'd. For it is either a dissipation of those elements of which it was a mixture; or a conversion of them: of the solid to the earthy, and the spirituous to the aerial. So that these too are taken into the plan of the whole, which is either to undergo * periodical conflagrations, or be renewed by perpetual changes. And don't think you had all the earthy and the aerial parts from your birth. They were late accessions of yesterday or the day before, by your food, and the air you breathed. These accessions, therefore, are changed, and not what your mother bore. Grant that this their change † into the peculiar nature of your body makes you cling earnestly to them, it alters nothing of what I was just now saying.

* See V. 13. and the note.

† This passage is extremely obscure, critics only guess at some sort of meaning to it.

8. If you take to yourself these names, a good man, one of a high sense of honour, modesty, veracity; one of attention of mind, conformity of mind, elevation of mind; take care you never change them for others. And if you happen to lose them at any time, run quickly back <236> to them. And remember, by attention of mind you meant to denote, that your knowlege, in every thing, be always founded on a thorough unbyassed inquiry into the true nature of the objects; and that nothing enter your mind without being carefully examined: By conformity of mind; a willing acceptance of every thing appointed by the common nature. By elevation of mind; the raising the thinking part superior to any pleasant or painful commotion of the flesh, to the little views of fame, to death, and all such things. If, then, you stedfastly keep to these names, without affecting or desiring these appellations from others, you will be quite another man; and enter into quite another life. For, to continue such a one as you have been till now, and subject to the distraction and pollution of such a life, is the part of * one extremely insensible, and fond of life; and who is like one of those half devoured combatants with the wild beasts [in the public shows] who, when covered with wounds and gore, yet beg to be preserved till to morrow; even to be exposed again to the same jaw and fangs. Resolutely force yourself into these few cha-<237>racters; and, if you are able to abide in them, abide, as one who has removed and settled in the † fortunate Islands. But if you perceive you fall from them, and succeed not thoroughly [in your intention to abide in them,] retire boldly into some corner, where you may prevail, [by meeting with less opposition] or, even, depart out of life altogether; yet not angry [that you could not prevail;] but with simplicity, liberty, and modesty; having at least perform'd this one thing well, in life, that you have in this manner departed out of it. Now, it will greatly assist you to keep in mind these names, if you keep in mind the Gods, and that they don't want ‡ adulation and flatte-<238>ry from their worshippers,

* Propter vitam vivendi perdere causas.[5]

† The poetical representations of the tranquillity and happiness of these islands of the blessed are well known.

‡ This sentiment, occurs often in the scriptures, particularly in the 50th psalm, and 1st chap. of Isaiah; and seems not to have been uncommon among the heathens them-

but that all beings indued with reason shou'd become * like unto themselves: Keep in mind too that that is a fig-tree, which performs the business of a fig-tree; a dog, which performs that of a dog; a bee, that of a bee; and a man who performs the business of a man.

9. The public diversions [which you must attend in Rome;] the Wars [abroad,] the consternation, stupidity, and slavery of those about you, will wipe <239> out daily, [if you take not heed,] those sacred maxims; unless † you have settled them upon a thorough consideration of nature, and laid them up in your mind. You ought so to think, and act, on every occasion, that, while you are discharging any external office, your contemplative powers may, at the same time, be exerting themselves, and ‡ your confidence

---

selves; as appears by the following fragment of a dramatic poet, which is no way aggravated in the translation.

> Is there, on earth, a man, so much a fool;
> So silly in credulity; who thinks
> That fleshless bones and the fry'd bile of beasts,
> Which were not food even for a hungry dog,
> Are offerings that the Gods delight to take;
> And these the honours, they expect from men:
> Or, on account of these, will favour shew,
> Tho' robbers, pyrates, nay tho' tyrants be
> The offerers. *See Clem. Alex. Strom. 7.*[6]

> *Compositum jus fasque animo, sanctosque recessus*
> *Mentis, et incoctum generoso pectus honesto;*
> *Haec cedo ut admoveam templis, et farre litabo.*
> Persius sat. 2.[7]

* This is the same with the grand Christian doctrine of the divine life. "(*a*) To be transformed into the same image with God. (*b*) To be conformed to the image of his Son. (*c*) Ye shall be holy as I the Lord your God am holy. (*d*) Pure as God your father is pure. Righteous even as he is righteous. (*e*) Merciful as your father also is merciful. (*f*) Be ye therefore perfect even as your father which is in heaven is perfect." Clemens Alex. testifies too, more than once, that he found the same doctrine in Plato: See Gataker on this place.[8]

Read numbers for these references by the small letters. (1) II. Cor. 3. 18. (2) Rom. 8. 29. (3) Levit. 19. 2. and I. Peter 1. 16. (4) I. John 3. 3, 7. (5) Luke 6. 36. (6) Matth. 5. 48.[9]

† The text is corrupt here. The translation is according to a conjecture of Gataker's.[10]

‡ This is the farthest that can be from what we commonly call self-sufficiency, or a stiff and self-willed temper. It is a virtue highly necessary in some of the sweetest characters; who, often, from too modest a diffidence of themselves, submit their own finer

in yourself, from your right knowledge of things, be preserv'd; unobserved perhaps, but not designedly concealed. For, then, you will enjoy simplicity; then, a dignity of deportment; then, an accurate inquiry into every thing which occurs; what it is in its real nature; what place and rank it has in the universe; how long it is naturally fitted to last; what <240> it is compos'd of; who may possess it; and who may give it, and take it away.

10. The spider exults if it has caught a fly: another, if he has caught a little hare; another, if a little fish in a purse-net; another, if he has hunted down wild-boars; another, if, bears; another, if he has conquered the Sarmatians.[11] Are not all these robbers alike, if you examine their sentiments? *

11. Acquire a method of contemplating how all things change into one another. Apply constantly to this part [of philosophy,] and exercise yourself thoroughly in it. For there is nothing so proper as this for raising you to an elevation and greatness of mind. He who does this, has already put off the body, and being sensible how instantly he must depart from among men, and leave all these things behind him, resigns himself entirely to † justice, in whatever he does him-<241>self; and to the nature of the whole, in every thing else which happens. What any one may say or think of him, or do against him, on this he spends not a thought. He satisfies himself with these two things: With acting justly in what he is at present doing; and with loving what is at present appointed for him. He has thrown off all hurry and bustle; and has no other will but this, to ‡ go on in the straight way § according to the law; and to ** follow God in the straight way.

---

sentiments, and allow themselves to be guided and led wrong, by men of far less genius and worth than themselves, whose low views their own candour makes them not suspect.

* This has probably been occasioned by the behavior of some of his officers, upon seizing parties of the Sarmatians, with whom the Romans were then at war; and designed to repress the vanity of conquerors.

† Justice is taken here in the extensive platonic sense, regarding not only what are called the rights of mankind, but comprehending resignation to God, and all the kindest social virtues. See, XI. 20. at the end; and, XII. 1.[12]

‡ See, V. 3.

§ See, II. 16. at the end.

** According to Gataker, Antoninus has here before his eye the following passage of Plato in the 4th book of the laws. "God, in whose hand is the beginning, end, and middle

12. What need of suspicions [about the event?] Since you can consider what ought to be done: and if you understand that surely, go on in the road to it, calmly, and inflexibly. * But if you are not sure, suspend, and consult the best advisers. If you meet with any obstacles in the way, proceed with a prudent caution, accord-<242>ing to the means you have; keeping close to what appears just. For that is the best mark to aim at. Since the failing in that is the only proper miscarriage. He who, in every thing, follows reason [or the law of his nature] is always at leisure, and yet ready for any business; always chearful, and yet composed.

13. As soon as you awake, immediately ask yourself. Will it be of consequence to you, if what is just and good be done by some other person? It will not. Have you forgot, those who assume such airs of importance in their praises and censures of others, what kind of men they are in bed, and at table? What their actions are; what they shun, and what pursue? What they steal, and what they rob? Not with feet and hands, but with their most precious part; by which one may, if he has the will, procure to himself faith, honour and modesty, truth, † law, and a good divinity within, [which is the supreme felicity or good-fortune.]

14. To [the presiding] nature, which gives and resumes again all things, the well-instructed mind, possessed of a sense <243> of honour and decency, says; "Give what thou willest: take back what thou willest." And this he says not with an arrogant ostentation, but with obedience alone, and good-will to her.

15. This remainder you have of life is small. Live, as if on a [lonely] mountain. For 'tis no matter whether there or here, if one, where ever he lives, considers the universe as a city. Let men see and know you to be a man indeed, living according to nature. If they cannot bear with you, let them put you to death. For better so than live as they do.

---

of all things, pursues the straight way; going about every where, according to nature. He is always attended by justice, who punishes those who come short in their observance of the divine law; The man who is about to live happy, keeps close by her, and follows God along with her."[13]

* The reading in the original here is uncertain.

† The grand law of promoting the perfection of the whole, obedience to which is the supreme happiness. B. VIII. 2. and X. 25.

16. Spend your time no longer, in discoursing on what are the qualities of the good-man; but in actually being such.

17. Frequently represent to your imagination a view of the whole of time, and the whole of substance: And that every individual thing is, in substance, as a grain of millet; and, in duration, as a * turn of a wimble.

18. Consider, with attention, each of the things around you as already dissolving, and in a state of change, and, as it were, corruption, or dissipation; or, as each formed by nature such as to die. <244>

19. What sort of men are they when eating, sleeping, procreating, easing nature, and the like! And, then, what sort of men when † distributing their largesses, and elate with pride; or angry, and sharply rebuking with a stately insolence! To how many were they, but lately, slaves, and on what accounts! and in what condition will they shortly be?

20. That is for the advantage of each which the nature of the whole brings to each. And for his advantage at that time, at which she brings it.

21. ‡ "Earth loves the rain";—"And the majestic Ether loves [the earth."][14] The universe, also, loves to do that which is going to happen. I say, then to the universe; § "What thou lovest I love." Is not our common ** phrase <245> according to fact, when we say "such a thing loves to be so," [to denote that it is usual or natural.]

22. Either you are living here, and now habituated to it: Or going hence, and that was your will: Or you are dying, and have finished your public offices in life. Now besides these there is nothing else. So, take courage.

* This a proverbial simile for things that pass in a moment.

† This word is uncertain in the original.

‡ From Euripides.

§ φιλει in Greek as *amat* in Latin for *solet.*[15]

** Thus Epictetus, Arrian II. 16. "Have the courage to lift up your eyes to God, and say: Use me, after this, for what purposes thou willest; my sentiments concur with thee. I plead against nothing which seems proper to thee." And IV. 7. "I adhere to him as a servant and attendant. His purpose, his desire, and in a word, his will, is mine also." Thus also Seneca in his antithetical way. Epist. 96, "I don't [barely] obey God, but [cordially] assent to him. I follow him from inclination, and not necessity." So that resignation to the will of God, in the highest sense, appears to have been a maxim universal among the Stoics.[16]

23. Let this be always manifest to you: That a country retirement is just like any other place; and that * all things are the same there as on the mountain-top, or at the wild sea-coast, or any where. For you may always meet with that of Plato, who says, "[The wise man ever enjoys retirement;] he makes the city-wall serve him for a shepherd's fold on a hill-top."[17]

24. What is my governing-part to me? and to what purposes am I now using it? Is it void of understanding? Is <246> it loosened and rent off from society? Is it glewed to, and incorporated with the flesh, so as to turn which way that pleases?

25. He who flies from his master is a fugitive-slave. Now, the law is our master; and so the transgressor of the law is the fugitive: and he, also, who is grieved, or angry, or afraid, because any thing has happened, or is happening, or formerly happened, of these things which are ordered by him who governs all: Who is † the law, appointing to every one what is proper for him. He, then, who is afraid, or grieved, or angry, is the fugitive-slave.

26. When one has cast the seed into the womb, he departs: another cause receives it, operates, and finishes the infant. Wonderful production from such a beginning! Again, the infant lets the food down its throat; and then another cause <247> receives it, and transforms it into [organs of] sensation, motion, and, in a word, life, and strength, and other things how many and surprising! Contemplate therefore, these things, tho' done so very covertly, and view the power [which produces them] in the same way as you view the power which makes bodies tend downwards or upwards: not with your eyes, indeed; yet no less manifestly.

27. Frequently reflect, how all things which happened formerly were just such as happen now. Reflect, also, that such too will those be which are to ensue. And place before your eyes the whole, which you have ever known, either from your own experience, or ancient history; dramas, and scenes,

* "To what place soever I go, there I can enjoy the sun, &c.—and there the society of the Gods." Epictet. II. 23.[18]

† This passage clears up many others where the same word occurs obscurely. See, VII. 31.[19]

Thus also, the author of the book de Mundo, which goes under Aristotle's name; chap. 6. "For our law, exactly impartial to all, is God; incapable of amendment or change; more excellent, I think, and stable, than those written on the tables of Solon."[20]

all of the same kind. Such as the whole court of Hadrian; the whole court of Antoninus; the whole court of Philip; of Alexander; of Croesus.[21] For all these were of the same kind [with your own] only composed of other persons.

28. Conceive every one, who is grieved, or storms, at any thing whatever, to be like the pig in a sacrifice, which kicks and screams, while under the knife. Such too is he, who, on his couch, deplores in silence, by himself, that we are <248> all tied to our fate. Consider, too, that, only to the rational animal it is given to follow * willingly what happens. But the bare following is a necessity upon all.

29. Look attentively on each particular thing you are doing; and ask yourself, if death be a terror because it deprives you of this.

30. † When you are offended at a fault of any one, immediately turn to yourself; and consider, what fault of a like kind you yourself commit. Such as judging money to be good; or pleasure; <249> or glory; and so of the rest. For, by fixing your attention on this, you will quickly forget your anger; taking this along, too, that he is ‡ forced. For, what else cou'd he do? or, if you can, remove what forces him.

31. When you consider § Satyrio the Socratic, think on Eutyches, or Hymen: and, when you consider Euphrates, think on Eutychio or Silvanus. And when Alciphron, think on Tropaiophorus; and when you consider Xenophon, think on Crito or Severus.[22] And when you look into yourself,

* Epictetus. II. 16. "All these, sorrow, fear, envy, desire, effeminacy, intemperance, it is impossible for you to throw off, otherways than by looking up to God, giving yourself up to him, piously embracing all he orders. Nay tho' your will be otherways, yet with all your wailing and groaning, you must still follow him, as the stronger."[23]

† It is recorded of Plato, that he practiced habitually this maxim. In Epictetus too the following divine passage is of the same kind, IV. 4. "I attend to what men say, and how they act, not with any bad intention, or that I may have matter of blaming, or laughing at them; but I turn into myself to see if I, too, commit the same faults. [My next inquiry is] how shall I get free of them? If I also was subject formerly to the same weakness, and am not now; 'TIS TO GOD I GIVE THE PRAISE."[24]

‡ See VI. 27. and IX. 42.

§ Of these names which follow, few are known; but it is plain, in general, his design here is, that, the sight of remarkable men should make one call to mind others like them in former ages, who are now gone. And that no man is of such importance, that he will be much missed in the universe; others as great are arising.

think on any one of the Cesars. And so analogously, when you see any body else. Then let this at the same time enter your mind. Where, now, are those? No where? Or who can tell? For thus you will constantly behold all human things as smoke and nothing. Especially if you recollect, that, what has once changed, will never exist again through all the infinity of time. How <250> soon, then, will your change come? And why is it not sufficient to you to pass this short space gracefully [in this universe.] How fine a * subject of employment to yourself are you shunning? For, what are all things but exercises for that rational power which hath viewed all things that occur in life, with accuracy, and according to their true natures? Stay, then, till you make all these things familiar to yourself: As the healthy stomach adapts all things to itself: As † the shining fire turns whatever you throw on it, into flame and splendor.

32. Let no-body have it in his power to say with truth of you, that you are not a man of simplicity, candour and goodness. But let him be mistaken, whoever has such an opinion of you. Now, all this is in your own power. For, what is he who hinders you to be good, and single-hearted? Only do you determine to live no longer if you are not to be such a man. For neither does ‡ reason, in that case, require you should.

33. In this present matter you are employ'd about, what can be done or <251> said in the soundest, [and most upright] manner? For, whatever that be, you are at liberty to do or say it. And don't make pretences, as if hindered. You will never cease from groaning [and repining,] till once you be so affected, that such as luxury is to the men of pleasure, such be to you the doing, in every subject of action that is thrown in your way, or falls into it, those things which are properly suitable to the frame and constitution of man. For, every thing, which you are at liberty to perform according to your own proper nature, you must conceive to be a delightfull enjoyment; and you have this liberty every where. Now, to the cylinder, it is not given to move every where in its proper motion: Nor to the water: Nor to the fire: Nor to any of those other things which are governed by a nature or a

* See VII. 68.

† See the same simile beautifully apply'd, IV. 1.

‡ See IX. 29.

soul irrational: For there are many things which restrain, and stop them. But intelligence and reason can pursue the course it is naturally fitted for, and wills, thro' every obstacle. Place before your eyes this easiness with which reason goes on through all obstacles, as the fire upward, as the stone downward, as the cylinder on the declivity; and seek for nothing further. For the other stops <252> are, either those of the insensible carcase, or such as don't hurt the man, or do him any evil, unless by opinion, and by Reason's own yielding itself to them, otherways he who suffered by them, wou'd himself presently have become evil. In all other fabrics, indeed, whatever evil happens to them, the sufferer itself thereby becomes the worse. But, here, if I may say so, the man becomes even the better, and the more praise-worthy, by making a right use of what falls across to him. Upon the whole, remember, nothing hurts him who is by nature a citizen, which hurts not the city. Nor hurts the city, which hurts not the law. Now none of these things called misfortunes hurt the law. So, what hurts not the law, neither hurts the city nor the citizen.[25]

34. To him, whose heart the true maxims have pierced, the shortest, the most common hint is a sufficient memorial to keep himself free of sorrow and fear. Such as,

> Some leaves the winds blow down: the fruitful wood
> Breeds more mean-while; which in spring-time appear.
> Of men, thus, ends one race, while one is born. * <253>

Your children, too, are little leaves; and these are leaves too, who declaim with such important airs of assurance, and sound forth the praises of others, or, on the contrary, curse them; or, who privately censure and sneer at them. In the same manner, these are leaves, also, who are to preserve your surviving fame. For all these, "in spring-tide appear." Then the wind shall presently throw them down. And the forest breed others in their stead. The short-lived existence is common to them all. Yet are you dreading or courting them, as if they were to be eternal. Nay, in a little, you will close your eyes. And him, who carries you out to your funeral, shall another bewail.

* Iliad VI. 148. Brevity is chiefly studied in the translation of these three lines of the Iliad; as designed for a short hint.[26]

35. The sound eye ought to behold [with ease] all the objects of sight; and not say, "I want the green": for that is like one who has sore eyes. The sound ear, and sense of smelling, ought to be ready for all the objects of hearing and smelling; and the sound stomach be equally disposed for all sorts of food, as a mill for all it is framed to grind. So also the sound mind ought to be ready for all things which happen. That mind which says, "Let my children be preserved; and let all men applaud whatever I do"; is an eye <254> which seeks the green objects; or teeth, which seek the tender food.

36. There is no man of so happy a lot, but that, when he dies, some of the by-standers will rejoice at the * evil which befalls him. Was he good and wise? Will there not be some-body, who, at his death, will say within himself? "I shall at last get breathing from this strict tutor. He was not indeed severe to any of us. Yet I was sensible he tacitly condemned us." Thus will they say of the good man. But, in my case, how many other reasons are there, for which, multitudes wou'd gladly get rid of me? This you may reflect on, when a-dying; † and depart with the less regret, when you consider, "I am going out of such a life, that, in it, my very partners, for whose sakes I underwent and struggled with so many labours, put up so many prayers, had so many cares, those very men are wishing me to be gone; hoping from thence, 'tis likely, for some other satisfaction." Who, then, would strive for a longer stay here? Don't, however, on this account, go off less benign toward <255> them. But preserve your own manners, and continue to them friendly, benevolent, and propitious: and, on the other hand, don't go off, as torn away; but as, when one dies a gentle death, the soul comes easily out of the body; such also ought your departure from these men to be. For nature had knit and cemented you to them: But now she parts you. I part, then, as from relations; not reluctant however, but peaceable. For death, too, is one of the things according to nature.[27]

37. Accustom yourself, as much as possible, in every thing any one is doing, to consider with yourself; What end does he refer this to? But, begin, at home; and examine yourself first.

* Death being in their opinion an evil.

† This is one of those he calls popular supports, which yet strike the heart: See IX. 3.

38. Remember, 'tis * that which lies hid within, which draws and turns you † as the wires do the puppet. 'Tis that, is eloquence: That, life: That, if I may say so, is the man. Never blend with it, in your imagination, this surrounding earthen vessel, and these little organs. They are but like the ax, [any tool of any artizan,] with this only difference, that they are <256> naturally united with us: since, none of these parts are of any more service, without the cause which moves and stops them, than the shuttle is to the weaver; the pen, to the writer; or the whip, to the charioteer. <257>

* Passions and opinions in the mind.

† See this term explained, at II. 2. in the note.

BOOK XI

1. These are the privileges of the rational soul: It contemplates itself: It forms or fashions itself in all parts: It makes itself such as it desires: * The fruit it bears, itself enjoys; whereas, others enjoy the fruits of vegetables and lower animals: It always obtains its end, whensoever the close of life may overtake it. In the dance, or the dramatic action, if by any thing interrupted, the whole action is made incomplete; but, as to the soul, in whatever part of action, or wheresoever, overtaken by death, the past action † may be a com-<258>plete whole, without any defect. So that, I may say, "I have obtained all which is mine." Nay, further, it ranges around the whole universe, and the void spaces beyond; views its extent; stretches into the immensity of duration, and considers and comprehends the periodical renovation of the whole. It discerns, also, that those who come after us shall see nothing new; and that our predecessors saw no more than we have seen. Nay, one who has lived but forty years, if of any tolerable understanding, has, because of the uniformity of all things, seen, in a manner, all that is past and future. These, too, are the properties of the rational soul: love to all around us; truth, and modesty; and the respecting nothing more than itself. Which,

* See IX. 10.

† As the supreme excellence of the rational soul is, according to the Stoics, an entire conformity to the will of the presiding mind, or agreement with nature; and this is their supreme and only happiness: He who acts well the part appointed to him, whether a long or a short one, has attained to the greatest happiness and perfection of his nature. Hence their paradox that "length of time is of no importance to happiness." All obstacles to our designs about external things, afford new occasions of the best actions, those which are most conformable to nature: Such as resignation to the will of God; good-will toward those who oppose us; submission to any distresses, or to an early death, happening by the divine providence. And thus our part may always be complete.[1]

too, is the property of the * law. Thus, there is no difference between right reason and the † reason of justice.

2. You may be enabled to despise the delightful song, or the dance, or the <259> admired exercises; if you divide the harmonious tune into its several notes, and ask yourself about each of them apart, "Is it this which so charms and conquers me?" For you would blush to own that. Do the like as to the dance, about each posture and motion; and the like about the exercises. In general, as to all things, except virtue, and the offices of virtue, remember to enure yourself to a low estimation of them, by running forthwith to their several parts, and considering them separately. Transfer the like practice to the whole of life.

3. How happy is that soul, which is prepared, either to depart presently from the body, or to be extinguished, or dispersed, or to remain along with it! But, let this preparation arise from its own judgment, and not from mere obstinacy, like that of the ‡ Christians;[2] that you <260> may die considerately, with a venerable composure; so as even to persuade others into a like disposition; and without noise, or ostentation.[3]

4. Have I done any thing social and kind? Is not this itself my advantage § ? Let this thought always occur; and never cease to do such actions.

5. What art do you profess? To be good. And, how else is this to be accomplished, but by the great maxims about the nature of the whole, and about the peculiar ** structure and furniture of human nature?

6. Tragedies were, at first, introduced, as remembrancers of the events which frequently happen, and must happen, according to the course of

* See X. 25.

† See X. 12. and the note.[4]

‡ It is no wonder an heathen emperor should thus speak of the Christians. It is well known that their ardour for the glory of martyrdom was frequently immoderate; and was censured even by some of the primitive fathers. This is no dishonour to christianity, that it did not quite extirpate all sort of human frailty. And there is something so noble in the stedfast lively faith, and the stable persuasion of a future state, which must have supported this ardour, that it makes a sufficient apology for this weakness, and gives the strongest confirmation of the divine power accompanying the Gospel.

§ See the end of the IX. book.

** This, as it was often mentioned already, is such as both recommends to us all pious veneration and submission to God, and all social affections; and makes such dispositions our chief satisfaction and happiness.

nature; and to intimate, that, such events, as entertain us on the stage, we should, without repining, bear upon the greater stage of the world. You see that such things must be accomplished; and, that those per-<261>sons could not avoid bearing them, who made the most dismal exclamations, " * Alas Cithoeron!" Our dramatic poets have many profitable sayings; such as that, especially,

Me and my children, if the Gods neglect,
It is for some good reason. ———

And again,

Vain is all anger at the external things.

And,

For life is, like the loaden'd ear, cut down.

And such like.[5]

To tragedy succeeded the antient comedy; using a very instructive liberty of speech; and, by open direct censure, humbling the pride of the great. To this end, Diogenes used something of the same nature. Next, consider well, for what purpose the middle comedy, and the new, was introduced;[6] which, by degrees, is degenerated, from the moral view, into the mere ingenuity of artifi-<262>cial imitation. 'Tis well known, however, that they, too, contain many useful admonitions. But, consider for what † purpose this whole contrivance of poetry, and dramatical pieces, was intended.

7. How manifest is it, that ‡ no other course of life was more adapted to the practice of philosophy than that you are engaged in?

* This relates to the celebrated tragedy of Sophocles, being the exclamation of Oedipus in his distress, wishing he had perished in his childhood when he was exposed on that mountain.[7]

† I suppose, to make us see, that many calamities, unlucky accidents, crimes, frauds, oppressions, and cunning artifices, are to be expected in the world; and to make them so familiar to us, that we shall not be much surprised, or lose presence of mind, and proper self-command and recollection, when they happen.

‡ This is an amiable notion of providence, that it has ordered for every good man that station of life, and those circumstances, which infinite wisdom foresaw were fittest for his solid improvement in virtue, according to that original disposition of nature which God had given him.[8]

8. A branch broken off from that branch to which it adhered, must necessarily be broken off from the whole tree. Even thus, a man broken off from any fellow-man, has fallen off from the social community. A branch must always be broke off by the force of something else: But, a man breaks off himself from his neighbour, by hatred or aversion; and is not aware that he thus tears off himself <263> from the whole political union. But, this is the singular gift of Jupiter, who constituted this community, to mankind, that we may again re-unite in this continuity, and grow together, and become natural parts, completing the whole. Yet, such separations, happening often, make the reunion and the restitution more difficult. In general, there is a considerable difference, between a branch which has always grown along, and conspired, with the tree; and one which has been broken off, and ingrafted again. Of these, say the gardeners, they may * make one tree in appearance with the stock, but not make an uniform whole with it.[9]

9. They who oppose you, in your progress according to right reason; as they cannot force you to quit the sound course of action; so, let them not turn you off from <264> your kind affections toward themselves. Vigilantly persist in both these; not only in the stable judgment and practice, but in all meekness toward those who attempt to hinder you, or otherwise give you trouble. 'Tis a sign of weakness, either to be enraged at them, or desist from the right practice, and give up yourself as defeated. Both are deserters from their post, the coward, and he who is alienated in affection from one by nature a-kin to him, and who ought to be beloved.

10. Nature cannot be inferior to art: The arts are but imitations of nature. If so, that nature which is of all others the most complete, and most comprehensive, cannot be inferior to the most artificial contrivance. Now, all arts subject and subordinate the less excellent to that which is more excel-

* There is great difficulty in ascertaining the text here, and apprehending well what is intended by the terms of gardening alluded to. In general, 'tis the author's intention to shew how much a continued innocence of manners is preferable to even the most thorough repentance after gross vices; as to the inward tranquillity, and uniform satisfaction, of the soul with itself. To this refer many thoughts in the former books, about the advantage of "being always straight and upright, rather than one rectified and amended."

lent. The universal nature must do the same. Hence the original of * Justice; and from Justice spring the other virtues. Justice cannot be preserved, if we are anxiously sollicitous about indifferent things, or are easily deceived, rash in assent, or inconstant. <265>

11. If those things which occasion you such disturbance in the keen pursuits or dread of them, don't advance to you, but you advance toward them; restrain your judgments about them, and they will stand motionless; and you will neither pursue nor dread them.

12. The soul is as a polish'd sphere, when it neither † extends itself to any thing external, nor yields inwardly to it, nor is compressed in any part; but shines with that light which discovers both the truth in other things, and that ‡ within itself.

13. Does any one despise me? Let him see to it. I shall endeavour, not to be found acting or speaking any thing <266> worthy of contempt. Does any one hate me? Let him see to it. I shall be kind and good-natured toward all; and even ready to shew to this man his mistakes: not to upbraid him, or make a shew of my patience; but from a genuine goodness; as § that of Phocion,[10] if he was truly sincere. Such should be your inward temper; so that the Gods may see you neither angry, nor repining at any thing. For

* The grand point of justice is the highest love to the supreme goodness and excellence, and resignation to infinite wisdom; and, next to this, a steddy obedience to his will, in all acts of beneficence and goodness to our fellows. See X. 12.[11]

† That is, as it were, stretching into length by desires, or admitting other things to stick to it by too eager and passionate fondness or anxiety, or yielding and sinking under the pressure of external evils. See VIII. 41.

‡ As the most important practical truths are found out by attending to the inward calm sentiments or feelings of the heart: And this constitution of heart or soul is certainly the work of God, who created and still pervades all things; it is just and natural to conceive all divine and social dispositions as the work of God: all the great moral maxims deeply affecting the soul, and influencing the conduct, are the illumination of God, and a divine attraction toward himself, and that way of life he requires.

Ille Deo plenus—
Haeremus cuncti superis. Temploque tacente,
Nil facimus non sponte Dei: nec vocibus ullis
Numen eget: dixitque semel nascentibus auctor
Quidquid scire licet. Lucan. lib. IX.[12]

§ The story alluded to, is uncertain. Phocion was of the sweetest and calmest temper.

what can be evil to you, if acting what suits your nature? Won't thou bear whatever is now seasonable to the nature of the universe, O man! Thou, who art formed to will that every thing should happen which is convenient for the whole.

14. Such as despise each other, yet are fawning on each other. Such as strive to surpass each other, are yet * subjecting themselves to each other. <267>

15. How rotten and insincere are these professions: "I resolve to act with you in all simplicity and candor." What are you doing, man? What need you tell us this? It will appear of itself. This profession should appear written in the fore-head: your temper should sparkle out in your eyes; as the person beloved discerns the affection in the eyes of the lover. The man of simplicity and goodness should, in this, resemble such as have a disagreeable smell in their arm-pits; his disposition should be perceived by all who approach him, whether they will or not. The ostentation of simplicity is like a dagger for insidious designs. Nothing is more odious than the friendship of the † wolf. Shun this above all things. The man of real goodness, simplicity, and kindness, bears them in his eyes, and cannot be unobserved.

16. The power of living well is seated in the soul; if it be indifferent toward things which are ‡ indifferent. It will <268> obtain this indifference, if it examines them well in their parts, as well as in the whole; and remembers that none of them can form opinions in us, nor approach to us; but stand still, without motion. These judgments we form ourselves, and as it were inscribe them in ourselves. We may prevent this inscription; or, if it lurks within, unawares, immediately blot it out. 'Tis but for a short time we shall need this vigilance. Our life shall presently cease. Where is the great difficulty of keeping these things right? If the opinions are according to nature, rejoice in them; they will sit easy. If they are contrary to nature, examine what it is that suits your nature; and quickly haste after it, tho'

* By desiring to obtain their applause, or fretting when disappointed: or by such passionate emulation or envy, as occasions a great deal of pain when another succeeds in his designs.

† Alluding to the fable of the treaty; in which, the sheep gave up their dogs as hostages to the wolf, upon his kind professions of friendship.[13]

‡ All external things or events; every thing beside virtue and vice. See B. II. 11.[14]

attended with no glory. A man is always excused, in pursuing his own proper good.

17. [Consider] whence each thing arose; of what compounded; into what changed; what the causes of the change; and that it suffers no evil.

18. [As to those who offend me, let me consider,] first, how I am related to them; that we were formed for each other; that, in another respect, I was set over them [for their defence,] as the ram over the flock, and the bull over the <269> herd. Ascend yet higher. There is either an empire of atoms, or an intelligent nature governing the whole. If this latter, * the inferior natures are formed for the superior, and the superior for each other.

Again, consider † what sort of men they are at table, in bed, and elsewhere; how necessarily they are influenced by their own maxims; and with ‡ what high opinions of their own wisdom they entertain them.

Thirdly, that, if they do right, you ought not to take it ill; if wrong, sure 'tis § unwillingly and ignorantly. 'Tis unwillingly, that any soul is deprived of truth, by erring; or of justice, by a conduct unsuitable to the object. How uneasy is it to them to be reputed unjust, insensible, covetous, or injuriously offensive to all around them? <270>

Fourthly, that ** you have many faults of your own, and are much such another. And, that, though you abstain from some such crimes, yet you have a like strong inclination; however from fear, or concern about your character, you abstain from them.

Fifthly, †† you are not sure they have done wrong. Many things may be done justly, with another intention than you imagine, on some singular occasions. A man must be well informed of many points, before he can pronounce surely about the actions of others.

* This consideration should have great power in restraining all anger, malice, or envy: As no event happens but by the permission of sovereign goodness: and as the great command of this supreme goodness, intimated in the very constitution of nature, is, that all intelligent beings should love and do good to each other.[15]

† This thought leads us to pity the mistakes and errors of others, because of their ignorance; and has frequently occurred before.

‡ See IX. 34.

§ See above, II. 1. and VIII. 14. with the places referred to there.

** See X. 30.

†† This explains IX. 38.

Sixthly, when your anger and resentment is highest, remember human life is but for a moment. We shall be all presently stretched out dead corpses.

Seventhly, that 'tis not the action of others, which disturbs us. Their actions reside in their own souls. Our opinions alone disturb us. Away with them; remove the notion of some terrible evil befallen you, and the anger is gone. How shall I remove it? By considering that what befalls you, has no moral turpitude: And, if you allow any thing else to be * evil, you must fall into <271> many crimes, may become a robber, or one of the worst character.

Eighthly, what worse † evils we suffer by anger and sorrow for such things, than by the things themselves, about which those passions arise.

Ninthly, that meekness is invincible, where it is genuine, and sincere without hypocrisy. For, what can the most insolent do to you, if you stedfastly persist in kindness to him, and, upon occasion, mildly admonish and instruct him thus, at the very time he is attempting to do you an injury? "Don't do so, my son! Nature formed us for a quite different conduct. You cannot hurt me; you hurt yourself, my son!" and shew him tenderly, and in general, that it is so; that bees, and other tribes of animals, don't thus behave to their fellows. But, this must be done without scorn or reproach; with a genuine good-will; and with a calm mind, not stung with the in-<272>jury, without ostentation of your philosophy, or any view to draw admiration from spectators; but as designed for him alone, altho' others may be present. Remember these nine topics, as gifts received from the muses; and begin at length to become a man, for the rest of life. But guard against flattering men, as well as being angry with them: Both are unsociable, and lead to mischief. And, in all anger, recollect, that wrath is not the manly disposition; that calm meekness, as it more becomes the rational nature, so, it is more manly. Strength, and nerves, and fortitude, attend this

* This reasoning is frequent among the Stoics. If other things are reputed evils beside vices, say they, some high degrees of these natural evils impending may overpower our virtuous resolutions. If we dread pain, poverty, or death, as great evils; in order to avoid them, we may be tempted to acts of injustice, to break our faith, or desert our duty to our friends or our country.

† That is moral evils, unkind affections, murmurings against providence.[16]

disposition, and not the wrathful and repining: the nearer this disposition approaches to an immunity from passion, the nearer is it also to strength and power. As sorrow is a weak passion, so is anger: Both have received the wound, and yield to it.

If you want a tenth gift from the president, [or, leader,] of the muses; take this: that, to expect bad men should not commit faults, is madness: 'Tis demanding an impossibility. To allow them to injure others, and demand they should not injure you, is foolish and * tyrannical. <273>

19. These † four dispositions of the soul you should chiefly watch against; and, if discovered, blot them out; by saying thus concerning each of them. "This appearance is not certain evidence. This disposition tends to dissolve the social community. You could not say this from the heart: Now you must repute it the most absurd thing, to speak not according to your own heart." And, fourthly, [suppress] whatever you are conscious is the part of one who is defeated, and subjects the diviner part to the more dishonourable and mortal, the body, and its grosser passions.

20. The aerial and etherial parts in your composition, tho' they naturally ascend; yet, obedient to the order of the whole, they are retained here in the compound. The earthy and humid parts, tho' they naturally descend; yet are raised, and stand erect, tho' not their natural situation. Thus, the elements, wheresoever placed by the superior power, obey the whole; waiting till the signal be given for their dissolution. Is it not grievous, that the intellectual part alone should <274> be disobedient, and fret at its situation? Nor is there any thing violent and opposite to its nature imposed upon it; but all according to its nature; and yet, it cannot bear them, but is carried away in a contrary course: For, all its motions toward injustice, debauchery, sorrows, and fears, are so many departures from its nature. And, when the soul frets at any event, it is deserting its appointed station. It is formed for holiness and piety toward God, no less than for justice. Nay,

* Denying the *jus aequum in populo libero;*[17] and raising yourself above the common lot of mankind, as tyrants and usurpers do; contrary to the laws of the state where they live.

† Rashness of assent, anger, insincerity, sensuality.

these are branches of * social goodness; yea, rather more venerable than any of the branches of justice toward men.

21. He who has not proposed one constant end of life, cannot persist one and the same in the whole of life. But, that is not enough: you must examine this also; what that end or purpose ought to be. For, as the same opinion is not entertained concerning all those things which to the vulgar appear good, but only concerning some of them, such as are of public utility; so, your end proposed must be of the social and political kind. For, he alone who directs all his pursuits to <275> such an end, can make all his actions uniform, and in this manner ever remain the same man.

22. Remember the † country-mouse, and the city-mouse; and the consternation and trembling of the latter.[18]

23. Socrates called the maxims of the vulgar hob-goblins, and terrors only for children.[19]

24. The Spartans, at their public shows, appointed the ‡ seats for foreigners in the shade; but sat themselves any where, as they happened.

25. Socrates made this excuse, for not going to Perdiccas upon his invitation: "lest," says he, "I should perish in the worst manner; receiving kindnesses, for which I cannot make returns."[20]

26. There is a precept even in the § writings of Epicurus, frequently to call to our remembrance some of those who were eminently virtuous.[21] <276>

27. The Pythagoreans recommended to us, in the morning, to view the heavens, to put us in mind of beings which constantly go on executing their proper work; and of order, and purity, and naked simplicity; for, no star hath a vail.

28. Consider what ** Socrates appeared, dressed in a skin; when Xantippe had gone abroad dressed in his cloaths; and with what pleasantries he

* The Stoics speak of the universe, as a great society or state made up of Gods and men, and therefore obedience and resignation is a piece of justice to the governours of this state, See B. V. 22.

† The fable is well known, representing the safety and tranquillity of a retired life, and a low station; and the dangers of ambition.[22]

‡ This shews how manly it is to be enured to hardships, and to bear heat or cold; or is designed as an instance of courtesy.

§ Or, in the Ephesian commentaries; the Greek text is suspected.

** This story is not preserved to us.

detained his friends, who seemed ashamed to see him in that dress, and were retiring.[23]

29. In writing, or in reading, be first taught yourself, before you pretend to teach others. Observe this much more in life.

30. * "Thou, since a slave, no freedom hast of speech."[24]

31. "And my heart laugh'd within me—."[25]

32. "Virtue herself they blame with harshest words."[26]

33. 'Tis madness to expect figs in winter; so it is, to expect to retain a child, when [fate] allows it not.[27] <277>

34. Epictetus advises that when a father is fondly kissing his child, he should say within himself, "he is, perhaps, to die to morrow."[28] Words of bad omen, say you. Nothing is of bad omen, says he, which intimates any of the common works of nature. Is it of bad omen, to say corn must be reaped in harvest?

35. The unripe grape, the ripe, and the dryed. All things are changes, not into nothing, but into that which is not at present.[29]

36. "None can rob you of your good intentions," says Epictetus.[30]

37. He tells us also,[31] we must find out the true art of assenting; and, when treating of our pursuits, that we must have a power of restraining them: That we may form every purpose with † reservation; take care they be kind and social, and proportioned to the worth of the object: That, for keen desires, we should restrain them altogether, and have no aversion to what depends not on our power.

38. 'Tis no small matter we contend for, says one,[32] ‡ whether we shall be mad-men, or not. <278>

39. What do you desire? Says Socrates, to have the souls of rational creatures, or brutes? Rational, surely. What sort of rational, of the virtuous or vicious? Of the virtuous. Why, then, don't you seek after them? Because we have them already. Why, then, are you fighting with each other, and at variance?[33] <279>

* The design of these citations is uncertain. The first may serve as an admonition to submit to providence. The second, to place our joy in virtue, and not in external things. The third, to make us easy under reproach.

† See above, B. IV. 1.[34]

‡ The Stoics had this paradox, that all who are not perfectly wise and virtuous are mad-men.[35]

BOOK XII

1. All you desire to obtain by so many windings, you may have at once, if you don't envy yourself [so great an happiness.] That is to say, if you quit the thoughts of what is past, and commit what is future to providence; and set yourself to regulate well your present conduct, according to the rules of holiness and justice. Of holiness, that you may embrace heartily what is appointed for you, since * nature hath produced it for you, and you for it. Of justice, that, with freedom, and without artifice or craft, you may speak the truth, and act according to † the law, and the merit of the matter. And, be not stopped in this course, by the wickedness of another, or his opinion or talk, or by any sensation of this poor carcase, which has grown up around you. Let that which suffers in such cases see to it. If, therefore, now that you are near your exit, you quit thought about other things, and honour only that governing and divine part <280> within you, and dread not the ceasing to live, but the not commencing to live according to nature; you will become a man, worthy of that orderly universe which produced you, and will cease to be as a stranger in your own country; both astonished, with what happens every day, as if unexpected; and in anxious suspence about this and t'other thing.

2. God beholds all souls bare, and stripped of these corporeal vessels, bark, and filth. For, by his pure intellectual nature, he touches only what flowed out, and was derived from himself. If you would enure yourself to do the like, you would be free from much distraction and solicitude. For, can he, who looks not to the surrounding carcase, be much hurried about dress, houses, glory, or any such external furniture or accomodation?

* That is the providence of the author of nature.

† X. 11. 25.

3. You consist of three things, this poor flesh, the animal breath of life, and the intellectual part. To the two former, * some care is due, to a certain degree, as they are your's. But the † third alone is properly your's. Separate, therefore, from yourself, that is, from the intellectual part, all which others do and say; or what yourself have formerly done or said; <281> and all those future events, about which you are disturbed; and all that may affect this encompassing carcase, or this animal life, which depends not on your power; and all these external events, which the eddy of fortune whirling around you, carries along; so that your intellectual power, kept disentangled from fate, pure and free, may live with itself; acting what is just; satisfied with what happens; and speaking truth: If, I say, you separate from the governing principle within you those things which are, as it were, appended to it by its vehement passions, and the times past and future, you make yourself like the firm World of Empedocles,

A sphere rejoicing 'midst the circling eddy.[1]

Be solicitous only to live well for the present; and you may go on till death, to spend what remains of life, with tranquillity, with true dignity, and complacence with the divinity within you.

4. I have often wondered how each man should love himself more than any other; and yet make less account of his own opinion concerning himself, than of the opinions of others. For, should God appear, or even any wise teacher, and <282> enjoin one to entertain no thought or design, but what, as soon as formed, he would publish to others, no man could endure to do so, even for one day: Thus, we stand in greater awe of what those around shall think of us, than of what we think of our selves.

5. How is it, that ‡ the Gods, who have disposed all other things in such comely order, and with such goodness toward men; yet, have neglected this

* X. 2.

† See B. II. 13. B. V. 19.

‡ This is plainly the objection of some others, not the author's own settled opinion against a future state. It was customary among the best philosophers, in imitation of Socrates, to speak upon this subject with such alternatives, even when they were persuaded that there would be a future existence. They thought this highly probable; and yet, as they had not full certainty, they suggested proper supports and consolations even

one point, to wit, the preventing that some of the very best of men, who have, as it were, lived with the Gods the great-<283>est part of life, and, by a course of holy and religious services, been, as it were, familiar with the Divinity, should have no further existence after they die; but be intirely extinguished. If this be truly the case, be well assured, had it been proper that the case should have been otherwise, they would have made it so. Had it been just, it would have been practicable. Had it been according to nature, nature would have effected it. From its not being so, if really it is not so, you may be assured it ought not to have been. You see, that, in debating this point, you are pleading a point of justice with God. Now, we would not thus plead a matter of justice with the Gods, were they not perfectly good and just. And, if they are so, they have left nothing unjustly and unreasonably neglected in their administration.

6. Enure yourself to attempt, even, what you despair of executing. For, the left hand, which, for its inability, through want of exercise, remains idle in many sorts of work; yet, can hold the bridle more firmly than the other, by being enured to it.

7. Consider, in what state shall death find you, both as to body and soul? <284> Observe the shortness of life; the vast immensity of the preceding, and ensuing duration; and the infirmity of all these materials.

8. To behold the active principle stripped of its bark; the references and intentions of actions; what pain is; what, pleasure; what, death; what, glory; who is to each one the cause of all his disturbance and trouble; how no man can be hindered by another; how all is opinion.

9. In the practising of the maxims, we should resemble the adventurers in the exercises; and not the gladiators. The gladiator, sometimes, lays by his sword, and takes it up again; but, the champion in the exercises carries always his arms and hands along with him. He needs nothing else for his work but to weild these skillfully.

---

upon the contrary supposition, and endeavoured to give strong motives to virtue independent upon future rewards. But we wrong them exceedingly, if we imagine that they were doubtful of such points as they often propose in such alternatives. See B. II. 11. and IV. 27. and B. XII. 14.[2] Where even the doctrine of a Deity and providence is proposed with such alternatives, tho' all know how firmly the Stoics were persuaded of both. Instances of this kind occur in every book of our author.

10. Consider well the natures of things, dividing them into the material and active principles; and their references.

11. What a glorious power is granted to man! never to do any action, but such as God is to commend; and to embrace kindly, whatever God appoints for him. <285>

12. As to what happens in the course of nature, the Gods are not to be blamed; They never do wrong, willingly or unwillingly. Nor are men; for they * don't willingly. There are none, therefore, to be quarrelled with.

13. How ridiculous, and like a stranger is he, who is surprised at any thing which happens in life!

14. There is either a fatal necessity, and an unalterably fixed order; or a kind and benign providence; or a blind confusion, without a governour. If there be an unalterable necessity, why strive against it? If there is a kind providence, which can be appeased; make yourself worthy of the divine aids. If there is an ungoverned confusion; yet compose yourself with this, that, amidst these tempestuous waves, you have a presiding intelligence within yourself. If the wave surrounds you, it can carry along the carcase, and the animal life; but, the intellectual part it cannot bear along with it.

15. When a lamp continues to shine, and loses not its splendor, till it be extinguished; shall your veracity, justice, and temperance, be extinguished before you are? <286>

16. When † you are struck with the apprehension, that one has done wrong; [say thus to yourself:] How are you sure this is wrong? Grant it to be wrong: You know not but he is deeply condemning himself: this is as pityable, as if he were tearing his own face. And then, one, who expects vicious men should not do wrong, is as absurd as one expecting a fig-tree should not produce the natural juice in the figs; or that infants should not cry; or a horse should not neigh; or such other necessary things. What can the man do, who has such dispositions? If you are a man of high abilities, cure them.

17. If not becoming, don't do it. If not true, don't say it. Let these be your fixed principles.

* B. II. 1.

† See IX. 38. and XI. 18, at the 5th precept.

18. Consider always what it is, which strikes your imagination; and unfold it, by distinguishing the cause, the matter, the reference, and the time within which it must necessarily cease.

19. Won't you, at last, perceive, that you have something more excellent and divine within you, than that which raises the several passions, and moves you, as the wires do a puppet,[3] without your <287> own approbation? What now is my intellectual part? * Is it fear? Is it suspicion? Is it lust? Is it any such thing?

20. First, let nothing be done at random, without a reference. Secondly, refer your actions to nothing else than some social kind purpose.

21. Yet a little, and you shall be no more; nor shall any of those things remain, which you now behold; nor any of those who are now living. 'Tis the nature of all things to change, to turn, and to corrupt; that others may, in their course, spring out of them.

22. All depends on your opinions: These are in your power. Remove, therefore, when you incline, your opinion; and then, as when one has turned the promontory, and got into a bay, all is calm; so, all shall become stable to you, and a still harbour.[4]

23. † Any one natural operation, ending at its proper time, suffers no ill by ceasing; nor does the agent suffer any ill, by its thus ceasing. In like manner, as to the whole series of actions, which is life; if it ends in its season, it suffers no ill by ceasing; nor is the person, who thus finishes his series, in any bad state. <288> The season and the term is limited by nature; sometimes even by your own, as in old age; but, always by the nature of the whole. 'Tis by the changes of its several parts, that the universe still remains new, and in its bloom. Now, that is always good and seasonable, which is advantageous to the whole. The ceasing of life cannot be evil to individuals; for, it has no turpitude in it; since it is not in our power; nor is there any thing unsociable in it. Nay, 'tis good; since 'tis seasonable to the whole, and advantageous, and concurring with the order of the whole. Thus, too, is he led by God, who goes the same way with God, and that by his own inclination.

* IX. 39, at the end.

† IX. 21.

24. Have these three thoughts always at hand: first, that you do nothing inconsiderately; nor otherwise than justice herself would have acted. As for external events, they either happen by chance, or by providence: now, no man should quarrel with chance, nor censure providence. The second, to examine what each thing is, from its seed, to its being quickened; and, from its quickening, till its death; of what materials composed, and into what it must be resolved. The third, that, could you be raised on high, <289> so as from thence to behold all human affairs, and discern their great variety; conscious, at the same time, of the crouds of aerial and etherial inhabitants who surround us: Were you thus raised on high, never so often, you would see only the same things, or things exactly uniform; all of short duration. Can we be proud of such matters?

25. Cast out your opinions; you are safe. Who, then, hinders you to cast them out?

26. When you fret at any thing, you have forgot that all happens according to the nature of the whole; and that the fault subsists not in you, but in another. And this, too, you forget, that, whatever now happens, has happened, and will happen; and the like now happens every where. And this, also; how great the bond of kindred is, between any man, and all the human race; not by common seed or blood, but a common intellectual part. You forget, too, that the * soul of each man is divine, an efflux from God; and this, also, that no man is proprietor of any thing: His dear children, his very body, and his life, proceeded from the same God. And this, too, <290> that opinion is all. And this, that † it is the present moment only, which one lives, or can lose.

27. Recollect frequently those, who, formerly, were transported with indignation; those, who, once, proceeded to the highest pitch in glory, or in calamities, or in enmities, or any other circumstance of fortune. Then stop, and ask, where are they all now? Smoke, and ashes, and an old tale; or, perhaps, not even a tale. Let every such instance occur. ‡ Fabius Catullinus in the country; Lucius Lupus, and Stertinius at Baiae: Tiberius at Capreae;

* See B. II. 1, and 13.

† See B. II. 14.

‡ Some of the persons here named as eminent, or singular in their fortunes, are not well known.

and Velius Rufus;[5] and, in general, all eminence attended with the high opinions of men. And, how mean are all the objects of our keen pursuits! How much more becomes it a philosopher, to shew himself, in the matters subjected to his management, a man of justice and temperance, following the Gods, and that with * simplicity. For, <291> the most intolerable pride is that displayed in an ostentation of humility, and contempt of pride.

28. To those who ask, "Where have you seen these Gods? or, whence are you assured they exist, that you thus worship them?" First, † they are visible, even to the eye: Again, my own soul I cannot see; and, yet, I reverence it; and thus, too, as I experience continually the power of the Gods, I both know surely that they are, and worship them.

29. The safety of life depends on this; to discern each object, what it is in whole, of what materials, what its form or cause; to do justice with all our heart; and, to speak truth. And, what further remains, but to enjoy life, adding one virtuous office to another; so as not to leave any vacant interval?

30. There is but one light of the sun, tho' divided by walls, mountains, and other objects. There is but one common substance, tho' divided among ten thousand bodies, with peculiar qualities. There is but one animal soul, tho' divided by ten thousand natures, with their peculiar <292> limitations; and ‡ one intellectual spirit, altho' it appears to be divided. The other parts of these mentioned wholes, such as the forms and matter, being void of sense, are void of affection to each other: And, yet, 'tis an intellectual being that preserves them, and a force of gravity, which makes them tend to the

* 'Tis plain from the reason subjoined, what this simplicity is, viz. A single view to act well the part apointed us by God, without aiming at glory, or any selfish advantage, or pleasure; but from love to God and moral goodness. This simplicity is opposite to the more subtile and refined sorts of selfishness.[6]

† This may relate to the heavenly bodies whom the Stoics deemed inferior deities.

‡ It is manifest he does not here intend proper numerical unity, but only specifical, or similitude: And this further, perhaps, that all individual natures are parts taken from some great mass, or whole of that kind. Nor can we conclude from their speaking of the re-union after death, that individuals cease to be distinct persons from the Deity and from each other; since it was the known tenet of the Stoics, that heroic souls were raised to the dignity of Gods, or immortal angels; and they mean no more than an entire moral union by resignation and complete conformity of will. Some degree of this union is attainable in this life, and strongly recommended by the Stoics: See B. VIII. 34. Such expressions are frequent in the New Testament.

same place. But, what is intellectual has a peculiar tendency to its kind, and is naturally recommended to it. And the social affection cannot be entirely repressed.

31. What do you desire? merely to be? or also to have sensation, and appetite? To grow, and to decay again; to speak, to think: Are any of these wor-<293>thy of your desire? If all these are despicable; go on to the last that remains, to follow reason and God. Now, it is opposite to the reverence due to them, if we repine that we must be deprived of all the former enjoyments by death.

32. How small a part is appointed to each one of the infinite immense duration? For, presently, it must vanish into eternity: How small a part of the universal matter? And, how small, of the universal spirit? On how narrow a clod of this earth do you creep? When all these things are considered, nothing will appear great, except acting as your nature leads; and bearing contentedly whatever the common nature brings along with it.

33. What use does the governing part make of itself? On this, all depends. Other things, whether dependent on your choice, or not, are but dead carcases, and smoke.

34. This must rouse you most powerfully to despise death, that, even * those who deemed pleasure the sole good, and pain the sole evil, yet despised it. <294>

35. To the person who reputes that alone to be good, which is † seasonable, and reckons it indifferent, whether he has opportunity of exerting a greater number of actions, according to right reason, or a smaller: whether he beholds this universe for a longer or a shorter space, death cannot appear terrible.

36. You have lived, O man, as a denizen of ‡ this great state: Of what consequence to you, whether it be only for five years? What is according to the laws, is equal and just to all. What is there terrible in this, that you are sent out, not by a tyrant, or an unjust judge, but by that nature, which at

* Epicurus.

† The peculiar meaning of this seasonableness is best explained in *Cicero de finib.* l. III. c. 14.[7]

‡ The universe.

first introduced you? As if * the praetor who employed the player, should dismiss him again from the scene. But, say you, I have not finished the five acts, but only three. You say true; but, in life, † three acts make a complete play. For, 'tis he who appoints the end to it, <295> who, as he was the cause of the composition, is now the cause of the dissolution. Neither of them are chargeable on you: Depart, therefore, contented, and in good humour; for, he is propitious and kind, who dismisses you. <296>

FINIS.

* The great magistrates at their own charge exhibited shows to the people, and among others gave plays, and for this purpose employed the actors.

† See above, B. XI. 1.

ERRATA

Page 51. line 8 [this edition: p. 27, line 22]. *for* confirming *read* arguing. 221. 13 [this edition: p. 114, line 17]. *for* perhaps, *read* who, perhaps. 223 *note. line ult.* [this edition: p. 115, the double-daggered note]. *others thus read the Text.* "Nay toward the Gods, too, behave with . . ." 239 [this edition: p. 123, 6 lines from bottom of page]. *read numbers for these references by the small letters.*

These errata to the 1742 edition have been incorporated into the Liberty Fund text—Eds.

MAXIMS OF THE STOICS

As Gataker, in the prefatory discourse to his excellent edition and commentary on ANTONINUS, *has given a very just* SUMMARY OF THE CHIEF MAXIMS OF THE STOIC PHILOSOPHY, *taken mostly from these Meditations; we thought it proper to translate it here; and give the references to the places he quotes; and the passages from some others, with a few additions.*

I

OF GOD, PROVIDENCE, and * the LOVE of GOD.

"The Divine Providence *a* takes care of human affairs; and not of the universe only, in general; but, of each <297> single man, and each single matter: Is present in all the affairs of men; and *b* aids mankind, not only in those things which are their true good and happiness, but in the external conveniencies and supports of life.

"GOD is, therefore, *c* above all to be worshipped; *d* in all undertakings to be invoked; *e* at all times to be remembered, and present to our thoughts;

* Tho' the Stoics have not used the term LOVE, for expressing our pious affections to GOD; yet, 'tis plain, they meant all that can be implied in that word, as used since with regard to the Deity. They seem to have abstained from this term, out of reverence: φιλειν, and φιλια, with them, carry a notion of equality.

a. II. 3, 11. and VI. 44. See also the *Dissert: of Epictet.* I. 12. 14. 16.

b. I. 14. and IX. 27.

c. V. 33.

d. VI. 23. III. 13. See also IX. 40. and the note.

e. VI. 7.

f in all things to be acknowledged, and *g* his conduct approved; *h* for all <298> things to be praised, and celebrated. *i* To HIM alone, we ought, in single-<299>ness of heart, to yield a willing obedience in all we do. *k* From HIM whatever comes to us, we ought to receive, and embrace, with a ready and hearty accord: and think *l* nothing better, *m* nothing more convenient, *n* more advantageous, *o* more fortunate, or more seasonable, than that,

f. III. 13.

g. VI. 18. "In all these things will I vindicate THEE before men." *Epictetus cited at* VII. 45.

h. "If I was subject formerly to the same weakness, and am not now, 'tis to God I give the praise." *Epictetus cited at* X. 30.

"In every event which happens in the universe, it is an easy thing to praise providence, if one has these two things within him: a power to comprehend and understand what happens to every one; and, a grateful heart." *Epictetus* I. 6.

"What words are sufficient to praise or declare these works of God as they deserve? Had we understanding, what else ought we to do, both in public and private, but sing hymns to God, and bless him, and pour out our thanks before him? Ought we not, while either digging, ploughing, or feeding, to sing this hymn to God: GREAT IS GOD! that he has given us hands, and organs for swallowing and digesting: That he makes us grow up insensibly; and breathe even while asleep. For each of these things we ought thus to bless him. But, of all to sing the greatest and most divine hymn, for his giving us the power of attaining the knowledge of these things, and the method of using them. What, then? Since you, the multitude, are blind, ought there not to be some one to perform this duty in your place; and pay this hymn to God for you all? For, what else can I do, a lame old man, but sing a hymn to God? Were I a nightingale, I would do the business of a nightingale. Were I a swan, I would do that of a swan. Now, that I am a rational creature, I ought to hymn the Deity. This is my business: this I perform. This is my post: while I am allowed I will never leave it. And you I will exhort to join with me in this my song." *Epictetus* I. 16.

These sentiments, says Gataker, *and others of the same kind in* Epictetus, *are not unworthy of* the best Christian: *had he but, only, to the subject of his hymn,* added God's *gift of* Christ *to* mankind.

i. "—I know to whom I owe subjection and obedience: it is to God." *Epictetus* IV. 34.

k. IV. 34. 25. III. 4.

"In fine, will nothing but that which God wills." *Epictetus* II. 17.

"To God I have subjected all my desires. What he wills, I will also. What he wills not, neither do I will." *Epictetus* III. 26. IV. 27.

l. "For I deem that better which God wills than that which I will." *Epictetus, ibid.*

m. VII. 57.

n. X. 20.

o. X. 20.

whatever it be, which HE has WILLED. *p* Wherever HE thinks fit to lead us, there we ought to follow; *q* without <300> turning our back, or murmuring. *r* Whatever place, or station, HE has assigned us; that we ought strenuously to keep, and with all our might maintain; were we, even, by that, to meet a thousand deaths."

II

OF MAN; and the SOCIAL DUTIES and AFFECTION TO MEN, as, by NATURE, our KINSMEN.

"Mankind we ought *a* from the heart to love, *b* have a tender care of, *c* and bear with their weakness; *d* abstain from all kind of injury, *e* that being even impiety: *f* do them all the good we can; *g* and not <301> believe, we are born, and to live, for ourselves alone; *h* but let all behold us dedicate ourselves, to the utmost of our strength and abilities, for the public good; *i* and kindly beneficent to all men.

p. XII. 27.

"I adhere to him, as a servant, and attendant. His purpose, his desire, and, in a word, his will, is mine also." *Epictetus* as cited at X. 21.

O Jove! and thou, O destiny! [by him
Establish'd thorough nature,] lead me on
Where e'er you have appointed me; and I
Will follow unreluctant.—

The prayer of Cleanthes
frequently quoted by Epictetus.[1]

q. "From God come all things; and it is best to follow him, without murmuring. He is a bad soldier who sighs while he follows his general." Seneca, *Epist.* 107.[2]

r. "Whatever station or rank thou shalt assign me, I will die ten thousand deaths sooner than abandon it." Epictetus III. 24. *after* Socrates, *in* Plato's apology.[3]

a. VIII. 13. IX. 27.

b. IX. 3.

c. V. 33.

d. V. 33.

e. IX. 1.

f. V. 33.

g. VII. 55. "Non sibi, sed, toti genitum se credere mundo." *Lucan.*[4]

h. VIII. 7.

k "We ought to live satisfied with acting our part well, and with the inward consciousness of having done so: *l* without concern for the reputation of it; *m* without witnesses; *n* without hope of reward; *o* without any view at all of our own advantage. *p* But go on from one good deed to another; *q* and never be weary of doing good; *r* esteeming it the true fruit of living, to make life one uninterrupted series of good actions, so closely linked to one <302> another, *s* that, thro' the whole, there be not found the *t* least break or interval: *u* deeming it our own good that we have done good to others; *x* and, that we have served ourselves, if we have been useful to any man: *y* and all, without catching at, or wishing for any external praise, or glory, among mankind.

z "The CULTURE of our own HEART deserves, of all other, the greatest and most reverential care."

a "To LOVE the MORAL CHARM, to act the FAIR, the LOVELY, the HONOURABLE PART, are, of all pursuits, the most excellent, the most precious.

b "From that which we are conscious is our DUTY, *c* no desires, neither of life, nor of any thing whatever, shou'd we allow to draw us away; no fears of death, or torture, much less of loss or harm, to deterr us."

i. III. 4.
k. IX. 6. & VII. 28.
l. V. 6. "Even while giving, forgetting that he gives." Seneca *de Beneficiis* II. 16.[5]
m. III. 5. "Let the motive, in all actions, be the deed itself, and not the observers of it." Cicero *de finibus.* B. II.[6]
n. " 'Tis Epicurus who says men love each other from hope of reward." Plutarch, *of the love of our offspring.*[7]
o. IX. *at the end.*
p. VI. 7. V. 6.
q. VII. 74.
r. XII. 29.
s. XII. 29.
t. IX. 23.
u. IX. *at the end.*
x. VII. 74.
y. VII. 73.
z. V. 21. II. 13.
a. III. 6. VI. 16.
b. VI. 22. VII. 15. VIII. 5.
c. VII. 44.

These (*says* Gataker,) *are the* MAXIMS *and* PRECEPTS *of the* STOICS; *perfectly agreeable to their principles: all* HOLY, RIGHTEOUS, STRICT, *and* <303> MANLY: *all breathing* PIETY, AFFECTION, HUMANITY, *and* GREATNESS OF SOUL.

GATAKER'S APOLOGY

To this we shall subjoin the following extract from the same preface: Being Gatakers apology *for employing, tho'* a Christian minister, *so many years' time and labour on these Meditations of a* Heathen Emperor, *under whose reign the Christians suffered persecution.*

In fine, says he, that I may return to what I at first advertised you of from St. Jerom; I think it may be boldly asserted, there are no remaining monuments of the ancient * strangers, which come nearer to the doctrine of CHRIST, than the writings and admonitions of these two; Epictetus, and Antoninus. 'Tis certain, whatever precepts OUR LORD HIMSELF has given, in those sermons and conversations of his, inserted and interwoven into the history of the gospel; <304> "*a* of abstaining from evil, even in thought: *b* of suppressing vicious affections: *c* of leaving off all idle conversation: *d* of cultivating the heart with all diligence *e* and fashioning it after the image of God: *f* of doing good to men from the most single disinterested view: *g* of bearing injuries with contentment: *h* of using moderation, and strict caution, in our admonitions and reproofs: *i* of counting all things whatever,

* So he calls the heathens after St. Paul.
a. Matth. XV. 19.
b. —V. 22, 28.
c. —XII. 36.
d. —V. 20. VI. 33.
e. —V. 45, 48.
f. —VI. 1, 3.
g. —V. 39.
h. —XVIII. 15, 16.
i. Luke XIV. 26, 33.

and even life itself, as nothing, when reason and the case demand them: and of undertaking and performing almost all the other duties of *k* PIETY, *l* AFFECTION, *m* EQUITY, *n* HUMANITY, *o* with the greatest diligence and ardour": All these same precepts are to be found in Antoninus, just as if he had habitually read them; they are every where interspersed through this collection of his thoughts and meditations; and continually inculcated with a surprising strength and life, which pierces to the <305> bottom of the heart, and leaves the dart deep fixed in the soul. This every attentive reader will perceive; every honest one confess.

But some may, perhaps, say: "to what purpose take those precepts from a stranger, and even an adversary to the Christian faith? When they can be had more readily from the sacred page, where they stand published to all. And as they come from the mouth of our MASTER himself, are inforced with the higher authority of his command, and attended to with a stricter necessity of obedience."

To this I answer, that a careful perusal and serious reflection on these meditations of Antoninus, are several ways useful.

For, in the first place, the sacred writers have given us only the chief heads of OUR LORD's discourses, concisely digested as a taste or specimen: and those maxims and precepts only summarily proposed, are in Antoninus more extensively applied, more fully explained; and, by a great variety of striking arguments, established, illustrated, inforced and inculcated upon us, and accommodated to practice in civil life. In all this, our Emperor particularly excells. <306>

And, then, another thing of no small moment is this. We discover the equity of the Christian doctrine, and its perfect agreement with reason, while we show it is approved and praised even by strangers and adversaries. *a* "A testimony from enemies is of great weight." And, says *b* DION PRU-

k. Matth. XXII. 37.
l. —XXII. 39.
m. —VII. 12.
n. —V. 44. and Luke X. 37.
o. —V. 19, 20.
a. Isidor. Pelus. II. *Epist.* 228. and III. *Epist.* 335.[1]
b. Oration 51.[2]

SAEUS, "the encomium of those who admire tho' they don't receive, must be the finest of all praises." The Apostle understood this very well, when he called in testimonies from *c* the inscriptions, and *d* writings of the strangers, for proof of the doctrine he brought and was publishing among them. Surely it must conduce not a little, to vindicate and implant in the breasts of any whatever, the precepts and lessons of OUR LORD, as perfectly agreeable to equity and *e* reason; that, a man, who was a stranger, and unfavourable to the Christian name, (for he neither knew our mysteries, nor understood the reasons of our faith), shou'd yet recommend and establish them with such vehemence and ardour, <307> and by so very forcible arguments. "Who is not sensible," says *f* an author of high character, "that those have had a good cause who gain'd it before judges who were indifferent?" What shall one say then of that cause which is gained even before the averse and prejudiced against it; nay, *g* when its very enemies sit judges.

Further, in these following books, the good providence and kindness of God shines forth; as he did not suffer his own image to be quite worn out and lost in man who had fallen off from him. But preserved some sparks alive, which he both excited by various methods, and improved even to a miracle. Partly, that the safety and good order of human society might be provided for: *h* lest men, turning quite savage, should like wild beasts, rush universally on each other's destruction. Since *i* "man, without education is the most savage of all the creatures which the earth nourishes." And, partly, that they might apply themselves to *k* know and *l* seek God, by the

c. Acts XVII. 23.

d. — 28.

e. Our reasonable service. *Rom.* XII. 1. To follow God and reason: *Antoninus,* XII. 31.

f. *Aug. Epist.* 170.[3]

g. *Deut.* XXXII. 31.

h. There is nothing more impious, more barbarous, than man once turned savage. *Polybius* Hist. B. 1. and Embass. 122.[4]

i. *Plato, in the laws,* B. VI.[5]

k. *Romans* I. 19. That which may be known of God. And, *verse* 21. When they knew God.

l. That they should see the Lord, if happy they might feel after him and find him. *Acts* XVII. 27.

<308> assistance of these helps; being plainly *m* without excuse if they either despised or neglected them. For that saying of St. Bernard, is undoubtedly true, *n* "The image of God in our hearts may be burnt, but not burnt out." Surely, to wear quite out that *o* image, originally stamped on the rational soul, to extinguish intirely *p* that torch, kindled from heaven in the human heart; has been beyond the power either of the vices of men or the malice of Devils: nay, according to him, "beyond the power of hell-flames." It was the will of the divine goodness that this image should, for the advantage of the human race, and the particular benefit of his people, be preserved and cherished amid the ruins and ashes, which followed the primitive defection.

FINIS.

m. Rom. I. 20.
n. *Bern. in annum Serm.* 1.[6]
o. *Genesis* I. 27. & IX. 6.
p. *Prov.* XX. 27. *Rom.* II. 15.

ENDNOTES

Editors' Notes to Hutcheson and Moor's *Life of the Emperor Marcus Antoninus*

1. Hutcheson and Moor normally refer to Marcus Aurelius Antoninus (emperor 161–80) as Antoninus rather than Marcus Aurelius, as he is commonly called today.

2. Casaubon, *Marcus Aurelius Antoninus the Roman Emperor, His Meditations Concerning Himselfe* (1634). See bibliography.

3. Collier, *The Emperor Marcus Antoninus His Conversation with Himself.* See bibliography.

4. Gataker, *Markou Antoninou tou Autokratoros* (1652/1697). See bibliography.

5. Dacier, *Reflexions morales de l'Empereur Marc Antonin avec des remarques de Mr. & de Mad. Dacier.* The Daciers added a prefatory "Life of Marcus," which is the ultimate source of the biographical material in Hutcheson and Moor's introduction. See the editors' introduction, pp. xii–xiii.

6. The chief literary sources for the life of Marcus Aurelius are Dio Cassius, *Roman History,* LXXI–LXXII, and the "Lives" of Marcus, Verus, and Avidius Cassius in the *Historia Augusta* (or *Scriptores historiae Augustae*). A full-length biography is Birley, *Marcus Aurelius;* and a short account of the reign by Birley may be found in the *Cambridge Ancient History,* vol. 11, pp. 156–86.

7. The emperor Hadrian (r. 117–38). For further information on persons and places, see *The Oxford Classical Dictionary,* 3rd ed., and *Brill's New Pauly.*

8. The second king of Rome, noted for his piety.

9. For Marcus's own account of his family, see bk. 1, art. 1, p. 25.

10. Sextus was a *nephew* of Plutarch (*Scriptores historiae Augustae,* "Life of Marcus" 3.2). See the endnotes, bk. I, p. 171n9.

11. For these persons, see the endnotes, bk. I, p. 170n6, p. 171nn13, 15.

12. Lucius Volusius Maecianus, eminent lawyer and imperial administrator under Hadrian and Antoninus Pius.

13. There is no paragraph corresponding to this in Dacier's "Life."

14. Valesius produced an edition of Eusebius's *Ecclesiastical History* in 1659. At bk. IV, chap. 11, Eusebius refers briefly to Justin Martyr's two "apologies" for the Christian religion, which Hutcheson mentions here; see note 21, below.

15. Eusebius, *Ecclesiastical History* 4.13.1–7 ascribes this letter to the emperor Antoninus Pius. It is generally regarded by historians as spurious.

16. Normally now spelled "Calpurnius."

17. Normally now called "Chatti."

18. After the assassination of Commodus, Pertinax was emperor for three months until he was himself assassinated in March 193.

19. Dio Cassius LXXII.3.3, in *Dio's Roman History* (Loeb ed., vol. IX, pp. 12–13).

20. This appears to be a paraphrase of Eusebius, *History of the Church* V.1.47: "For Caesar had written that they should be tortured to death, but that if any should recant they should be let go."

21. Justin Martyr, author of two *Apologies* for the Christian religion addressed to Antoninus Pius and Marcus Aurelius jointly, was executed in 165. The Greek text of the *Apologies* is found in *Justini Martyris Apologiae,* ed. Marcovich, 1994, and a translation in Justin, *The First Apology,* ed. and trans. Falls, 1948.

22. Athenagoras, Christian apologist; his *Presbeia peri Christianōn* (A Plea for Christians), addressed to Marcus Aurelius and his son Commodus, is a defense of Christians from the charges of immorality frequently leveled against them. See Athenagoras, *Legatio and De resurrectione.*

23. The "Marcomannic Wars" continued for much of the 170s.

24. In 171 occurred the Moorish inroads into Spain and the revolt of the Bucoli (Herdsmen) in Egypt.

25. The incident is related by Dio Cassius LXXII.8–10, in *Dio's Roman History* (Loeb ed., vol. IX, pp. 26–33). Dio ascribes the miracle to an Egyptian "magician" invoking Hermes Aetios. The "Life of Marcus" 24.4 in *The Scriptores historiae Augustae* (Loeb ed., vol. I, pp. 192–93) describes thunderbolts hurled against the enemy by Jupiter in response to Marcus's prayer. See the account in the *Cambridge Ancient History,* vol. 11, p. 170.

26. The Christian interpretation is preserved in Eusebius, *History of the Church* V.5, who gives Tertullian as his source (see the endnotes, "The Life of the Emperor," pp. 168–69n45).

27. Legio XII Fulminata was descended from Julius Caesar's twelfth legion, and, as Hutcheson and Moor say, already had the name Fulminata in the first century. In Marcus's time, this legion was recruited in the regions of Melitene, where there were many Christians, according to Bury (Gibbon, *Decline and Fall,* ed. Bury [1909], vol. II, p. 116n107).

28. This letter purporting to be by Marcus, but certainly spurious, is appended to Justin Martyr's *First Apology* (Greek text in Marcovich, ed., pp. 165–68; English translation in Falls, pp. 110–11). The incident and the letter are also referred to by Tertullian, *Apology* V.6, in Tertullian, *Apology, De spectaculis* (Loeb ed., p. 31).

29. Gaius Cassius Longinus, one of the assassins of Julius Caesar.

30. The letter of Verus about Cassius, and Marcus's reply to it, are found in the "Life of Avidius Cassius" 1.7–9 and 2.1–8 in *Scriptores historiae Augustae* (Loeb ed., vol. I, pp. 234–37). These letters are forgeries. Indeed the whole of this "Life of Avidius Cassius" has been described as "mainly fictional, except for a few passages dealing with the revolt in 175" (*Cambridge Ancient History,* vol. 11, p. 157n52).

31. "Life of Avidius Cassius" 14.8, in *Scriptores historiae Augustae* (Loeb ed., vol. I, pp. 262–63).

32. Dio Cassius LXXII.23.3–26.4, in *Dio's Roman History* (Loeb ed., vol. IX, pp. 39–45). This speech may contain the gist of what Marcus actually said (*Cambridge Ancient History,* vol. 11, p. 177).

33. This purported correspondence between Marcus Aurelius and Faustina, found in the "Life of Avidius Cassius" 9.5–10.10, is spurious. See *Scriptores historiae Augustae* (Loeb ed., vol. I, pp. 252–55).

34. The sophist Herodes Atticus, the friend and teacher of Marcus Aurelius and of Lucius Verus (Dio Cassius LXXII.35.1, in *Dio's Roman History,* Loeb ed., vol. IX, pp. 64–65). He is not mentioned in *The Meditations,* but he is the subject of five letters between Marcus and Fronto (Fronto, *Correspondence,* Loeb ed., pp. 59–71). For his life see Philostratus, *Lives of the Sophists* II.1 (Philostratus and Eunapius, *The Lives of the Sophists,* Loeb ed., pp. 139–83).

35. Philostratus, *Lives of the Sophists* II.1 (563) (Loeb ed., pp. 175–77).

36. A forged letter from "Life of Avidius Cassius" 11.3–8, in *Scriptores historiae Augustae* (Loeb ed., vol. I, pp. 254–57).

37. "Life of Avidius Cassius" 8.2–5, in *Scriptores historiae Augustae* (Loeb ed., vol. I, pp. 248–51).

38. A forgery in "Life of Avidius Cassius" 12.1–10, in *Scriptores historiae Augustae* (Loeb ed., vol. I, pp. 256–59).

39. Dio Cassius LXXII.30.2, in *Dio's Roman History* (Loeb ed., vol. IX, pp. 52–53).

40. Aelius Aristides, a prominent sophist, to whom Marcus gave an audience at Smyrna in 176. Among his many surviving speeches is a panegyric of the Roman empire ("To Rome"); he also composed *Sacred Teachings,* an account of the revelations made by Asclepius, god of healing, with regard to his medical problems.

41. Marcus was initiated into this ancient cult of Demeter at Eleusis near Athens in 176. The emperor Hadrian had also been initiated.

42. The source of this purported deathbed speech of Marcus is Herodian I.4., in *Herodian* (Loeb ed., pp. 14–21).

43. Maximus of Tyre, a "middle Platonist," who was popular among humanists of the Renaissance and later; the conception of God articulated in Oration 11 "Plato on God" was particularly influential. See Maximus Tyrius, *Philosophical Orations,* pp. 93–106.

44. See also bk. V, art. 22, p. 65n: "God, the great governour of this city"; bk. VIII, art. 19, p. 98n: where the inferior gods of "the heathen philosophers" are compared with the angels believed in by "many Christians"; and bk. IX, art. 1, the asterisked note: "This is a clear acknowledgement of the one supreme God."

45. Marcus was regarded by Christians as one of the major persecutors. The highly influential *History of the Church* by Eusebius (composed early in the fourth century at a time of widespread persecution) devotes most of its account of the Church in the reign of Marcus (IV.14.9–V.10.3) to the persecutions of the reign, beginning: "In this period Asia was thrown into confusion by the most savage persecutions." Eusebius assigns the celebrated martyrdom of Polycarp to Marcus's reign, though it actually occurred in 156. He gives an account of the execution of the Christian apologist Justin Martyr and of many other Christians in Asia. He also describes the martyrdoms in Gaul in graphic detail. Eusebius left to succeeding centuries the impression that persecution was general throughout the empire in the reign of Marcus, summarizing as follows (V.2.1): "Such were the experiences of the Christian churches [in Gaul] under Marcus Aurelius: from them one can easily guess what happened in the other provinces of the Empire." (The quotations in this note are from Eusebius, *History of the Church,* trans. Williamson, 168, 203.) A recent historian, however, expresses the widely accepted view that Marcus simply followed the policy of his predecessors since Trajan of permitting prosecution of Christians if initiated by private citizens:

"Marcus's own conduct appears to me at all points traditionalist, not least in the scrupulous respect for Roman religious ceremonial, and it would not be astonishing if he simply assumed without examination that the measures taken by his predecessors against sectaries who spurned the ancestral cults were correct" (Brunt, "Marcus Aurelius and the Christians," 499).

Editors' Notes to Marcus's Text and to Hutcheson and Moor's Notes

BOOK I

1. Hutcheson and Moor's first paragraph contains the first three paragraphs of all other editions, including Gataker's, who first established the numbering for Marcus. Hence all their numbers in the first book from paragraph 2 onward are three lower than in other editions and translations.

2. Hutcheson and Moor are paraphrasing here; they omit the names of "the contending parties."

3. Gataker prints the negative particle in his Greek text, discusses a proposal to delete it in his annotation to this passage (p. 3), and omits it from his Latin translation. All references to Gataker are to the 1697 edition.

4. This Diognetus was Marcus's painting instructor, as Gataker, p. 5, reports from the "Life of Marcus," chap. 4, sec. 9, in *Scriptores historiae Augustae* (Loeb ed., vol. I, p. 143). See also Birley, *Marcus Aurelius,* pp. 37–38.

5. Baccheios was "a Platonic philosopher of the day" (*The Meditations of Marcus Aurelius Antoninus,* trans. Farquharson, 146); the others are unknown.

6. Quintus Junius Rusticus (cos. II, 162) was the man primarily responsible for arousing Marcus's devotion to philosophy (see I.14). He was descended from the Rusticus who was executed by Domitian in 93 A.D. as a member of a group of aristocratic Stoics who opposed tyranny. Marcus mentions him in I.17 as one of the three men whom he is most grateful to the gods to have known (the others being Apollonius [endnote 8, below] and Maximus [endnote 15, p. 171]).

7. Epictetus (ca. 55–ca. 135), a freed slave, who taught Stoic philosophy. His lectures and discussions were written up by Arrian in the *Discourses,* to which Marcus refers here, and an outline of his principles is given in his *Manual* (*Encheiridion*). He and Marcus are bracketed together in the revival of interest in Stoicism in the early eighteenth century (see, for example, Rivers, *Reason, Grace, and Sentiment,* vol. II, pp. 91–92, 118–19, 184–86).

8. Apollonius of Chalcedon was invited to Rome by the emperor Antoninus to instruct the young Marcus in philosophy. Gataker, p. 12, repeats the story found in the "Life of Marcus" in the *Historia Augusta* that even when Marcus had been adopted into the imperial family, he used to visit the house of Apollonius for philosophical instruction ("Life of Marcus," chap. 3 in *Scriptores historiae Augustae,* vol. I, p. 137).

9. Stoic philosopher, nephew of Plutarch.

10. Alexander was a sophist and grammarian from Cotiaeon, a great authority on Homer, who taught Marcus literature.

11. Marcus Cornelius Fronto taught Marcus rhetoric. Some of the correspondence between Marcus and Fronto survived in a manuscript that had been overwritten with another text (a palimpsest). This was not discovered until the early nineteenth century and would not have been known to Hutcheson and Moor. The correspondence is translated in Fronto, *Correspondence.*

12. Philosopher and orator, Marcus's Greek secretary.

13. Cinna Catulus, reported to have been a Stoic.

14. Athenodotus was a Stoic, a pupil of the famous Musonius Rufus, who also taught Fronto, Marcus's tutor in rhetoric and correspondent (Birley, *Marcus Aurelius,* pp. 97–98, 105).

15. Claudius Maximus, Stoic senator, consul ca. 142, provincial governor; described as "a man of austere principles and long military service" (Apuleius, *Apology,* 19). See Birley, *Marcus Aurelius,* pp. 96–97.

16. Gnaeus Claudius Severus Arabianus, consul 146; his son married one of Marcus's daughters (Birley, *Marcus Aurelius,* pp. 96–97).

17. These were all men who won fame by opposing tyranny. Most of them were Stoics. Thrasea Paetus was forced to commit suicide by Nero. Helvidius Priscus was executed by Vespasian; his son, also Helvidius, by Domitian. M. Porcius Cato committed suicide after the battle of Thapsus rather than submit to Julius Caesar. Brutus is the assassin of Julius Caesar who killed himself after being defeated by Octavian at Philippi. Dio is probably the disciple of Plato who deposed the tyrant Dionysius II of Syracuse; he is usually now called Dion.

18. An error for *Lanuvium;* it is spelled correctly in Gataker's Greek text and in his Latin translation (1697, p. 6).

19. The river Gran or Hron, a tributary of the Danube in Slovakia. Marcus had his winter quarters here during his campaign against the Quadi, a Germanic tribe.

BOOK II

1. See also bk. IV, art. 1, p. 47n; bk. VI, art. 16, pp. 73–74 and note; bk. IX, art. 12, p. 111; and especially bk. VI, art. 7, p. 71, and the endnotes, bk. VI, p. 178n1.

2. See bk. II, art. 13, p. 37n, on the rational soul as the seat of knowledge and virtue; bk. V, art. 19, p. 65n, on the rational soul as a being or substance distinct

from the body and the animal soul: "The rational soul, say they, is the man; the seat of true perfection and happiness"; bk. VI, art. 24, p. 75, the asterisked note, bk. VIII, art. 54, p. 105n, bk. XI, art. 12, p. 137, the double-daggered note, on the identification of the soul and the heart; bk. VI, art. 24, p. 75, bk. XII, art. 5, pp. 145–46n, and bk. XII, art. 30, p. 150n, on the soul and the possibility of a future state.

3. See also bk. X, art. 38, p. 132, and bk. XII, art. 19, p. 148.

4. See bk. II, art. 17, p. 39, the asterisked note; bk. IV, art. 46, p. 56; bk. V, art. 13, p. 63, the asterisked note.

5. Theophrastus succeeded Aristotle as head of the Peripatetic school in 322 B.C. The passage is from a lost work.

6. See also bk. IV, art. 19, p. 50n; bk. IV, art. 38, p. 54n; and bk. XI, art. 14, p. 138. In these passages Hutcheson reminds the reader of the limitations that the Stoics placed upon the desire for fame, esteem, and popular applause. In *An Essay on the Nature and Conduct of the Passions and Affections* (1728), sec. IV, art. 4, pp. 109–11 (Liberty Fund ed., pp. 78–79), Hutcheson expressed similar reservations concerning desires for honor, wealth, and power.

7. A Cynic philosopher of the fourth century B.C.

8. East of Vienna, where Marcus had his winter quarters for three successive years while on campaign against the Marcomanni, a Germanic tribe, in the early 170s.

BOOK III

1. Hutcheson referred to this section of *The Meditations* and to others in the third edition of *An Essay on the Nature and Conduct of the Passions and Affections* (1742), V.III, p. 137 (Liberty Fund ed., p. 93). Hutcheson's use of this section in *An Essay* had a strictly moral application. It was that we must separate ideas of wealth and other external things from ideas of friendship, generosity, and public spirit: "consider things barely and apart from each other: and in opposition to these Desires, set but the weakest moral Species, and see if they can prevail against it." Marcus's point in this section appears rather to have been an aesthetic observation: he was reminding himself and his readers that everything in nature, however rugged or aging or deformed, is beautiful if one considers the nature of things as a whole. See also Adam Smith, *Theory of Moral Sentiments,* VII, ii, 1, p. 288: "The good-natured Emperor . . . delights in expressing contentment with the ordinary course of things, and in pointing out beauties even in those

parts of it where vulgar observers are not apt to see any." Hutcheson returns to the moral significance of separating images in the imagination in bk. VII, art. 54, p. 90n. It may be added that Marcus, like Shaftesbury and Hutcheson, linked the beautiful and the moral. See bk. IV, art. 20, pp. 50–51.

2. Hippocrates of Cos, the great physician and author of some of the medical treatises in the *Hippocratic Corpus.*

3. The Babylonians (or Chaldeans) were the source of the astrology that was very popular in Rome in the imperial period.

4. Gaius Julius Caesar.

5. Heraclitus of Ephesus, Greek philosopher of the sixth century B.C., from whom the Stoics derived their doctrine of the periodic conflagration of the universe. For his death, see Diogenes Laertius, *Lives of the Philosophers,* bk. IX, chap. 1, sec. 3 (Loeb ed., pp. 410–11).

6. Democritus of Abdera, atomist philosopher of the fifth century B.C. Gataker, p. 93, notes that this death story is told of Pherecydes of Syros rather than of Democritus (from Diogenes Laertius, *Lives,* bk. I, chap. 11, sec. 118 [Loeb ed., pp. 124–25]).

7. The reference to "vermi' here seems to be to the accusers of Socrates, as Gataker suggests (Gataker 1697, p. 93).

8. It was one of the dominant themes of Hutcheson's moral philosophy that all mankind would be naturally sociable if it were not for misleading associations of ideas and "falsely imagined interests." See especially his inaugural lecture as Professor of Moral Philosophy at the University of Glasgow (1730) in Francis Hutcheson, *Logic, Metaphysics, and the Natural Sociability of Mankind* (2006).

9. See also bk. VII, art. 59, p. 91, where Hutcheson writes: "the dissipating pursuits of external things, stupify the nobler powers"; and bk. XI, art. 1, p. 133, the daggered note, and bk. XI, art. 6, p. 135, the daggered note, where obstacles encountered in the pursuit of external things or things indifferent are taken to be opportunities for actions which may be more properly denominated virtuous or good. In his dedication "to the students in universities," prefaced to *A Short Introduction to Moral Philosophy,* p. 111, Hutcheson summarizes the Stoic position on this matter: "Now 'tis well known that the Stoicks made such difference between virtue, which they counted the sole good, and the *officia,* or external duties of life, that they counted the duties among the things indifferent, neither good nor evil." In this assertion, Hutcheson was expressing a reservation about the subject matter of Cicero's *De officiis* and explaining why it should not be mistaken for a complete system of morals.

10. Phalaris, tyrant of Acragas (Agrigento) in Sicily in the sixth century B.C. and a byword for cruelty and sensuality. The supposed *Letters* of Phalaris had given rise to a celebrated controversy between Richard Bentley, who first definitively proved that they were spurious (*A Dissertation upon the Epistles of Phalaris,* 1699), and Charles Boyle, who had edited the *Letters* and was inclined to accept their authenticity. See Jebb, *Bentley,* 40–85.

11. The translation here omits a clause in the Greek text, which is itself mutilated: "and those who . . . when they have closed their doors." Some phrase like "commit all sorts of depravity" seems to be missing from the Greek, and some commentators have seen here a derogatory reference to the Christians, who were believed to commit all kinds of depravity behind closed doors. Others, including Gataker (1697, p. 119), apply it to evil men generally; Gataker quotes Ephesians 5:12, "For it is a shame even to speak of the things that they do in secret."

BOOK IV

1. The Greek terms *hypexairesis,* translated by Hutcheson as "reservation," and *hegemonikon,* as "the governing part," were technical terms in the vocabulary of the Stoics. On Marcus's employment of this technical language and its significance for his thought, see Hadot, *The Inner Citadel,* pp. 52, 122–23, and 193. See also bk. V, art. 20, p. 65, and bk. XI, art. 37, p. 143, where Marcus cites Epictetus: "That we may form every purpose with reservation; take care they be kind and social, and proportioned to the worth of objects." On Hutcheson's use of the term *hegemonikon,* see also "On the Natural Sociability of Mankind," in Hutcheson, *Logic, Metaphysics, and Natural Sociability* (2006), 199n25.

2. See also bk. VIII, art. 57, p. 105n.

3. On the Stoic citizenship of the world, see also bk. IV, art. 29, p. 52. See also the editors' introduction, p. xxi.

4. Gataker's Greek text differs from his Latin translation here (1697, p. 26). His Greek text has *to agathon* ("the good"), whereas his Latin translation, following Xylander's emendation *kata ton Agathona,* takes *Agathon* as a personal name, and in his annotation to the text (1697, p. 137) Gataker says that he approves of Xylander's emendation.

5. See also note to bk. II, art. 6, p. 35, and other references noted there.

6. This section was quoted in part by Henry More, *An Account of Virtue* (1690), bk. III, chap. 9, sec. xviii, p. 251, in support of a theory of liberty, properly

understood, where the will is resigned to Divine Providence. The same section was quoted in full by Adam Smith, *Theory of Moral Sentiments,* pt. VII, sec. ii.1, p. 289, as illustrative of a moral system "too absurd to deserve any serious consideration." See the editors' introduction to this edition, p. xxvii.

7. See also bk. V, art. 13, p. 63n.

8. Shaftesbury took this article to be an expostulation directed against Lucretius: "Miscellany II," chap. 1, in *Characteristics,* ed. Klein, p. 353n.

9. Vespasian, emperor 69–79.

10. Trajan, emperor 98–117.

11. Marcus proceeds from some mostly obscure figures of early Roman history through Scipio and Cato, heroes of the Republic, to Augustus, the first Roman emperor, and ends with Hadrian and Antoninus Pius, his immediate predecessors.

12. See also bk. V, art. 14, p. 63; bk. VI, art. 17, p. 74n; bk. X, art. 1, p. 119; and bk. XII, art. 27, p. 150n. Henry More, *An Account of Virtue,* bk. II, chap. III, sec. II, p. 105, and bk. II, chap. VIII, sec. XX, p. 145, took the simplicity or sincerity of the soul, as represented by Marcus Aurelius, to be one of the three primitive virtues, together with prudence and patience.

13. In Cicero, *De finibus,* bk. III, chaps. 5 and 6, secs. 16–22 (Loeb ed., pp. 233–41), Cato defends the Stoic theory that all creatures must first preserve themselves, but they must then proceed to live in conformity with nature: "It is only at this final stage that the Good first emerges and comes to be understood in its true nature."

14. This article is attributed to Epictetus on the authority of Marcus and reproduced among the otherwise unauthorized fragments in Epictetus, *Discourses* (Loeb ed., vol. II, pp. 470–71).

15. Cicero, *On the Ends of Good and Evil,* III.v–vi, 16–22 (Loeb ed., pp. 232–41).

16. Heraclitus, fragments B76, 71–74 (Diels-Kranz). Diels, *Die Fragmente der Vorsokratiker,* vol. I, pp. 167–68.

17. Helice, a town in the district of Achaea in Greece, was overwhelmed by the sea in 373 B.C. (*Brill's New Pauly,* vol. 6, p. 70, s.v. "Helice"). Pompeii and Herculaneum (as it is usually now spelled) were destroyed by the eruption of Vesuvius in A.D. 79.

18. The sentences placed within square brackets have also been attributed to Epictetus. See Epictetus, *Discourses,* fragment 28 (Loeb ed., vol. II, pp. 470–73).

19. These cannot be identified.

20. The legendarily long-lived king of Homer's *Iliad.* See *Iliad* I.250ff.: "In his time two generations of mortal men had perished, / those who had grown up with him and they who had been born to / these in sacred Pylos, and he was king in the third age" (trans. Lattimore).

BOOK V

1. Aesculapius, the god of healing, also known as Asclepius. A noted recipient of Asclepius's medical advice, usually given in dreams, was Marcus's contemporary, the sophist Aelius Aristides. See the endnotes, "Life of the Emperor," p. 168n40.

2. "happen."

3. Menander, *The Ghost* 17: "You're so well off you don't / Have anywhere to shit, I'd have you know." (In *Menander,* Loeb ed., vol. 3, p. 379).

4. See bk. IV, art. 21, p. 51, and bk. V, art. 27, p. 67n, on the divine ether.

5. See also bk. IX, art. 9, p. 110, the asterisked note, on "the present degenerate state [of the soul], as it is often counteracting its original destination."

As Hutcheson explains it, the present degenerate state of the soul has been brought about by confused imaginations, present opinions, dispositions, and habits. But this lapse of the soul into degeneracy has happened in accordance with the divine plan, in which it was foreseen that there must be different orders of beings, some of them less perfect than others. Many evils are necessary to reclaim the less perfect from their vices. And other evils are necessary for the exercise of "the most divine virtues, in the more perfect orders of beings." When one understands that imperfection is part of the divine plan or system, one also understands why the more imperfect orders behave badly. And one no longer feels anger or ill will toward the vicious, although one can still recognize vice in all its ugliness.

Hutcheson had alluded to a similar theodicy outlined in the comments of Simplicius on the morals of Epictetus in *An Essay* (1728), sec. II, art. 6, pp. 50–51 (Liberty Fund ed., pp. 43–44), where the relevant passage from Simplicius is reproduced. Hutcheson also refers on the same pages to the theodicy of William King, *De origine mali* (1702). The unavoidability of imperfection in the divine plan was elaborated most fully by Hutcheson in *A System of Moral Philosophy* (1755): for discussion, see Moore, "Hutcheson's Theodicy," pp. 239–66, in *The Scottish Enlightenment: Essays in Reinterpretation.* It is also interesting that Hutcheson should conclude this note with the sentence: "And the Stoic allows the vicious could refrain from their vices, if they heartily inclined to do so." This is consistent with the assertion made in bk. VII, art. 56, p. 91n, that: "the law of God [is] written in the heart." There is a law of nature but it is known by the immediate promptings of the heart. And even those imperfect degenerate natures who have been misled by confused imaginations or present opinions might behave otherwise "if they heartily wished to do so."

6. See note to bk. II, art. 1, pp. 171–72n2.

7. See bk. IV, art. 4, pp. 48–49: "We are all fellow-citizens: and if so, we have a common city. The universe, then, must be that city; for of what other common city are all men citizens?"

8. Horace, *Satires* II.2.79 (Loeb ed., pp. 142–43): "a portion of the divine spirit."

9. Virgil, *Georgics* IV.220–26, in *Virgil* (Loeb ed., vol. I, pp. 234–35): ". . . some have taught that the bees received a share of the divine intelligence, and a draught of heavenly ether; for God, they saw, pervades all things, earth and sea's expanse and heaven's depth; from him the flocks and herds, men and beasts of every sort draw, each at birth, the slender stream of life; to him all beings thereafter return, and when unmade, are restored."

10. Virgil, *Aeneid* VI.724–46 (Loeb ed., vol. I, pp. 582–85), explains that an "inner spirit" pervades all things, including human beings, but that human beings need to be purged of the sinful elements they have acquired in life before they can rejoin the heavenly spirit after death.

11. Marcus is here paraphrasing Homer, *Odyssey* IV.690.

12. The modern reference is Hesiod, *Works and Days,* 197–200 (Loeb ed., pp. 234–35): "Then indeed will Reverence and Indignation cover their beautiful skin with white mantles, leave human beings behind and go from the broad-pathed earth to the race of the Immortals, to Olympus."

13. Marcus's language here is an adaptation of the famous phrase of Epictetus, *ἀνέχου καὶ ἀπέχου*, fragment 10.6 (Epictetus, *Discourses,* Loeb ed., vol. II, p. 455).

14. The comedy is not known, if indeed this is a reference to a comedy, which the Greek does not necessarily imply.

15. Virgil, *Aeneid* IX.252–54 (Loeb ed., vol. I, pp. 132–33): "What reward, men, shall I deem worthy to be paid you for deeds so glorious? The first and fairest the gods and your own hearts shall give."

16. Virgil, *Aeneid* I.603–5 (Loeb ed., vol. I, pp. 304–5): "The gods . . . and the consciousness of right will bring you worthy rewards!"

BOOK VI

1. This sentence was cited by Hutcheson (in the original Greek) as one of the epigraphs prefaced to *Philosophiae moralis* (1745). In the translation of that work, *A Short Introduction to Moral Philosophy* (1747), this adage is rendered: "In this one thing delight and rest yourself, in going on constantly from one social action to another with remembrance of the Deity."

2. The sentences from here to the end of this article were cited by Shaftesbury to reinforce his view that wit is sometimes needed to explode pomposity: "Soliloquy or Advice to an Author," in *Characteristics* (1999), ed. Klein, p. 113n38. See also bk. IV, art. 27, p. 52, and bk. XI, art. 6, p. 135n.

3. Homer, *Iliad* 7.99 in modern editions.

4. See bk. II, art. 2, p. 34n; bk. X, art. 38, p. 132; and bk. XII, art. 19, p. 148.

5. Here and elsewhere Hutcheson inserts into his translation a number of phrases in square brackets, which correspond to nothing in the Greek text. They seem to be interpretative additions. For Nestor, see the endnotes, p. 176n20.

6. See also bk. VIII, art. 19, p. 98n, and bk. XII, art. 5, pp. 145–46. Hutcheson's strongest arguments for a future state of the soul are found in "A Synopsis of Metaphysics," pt. II, chap. 4, sec. 3, in *Logic, Metaphysics, and Natural Sociability,* pp. 147–49.

7. Like the Stoics, Hutcheson thought that one may have ideas of virtue and moral goodness and be motivated to act virtuously without "any Thoughts of future Rewards." See *Inquiry,* sec. I, art. 5, and sec. II, art. 7 (Liberty Fund ed., pp. 96 and 108–10).

8. Emperor, 138–161; Marcus's adoptive father. See also bk. I, art. 13, pp. 28–30.

9. Athos, a mountain headland at the end of the Chalcidic peninsula, through which Xerxes notoriously cut a canal in preparation for his invasion of Greece in 480 B.C.

10. Fragment B75 (Diels-Kranz). Diels, *Die Fragmente der Vorsokratiker,* vol. I, p. 168.

11. Von Arnim, *Stoicorum veterum fragmenta,* vol. II, fragment 1181 (from Plutarch, *Moralia* 1065e). Chrysippus was head of the Stoic school in the third century B.C. and was recognized as the "second founder" of Stoicism.

12. Aesculapius (Asclepius), god of healing (see the endnotes, bk. V, p. 176n1); Ceres, goddess of the corn.

13. See also bk. V, art. 17, p. 64n; bk. VIII, art. 14, p. 97; and bk. IX, art. 27, pp. 112–13.

14. These three figures are unknown.

15. Eudoxus, mathematician and astronomer (fourth century B.C.); Hipparchus, astronomer (second century B.C.); Archimedes, mathematician (third century B.C.).

16. Influential Cynic writer of the third century B.C., author of satirical works thought to have been imitated by Lucian (born about A.D. 120).

17. This sentiment and the parallel theme in the New Testament are a repeated refrain in the notes provided by Hutcheson and Moor. See bk. V, art. 31, p. 68; bk. VII, art. 22, p. 86; bk. VII, art. 70, p. 94; bk. IX, art. 3, p. 108; bk. IX, art. 8, p. 109; bk. IX, art. 27, pp. 112–13.

BOOK VII

1. For Chrysippus see the endnotes, bk. VI, p. 178n11. For Epictetus see the endnotes, bk. I, p. 170n7.

2. "Father, forgive them; for they know not what they do."

3. Cicero, *De officiis,* bk. I, chap. 29 (Loeb ed., pp. 104–5): "We need only to look at the faces of men in a rage or under the influence of some passion or fear or beside themselves with extravagant joy: . . ." Hutcheson had cited the same observation from Cicero in *A System of Moral Philosophy,* bk. I, chap. V, sec. V, vol. I, p. 87.

4. Hutcheson's remark may indicate that he found Marcus's writing obscure in this article; or he may have been suggesting that Marcus was proposing a doubt on this subject in the same dialectical spirit that Hutcheson perceived in bk. XII, art. 5, pp. 145–46. See the endnotes, bk. V, p. 177n16.

5. Antisthenes, fragment 20b. *Antisthenis fragmenta,* ed. Caizzi.

6. Euripides, *Bellerophon,* fragment 287, ll. 1–2 (*Tragicorum Graecorum fragmenta,* vol. 5, pt. 1, ed. Kannicht, p. 357).

7. This quotation was used as an epigram prefaced to *Philosophiae moralis* (1745). In *A Short Introduction to Moral Philosophy* (1747) it is translated as "Give joy to the immortal gods and those that love you," and it is attributed to "An unknown poet in Antonin." The source remains unknown.

8. Euripides, *Hypsipyle,* fragment 757, ll. 925–26 (*Tragicorum Graecorum fragmenta,* vol. 5, pt. 2, p. 777).

9. Euripides, *Antiope,* fragment 208, ll. 1–2 (*Tragicorum Graecorum fragmenta,* vol. 5, pt. 1, p. 299).

10. Euripides, fragment 918, ll. 3–4 (*Tragicorum Graecorum fragmenta,* vol. 5, pt. 2, p. 924).

11. Plato, *Apology* 28b (Loeb ed., pp. 102–5).

12. Plato, *Republic* 486a–b (Loeb ed., vol. II, pp. 8–11).

13. Epictetus, *Discourses,* bk. II, chap. 16, sec. 42 (Loeb ed., vol. I, p. 335).

14. Plato, *Apology* 28d (Loeb ed., pp. 104–5).

15. Plato, *Gorgias* 512d–e (Loeb ed., pp. 484–85).

16. The words "This is beautiful in Plato," which are found in some manuscripts, are excluded from modern editions; Gataker, however, printed them (1697, p. 65). A close approximation to this passage is found in Plato's *Sophist* 216c (Loeb ed., pp. 266–67); similar sentiments appear in Plato's *Republic* 500b–c (Loeb ed., vol. II, pp. 66–67).

17. Euripides, *Chrysippus,* fragment 839, ll. 9–11 (*Tragicorum Graecorum fragmenta,* vol. 5, pt. 2, p. 924).

18. Euripides, *Suppliants* 1110–11 (Loeb ed., pp. 124–25); and a quotation of unknown authorship, fragment 303 (*Tragicorum Graecorum fragmenta,* vol. I, p. 95).

19. See the endnotes, bk. III, pp. 172–73n1.

20. See the editors' introduction, p. xx. Also see bk. VI, art. 24, p. 76n, and bk. VIII, art. 54, p. 105n.

21. Hutcheson was referring to the citation from Epictetus at art. 45, pp. 88–89; there is no note at bk. VIII, art. 46.

22. See the endnotes, bk. III, p. 173n9.

23. A characteristic doctrine of Plato's found, for instance, at *Republic* 412e–13a (Loeb ed., vol. I, pp. 296–97), but Marcus's version closely follows Epictetus's paraphrase at *Discourses,* bk. I, chap. 28, sec. 4 (Loeb ed., vol. I, pp. 178–79).

24. Epicurus, fragment 447, *Epicurea,* ed. Usener, p. 447.

25. Hutcheson's translation is consistent with Gataker's text (p. 68), "ei tēlaugēs Sōkratēs," but modern editions treat "Tēlaugēs" as the proper name of an obscure contemporary of Socrates and add a negative, in which case the meaning of the sentence is, "How do we know that Telauges was not in character superior to Socrates?" See *The Meditations of the Emperor Marcus Aurelius Antoninus,* ed. Farquharson, vol. I, p. 143, vol. II, pp. 749–50.

26. Hutcheson's translation, "in the Areopagus," is a mistranslation of "en tōi pagōi" (in Gataker's text, p. 68). It is an understandable mistranslation since in earlier Greek, at least, "pagos" could mean "rock" or "hill," and does have this meaning in "Areopagos," "the hill of Ares" in Athens. In this passage of Marcus, however, "en tōi pagōi" means "in the frosty cold," and alludes to the story Plato tells at *Symposium* 220b–d (Loeb ed., pp. 232–35) of how Socrates slept in the open through the frosty nights during the campaign against Potidaea.

27. Plato, *Apology* 32c–d (Loeb ed., pp. 116–19); *Epistle* VII, 324c–325a (Loeb ed., pp. 478–81). The "thirty tyrants" conducted a reign of terror at Athens in 404–403 B.C. The charge mentioned in the text that Socrates assumed "stately airs or gate" seems to be a reference to Aristophanes, *Clouds,* 222ff.

28. The reference to Matthew 5:45–47 is to the Sermon on the Mount where Christ urges his followers not to follow the example of the Roman tax collectors ("the publicans") who love only those who love the Romans. He exhorts his followers to love their enemies, bless those that curse them, and so on.

The reference to "Cambray's dialogue of Socrates, Alcibiades and Timon" is to François de Salignac de la Mothe-Fénelon (1651–1715), Archbishop of Cambrai (1696–1715), *Fables and Dialogues of the Dead,* Dialogue XVII: "Socrates, Alcibiades and Timon: A Just Medium between the Man-Hating Character of Timon, and the Corrupt Character of Alcibiades," pp. 187–201. At p. 194, Socrates declares "we must love Mankind, in spite of their Defects, endeavour to do 'em good; we must serve 'em without any view of interest."

29. See bk. V, art. 17, p. 64n.

BOOK VIII

1. See bk. VII, art. 56, p. 91n; bk. IX, art. 10, p. 110; bk. X, art. 13, p. 125n; and bk. X, art. 25, p. 127.

2. Gaius Julius Caesar.

3. Diogenes of Sinope, founder of the Cynic sect in the fourth century B.C., appropriated by the Stoics as one of the intellectual precursors of Zeno, the founder of Stoicism.

4. For Heraclitus see the endnotes, bk. III, p. 173n5.

5. Emperor, 117–38.

6. The first Roman emperor (d. A.D. 14).

7. In *A System of Moral Philosophy,* bk. I, chap. 9, sec. XV, vol. I, p. 206,

Hutcheson deplored "the vanity of *Polytheism,* if any ever believed a plurality of *original beings.* The wiser *Heathens* had a different *Polytheism.*" Marcus was clearly one of those "wiser Heathens." It is also notable that whereas Marcus usually refers in the text to "the Gods," Hutcheson and Moor typically find in the text evidence of Marcus's belief in one God. See bk. V, art. 27, p. 67n; bk. IX, art. 1, p. 107, the asterisked note; bk. XII, art. 1, p. 144, the daggered note.

8. Insofar as these persons are identifiable, they are members of the imperial family and court.

9. These persons are unknown, except that Demetrius the Platonist may be the person mentioned by Lucian, *On Not Listening to Slander* 16 (Loeb ed., vol. I, p. 379), as a victim of slander at the court of Ptolemy XII, who came to power at Alexandria in 80 B.C. (*Real-Encyclopädie,* vol. 4, column 2844, s.v. "Demetrios 92").

10. Emperor from 138 to 161.

11. Marcus Vipsanius Agrippa, general and minister to Augustus; Areios, a Stoic who was a confidant of Augustus (*Brill's New Pauly,* vol. I, column 1158); Maecenas, friend and minister of Augustus and the patron of Virgil, Horace, and Propertius.

12. See bk. III, art. 11, p. 45, and bk. XI, art. 1, pp. 133–34.

13. At bk. IV, art. 19, p. 50n, Hutcheson had remarked that "the Stoics denyed fame to be desirable, except as it gave opportunities of more extensive good offices." Hutcheson was observing that desires for fame and other external goods were rational and good only if such desires were directed to the good of others and the whole. Hutcheson had insisted elsewhere that the Stoics made provision for rational longing or desires of the soul. See *A System of Moral Philosophy,* bk. I, chap. I, sec. V, vol. I, p. 8.

14. This footnote does not appear in later editions. Hutcheson's note makes it clear that he considered this article (bk. VIII, art. 32) to be another use of the Stoic concept of *reservation* explained above at bk. IV, art. 1, p. 47n, and again at bk. V, art. 20, p. 65, and bk. XI, art. 37, p. 143. Also see the endnotes, bk. IV, p. 174n1.

15. These persons are not certainly known, except for Panthea, who was a mistress of Marcus's co-emperor, Verus, and is celebrated by the contemporary satirist Lucian in "Essays in portraiture" and "Essays in portraiture defended," in *Lucian,* ed. and trans. Harmon, vol. IV (Loeb ed., pp. 255ff. and 297ff.).

16. Horace, *Satires* II.7.86–87 (from Horace's description of the wise man): "who in himself is a whole, smoothed and rounded, so that nothing from outside

can rest on the polished surface." *Satires, Epistles, and Ars Poetica* (Loeb ed., pp. 231–33).

17. In this note, Hutcheson appears to find in Marcus's thinking intimations of the scholastic notion that certain of God's attributes are communicable or may be shared with human beings. Hutcheson had described the communicable attributes in "A Synopsis of Metaphysics," pt. III, chaps. 2 and 3, in *Logic, Metaphysics, and Natural Sociability* (2006), pp. 162, 174–75; in *A Short Introduction to Moral Philosophy* (1747), bk. I, chap. 7, sec. III, pp. 105–7; and in *A System of Moral Philosophy,* bk. 1, chap. 10, sec. II, vol. I, pp. 210–11. This was a characteristic of Hutcheson's moral philosophy that made a particular impression upon Adam Smith; see *The Theory of Moral Sentiments,* pt. VII, chap. 3, pp. 300–301. Smith identified this theory with the Platonists, notably with the work of the Cambridge Platonists and with the Eclectics of the early Christian centuries. It is interesting that Hutcheson should have found this theory in the thinking of a philosopher whom he took to be a Stoic, albeit a Stoic who incorporated Platonic insights in his thought.

18. See also bk. III, art. 15, p. 45n. The Stoics' interest in etymology derives from their view that the meanings of words are in some sense natural rather than conventional. See Long, *Hellenistic Philosophy,* 131–39. Cicero criticizes the Stoics' etymologies of the gods' names in *On the Nature of the Gods,* bk. III., sec. 62ff.

BOOK IX

1. See *A System of Moral Philosophy,* bk. I, chap. 9, sec. V, pp. 174–80, under the heading "The Original Mind is benevolent or good."

2. See bk. X, art. 36, p. 131.

3. Source not known.

4. The three notes appended to this article summarize succinctly the three duties distinguished by Hutcheson in *A Short Introduction to Moral Philosophy,* bk. I, chaps. 4, 5, and 6; and by Carmichael in his notes and supplements to Pufendorf's *De officio.* See Carmichael, *Natural Rights on the Threshold of the Scottish Enlightenment,* chaps. 6, 7, and 8, pp. 54–76.

5. See bk. V, art. 17, p. 64n.

6. See "On the Natural Sociability of Mankind" in *Logic, Metaphysics, and Natural Sociability* (Liberty Fund ed., p. 204) and *A Short Introduction to Moral Philosophy,* bk. I, chap. 1, sec. 9, p. 14 (Liberty Fund ed., p. 33): "that *sympathy*

or fellow-feeling by which the state and fortunes of others affect us exceedingly." Shaftesbury provides an account similar to Marcus's of the sympathy that brings together families, friends, and assemblies in "Sensus Communis," pt. III, sec. 2, in *Characteristics,* ed. Klein, p. 51. See also the editors' introduction, pp. xiv–xv.

7. "You shall love the Lord your God with all your heart, and with all your soul, and with all your mind. This is the first and great commandment. And the second is like it, You shall love your neighbour as yourself" (Matthew 22:37–39).

8. See bk. VI, art. 7, p. 71, and the endnotes, bk. VI, p. 178n1.

9. See also bk. VII, art. 13, pp. 84–85, and *A System of Moral Philosophy,* bk. II, chap. 16, vol. II, pp. 104–16.

10. "Representations of the shades" interprets Marcus's words, *to tēs Nekuias,* which refer to the account of the Underworld in Homer, *Odyssey* XI, the abode of the "shades" of the dead.

11. See the previous endnote (10).

12. See also bk. V, art. 13, p. 63, and bk. IX, art. 31, p. 114. The active principle is the soul, the divine fire within things themselves. Marcus invites us to consider how long this active principle will last, and how transient are the things comprehended in the material principle: external things, the imagination, the passions, and so forth.

13. While Marcus warned against Plato's idealism, others have taken Marcus's style of governing to have been the opposite of Machiavellian realism: "Let Caesar Borgia be the Pattern of Machiavelli's Hero, that of all virtuous Princes will be Marcus Aurelius": *Anti-Machiavel* (1741), p. 59n.

14. Philip II, king of Macedon, father of Alexander.

15. Demetrius of Phalerum, a Peripatetic philosopher by training, was ruler of Athens from 317 to 307 B.C. on behalf of Macedonia.

16. Gataker translates as "rerum praeteritarum, praesentium, decedentium differentias": "the differences of things past, things present, and things that are passing away."

17. See bk. V, art. 17, p. 64n, on the necessity of evil in the best-formed systems.

18. Epictetus, *Discourses,* bk. II, chap. 18, secs. 28–29 (Loeb ed., vol. I, p. 357).

19. Fragment 191 (Usener). Epicurus, *Epicurea,* ed. Usener, p. 158.

20. Epictetus, *Manual* (*Encheiridion*), 10, in Epictetus, *Discourses* (Loeb ed., vol. II, p. 491).

21. Epistle of Paul to Titus 3:1 and 3.

BOOK X

1. Epistle of Paul to the Philippians 4:11.

2. Epictetus, *Manual* (*Encheiridion*), 15, in Epictetus, *Discourses* (Loeb ed., vol. II, p. 495).

3. The quotations on this and the next page are all from the Epistles of Paul: Second Corinthians; Romans; Philippians; Romans again.

4. See the endnotes, bk. IX, p. 184n9.

5. "For the sake of life, to lose the reasons for living."

6. Clement of Alexandria, *Stromateis,* bk. VII, chap. 34, sec. 3, pp. 26–27.

7. Persius, *Satires* II.73–75 (Loeb ed., pp. 70–71): "[Let us offer to the gods] justice and right blended in the spirit, the mind pure in its inner depths and a breast imbued with noble honour. Let me bring these to the temples, and with a handful of grits I shall make acceptable sacrifice."

8. Gataker, 1697, pp. 359–60.

9. The biblical books in this note are, respectively, the Second Epistle of Paul to the Corinthians, Romans, Leviticus, the First Epistle of Peter, the First Epistle of John, and the Gospels of Luke and Matthew.

10. Moor is translating the conjecture ἀφυσιολογήτως, which Gataker proposes in his annotation on p. 361 (1697). This conjecture is generally accepted by modern editors.

11. During the final years of his life, Marcus was engaged in warfare against the Sarmatians, a nomadic people who had advanced to the river Danube.

12. See also bk. XI, art. 10, pp. 136–37n. It will be evident that the two principles of justice defined in these two notes correspond with the two parts of Thomas Gataker's "Maxims of the Stoics," appended here, pp. 155–58.

13. Gataker, 1697, p. 363; Plato, *Laws,* bk. IV, 715e–716a (Loeb ed., vol. I, pp. 292–95).

14. Euripides, fragment 898, lines 7–9 (*Tragicorum Graecorum fragmenta,* vol. 5, pt. 2, p. 908).

15. There is a play on words in the text. Both φιλει (*philei*) and *amat* normally mean "loves" but are also used to mean the same as *solet* (i.e., "is accustomed to").

16. Epictetus, *Discourses,* bk. II, chap. 16, sec. 42 (Loeb ed., vol. I, p. 335) and bk. IV, chap. 7, sec. 20 (Loeb ed., vol. II, p. 367); Seneca, *Epistulae morales,* 96.2 (Loeb ed., vol. II, pp. 104–7).

17. Plato, *Theaetetus* 174e (Loeb ed., 122–23).

18. Epictetus, *Discourses* III.22 (Loeb ed., vol. II, p. 137).

19. See also bk. XI, art. 1, pp. 133–34, the daggered note, and bk. XII, art. 1, p. 144.

20. [Aristotle], *On the Universe* 6 (400b27–30), in *The Complete Works of Aristotle,* ed. Barnes, vol. I, p. 639.

21. Hadrian, emperor A.D. 117–38; Antoninus, emperor A.D. 138–61; Philip II, king of Macedon 359–336 B.C.; Alexander, his son, king 336–323 B.C.; Croesus, legendarily wealthy king of Lydia ca. 560–546 B.C.

22. The known persons here are Xenophon, the Athenian general and author (born about 430 B.C.); Crito, who attempted to persuade Socrates to escape from prison (see Plato's *Crito*); and Euphrates, a sophist for whom Pliny the Younger wrote a letter of recommendation (*Letters* bk. 1, letter 10, in Pliny, *Letters and Panegyricus,* Loeb ed., vol. I, pp. 30–35).

23. Epictetus, *Discourses,* bk. II, chap. 16, secs. 46–47, in Epictetus, *Discourses* (Loeb ed., vol. I, p. 337).

24. Epictetus, *Discourses,* bk. IV, chap. 4, sec. 7 (Loeb ed., vol. II, p. 315).

25. The Stoic theory of liberty of acting in accordance with reason and the law that governs all things was reviewed by Hutcheson in "A Synopsis of Metaphysics," in *Logic, Metaphysics, and Natural Sociability* (Liberty Fund ed., pp. 97–98, 129–30, and 171 and in the editors' introduction, p. xxv).

26. Homer, *Iliad* VI, 147–49 (Lattimore trans., p. 157).

27. See also bk. IX, art. 3, pp. 108–9.

BOOK XI

1. See the editors' introduction, pp. xxi–xxii.

2. This is Marcus's only explicit reference to Christians in the *Meditations* (if it is not a later interpolation). As Gataker recognized (1697, p. 386), Marcus is referring to the stubbornness with which Christians refused to sacrifice to the emperor, which seemed to be tantamount at times to voluntary martyrdom.

3. See also "The Life of the Emperor Marcus Antoninus," pp. 19–23, for further considerations by Hutcheson in mitigation of the charge made against Marcus Aurelius that he was guilty of persecuting Christians. See also the editors' introduction, p. xxiv.

4. The relevant note is found at bk. X, art. 11, pp. 124–25.

5. For the sources of these quotations, which Marcus also quotes in bk. VII, arts. 38–41, see the endnotes, pp. 179–80nn6–9.

6. The major surviving figure of Old Comedy is Aristophanes; Middle Com-

edy is almost entirely lost; New Comedy is represented by Menander. Diogenes is the Cynic philosopher of the fourth century (see the endnotes, bk. VIII, p. 181n3). Shaftesbury juxtaposed the first sentence of this article with the three sentences preceding this note to illustrate the "natural and gradual refinement of styles and manners among the ancients," in "Soliloquy or Advice to an Author," in *Characteristics,* ed. Klein, p. 21. Moreover, the writers of comedy served "as a sort of counter-pedagogue against the pomp and formality of the more solemn writers": Ibid., p. 113n. Hutcheson's understanding of this article was different and more Stoical. It was that poetry and drama make us familiar with calamities so that we will not lose self-command when they happen. See bk. XI, art. 6, the daggered note on p. 135.

7. Sophocles, *Oedipus Tyrannus* 1391 (Loeb ed., vol. I, pp. 468–69).

8. See bk. VII, art. 57, p. 91n, where Hutcheson writes: "For, a man who desires only what God destines him, can never be disappointed; since infinite power, wisdom, and goodness, must always accomplish its designs; and, as he [God] loves all his works, every event ordered by him, must be best for the whole, and for the individuals to which it happens." Hutcheson had not replaced fate (or predestination) with benevolence: he thought rather that acting in a manner consistent with predestination or the divine plan was the most effective way to promote benevolence or the universal happiness. See also bk. XI, art. 18, p. 139, and the editors' introduction pp. xxi–xxii.

9. See bk. I, art. 12, p. 28: "He [Claudius Maximus] taught me, not to be easily astonished or confounded with any thing, never to seem in a hurry, nor yet to be dilatory, or perplexed, without presence of mind, or dejected, fretful, angry, or suspicious; and to be ready to do good to others, to forgive, and to speak truth; and in all this, to appear rather like one who had always been straight and right, than ever rectified or redressed."

10. Phocion "the good," fourth-century Athenian general and politician, noted for his uprightness, condemned to death by the Athenians in 318 B.C. From the many anecdotes about Phocion's forbearance, Marcus may be referring to his injunction, just before he drank the hemlock, to his son, that he should "cherish no resentment against the Athenians" (Plutarch, *Phocion,* chap. 36, sec. 3). *Plutarch's Lives,* Loeb ed., vol. VIII, pp. 228–31.

11. The correct reference is bk. X, art. 11, p. 124.

12. Lucan, *The Civil War,* IX.564 and 573–76 (Loeb ed., pp. 546–49): "Cato, inspired by the god whom he bore hidden in his heart" [said] "We men are all inseparable from the gods, and, even if the oracle be dumb, all our actions are

predetermined by Heaven. The gods have no need to speak: for the Creator told us once for all at our birth whatever we are permitted to know."

In Lucan's *Pharsalia,* a narrative epic of the civil war between the legions of Pompey and of Julius Caesar, the above lines contain the Stoical response of Cato to a request put to him by his lieutenant, Labienus, who had urged Cato to consult an oracle to learn what virtue is and to obtain from the oracle a description of an honorable man. Cato was offended by the request; he was himself the model of virtue and honor that Labienus hoped the oracle would describe. David Hume had quoted Labienus's request to Cato in an epigraph prefaced to book III of *A Treatise of Human Nature* (1740).

Hutcheson in turn found it apposite to quote Cato's response to that question in this context and identify Cato's response with Marcus's moral philosophy and with his own.

13. Aesop, *Fables,* "The Wolves and the Sheep," no. 217 in the Budé ed. (ed. Chambry, 96–97).

14. The correct reference is bk. III, art. 11, pp. 44–45.

15. See bk. XI, art. 7, p. 135.

16. On the distinction between natural and moral evil, see Hutcheson, *An Inquiry into the Original of Our Ideas of Beauty and Virtue* (2004), sec. I, art. 1, pp. 90–91.

17. "Equal law among a free people."

18. See bk. XI, n22, below.

19. Similar to Epictetus, *Discourses,* bk. II, chap. 1, sec. 15 (Loeb ed., vol. I, pp. 216–17).

20. Aristotle, *Rhetoric,* bk. II, chap. 23, sec. 8 (1398a24); Hutcheson and Moor write "Perdiccas" following Gataker's text (1697, p. 113), but Aristotle makes Socrates' remark refer to Perdiccas's son, Archelaus, rather than to Perdiccas himself. Both were kings of Macedon contemporary with Socrates. Gataker discusses the passage on p. 409. Aristotle, *The Complete Works of Aristotle,* vol. II, p. 2228.

21. It is Epicurus, fragment 210, in Epicurus, *Epicurea,* p. 163.

22. Aesop, *Fables,* "The Country Mouse and the City Mouse," no. 243 in the Budé ed., pp. 107–8; no. 41 in the Penguin Classics trans. (*Fables of Aesop,* trans. Handford, p. 43); there is a classic treatment of the story in Horace, *Satires,* bk. II, Satire 6.77–117 (Loeb ed., 216–19).

23. Xanthippe was Socrates' wife, reputedly shrewish.

24. Source unknown.

25. Homer, *Odyssey* bk. IX.413 (Loeb ed., pp. 346–47).

26. Hesiod, *Works and Days* 186 (Loeb ed., pp. 102–3). Hutcheson and Moor translate Gataker's Greek text (though ignoring the future tense of the verb). That text, however, is corrupt and quotes Hesiod inaccurately (*aretēn* instead of *ara tous*). Gataker's Latin translation quotes Hesiod correctly (1697, p. 114).

27. Epictetus, *Discourses,* bk. III, chap. 24, secs. 86–87 (Loeb ed., vol. II, p. 213).

28. Ibid., secs. 88–91 (Loeb ed., vol. II, p. 213).

29. Ibid., secs. 91–93 (Loeb ed., vol. II, p. 215).

30. Ibid., chap. 22, sec. 105 (Loeb ed., vol. II, p. 167).

31. Epictetus, fragment 27 (Loeb ed., vol. II, p. 471).

32. Epictetus, fragment 28 (Loeb ed., vol. II, p. 471).

33. Marcus does not seem to be referring to any specific passage of Plato or Xenophon.

34. See also the editors' introduction, p. xiii.

35. See bk. VII, art. 73, p. 94.

BOOK XII

1. See Empedocles, fragments B27–28. Diels, *Die Fragmente der Vorsokratiker,* vol. I, pp. 323–24.

2. See also the endnotes, bk. VI, p. 178n7.

3. This article was cited by Henry More, in *An Account of Virtue* (1690), p. 120, in corroboration of his theory that "there is so much of Divinity interwoven in a virtuous Mind; . . ."

4. This article was cited by Shaftesbury in Miscellany IV, chap. 1, in *Characteristics,* ed. Klein, p. 423, in the context of a Stoical reflection, supported by sayings of Marcus, Epictetus, and Horace, to the effect that we should withdraw our admiration and desire from the merely pleasurable and direct them to "objects, whatever they are, of inward worth and beauty (such as honesty, faith, integrity, friendship, honor)."

5. Little is known of these persons, except that Tiberius is the emperor of that name (A.D. 14–37), whose final years, spent in retirement on the island of Capri, were supposed to have reached unexampled depths of depravity.

6. See also bk. IV, art. 37, p. 54, the asterisked note; and the endnotes, bk. IV, p. 175n12, and other references cited there.

7. In Cicero's *On the Ends of Good and Evil,* bk. III, xiv, 45–48 (Loeb ed.,

pp. 216–19), Cato defended the Stoic theory that actions inspired by goodness and virtue are not enhanced by prolongation or duration; such actions are seasonable or opportune or they are not. Hutcheson's term "seasonableness" is a translation of *eukairia,* which Cicero translated *opportunitas.* In *A System of Moral Philosophy,* bk. I, chap. 4, sec. 6, vol. I, p. 61, Hutcheson quoted "the Stoick in *Cicero de fin.* l. iii c. 10" to reinforce his claim that moral good cannot be estimated by degrees: "nor can such matters of immediate feeling be otherways proved but by appeals to our hearts."

Editors' Notes to *Maxims of the Stoics*

1. Cleanthes (331–232 B.C.) was the second head of the Stoic school. A translation of his Hymn to Zeus may be found in *The Hellenistic Philosophers,* ed. Long and Sedley, vol. 1, pp. 53–54.

2. Seneca, *Epistulae morales,* letter 107, sec. 9 (Loeb ed., vol. III, pp. 226–29).

3. Plato, *Apology,* 28d–e (Loeb ed., pp. 74–77).

4. "to believe that he was born to serve the whole world and not himself" (of Cato). Lucan, bk. II, line 383, in Lucan, *The Civil War* (Loeb ed., pp. 84–85).

5. This does not appear to be a correct reference.

6. Cf. Cicero, *De finibus,* bk. II, chap. 15, secs. 49–50 in Loeb ed., pp. 136–39.

7. Plutarch, "On Affection for Offspring," in Plutarch's *Moralia,* trans. Humbold (Loeb ed., vol. VI, pp. 342–43).

Editors' Notes to *Gataker's Apology*

1. The *Epistles* of Isidore of Pelusium can be found in Migne, *Patrologiae Graecae,* vol. 78, pp. 178–1646.

2. Dio of Prusa (Dio Chrysostom), Oration 51 "Against Diodorus," chap. 9.

3. Augustine, Epistle 170. *S. Aureli Augustini Hipponensis episcopi Epistulae,* ed. Goldbacher, in *Corpus scriptorum ecclesiasticorum Latinorum,* vol. 44, pt. 3, pp. 622–31.

4. Gataker seems to be referring to Polybius, *Histories,* I.81.5–11 (Loeb ed., vol. I, pp. 218–21): "No beast becomes at the end more wicked or cruel than man"; and *Histories,* XXXII.3.7 (Loeb ed., vol. VI, pp. 236–37): "There is nothing more terrible in body and soul than a man once he has become absolutely like a beast." The latter passage is preserved in the *Excerpta de legationibus,* which consists of passages about *Embassies* culled from Polybius on the orders of Constantine Porphyrogenitus and which was printed as a separate text in the early modern period.

5. Plato, *Laws,* bk. VI, 766a, in Plato, *Laws,* trans. Bury (Loeb ed., vol. I, pp. 438–39).

6. Bernard of Clairvaux, "Sermones per annum," in vol. 4 of *Sancti Bernardi Opera,* p. 161ff.

BIBLIOGRAPHY

Editions of *The Meditations of the Emperor Marcus Aurelius Antoninus.* Translated by Francis Hutcheson and James Moor and Published in Glasgow by Robert and Andrew Foulis and in Dublin for Robert Main

The Meditations of the Emperor Marcus Aurelius Antoninus. Newly Translated from the Greek: With Notes, and an Account of His Life. Glasgow: Printed by Robert Foulis; and sold by him at the College; by Mess. Hamilton and Balfour, in Edinburgh; and by Andrew Millar, over against St. Clements Church, London. 1742.

The Meditations of the Emperor Marcus Aurelius Antoninus. Newly Translated from the Greek: With Notes, and an Account of His Life. 2nd ed. Glasgow: Printed by Robert and Andrew Foulis, Printers to the University, 1749.

The Meditations of the Emperor Marcus Aurelius Antoninus. Newly Translated from the Greek: With Notes, and an Account of His Life. 3rd ed. Glasgow: Printed by Robert and Andrew Foulis, Printers to the University, 1752.

The Meditations of the Emperor Marcus Aurelius Antoninus. Newly Translated from the Greek: With Notes, and an Account of His Life. 4th ed. Dublin: Printed for Robert Main at Homer's Head in Dame-Street, 1752.

The Meditations of the Emperor Marcus Aurelius Antoninus. Newly Translated from the Greek: With Notes, and an Account of His Life. 4th ed. Glasgow: Printed by Robert and Andrew Foulis, Printers to the University, 1764.

Other Editions of *The Meditations of Marcus Aurelius Antoninus* Referred to in the Notes to This Edition

Marcus Aurelius Antoninus the Roman Emperor, His Meditations Concerning Himselfe: Treating of a Naturall Mans Happiness; Wherein It Consisteth, and of the Meanes to Attain unto It. Translated out of the originall Greeke; with notes by Meric Casaubon, B. of D. and Prebendarie of Christ Church Canterbury. London, 1634.

Markou Antoninou tou Autokratoros tōn eis heauton biblia 12 = Marci Antonini Imperatoris de rebus suis, sive de eis quae ad se pertinere censebat, Libri XII, locis haud paucis repurgati, suppleti, restituti: versione insuper Latina nova; lectionibus item variis, locisque parallelis, ad marginem adjectis; ac commentario perpetuo, explicati atque illustrati; studio operaque Thomae Gatakeri Londinatis. Cantabrigiae, 1652.

Réflexions morales de l'Empereur Marc Antonin avec des remarques de Mr. et de Mad. Dacier. 2 vols. Paris: Barbin, 1691.

Markou Antoninou tou Autokratoros tōn eis heauton biblia 12 = Marci Antonini Imperatoris de rebus suis, sive de eis quae ad se pertinere censebat, Libri XII, locis haud paucis repurgati, suppleti, restituti: versione insuper Latina nova; lectionibus item variis, locisque parallelis, ad marginem adjectis; ac commentario perpetuo, explicati atque illustrati; studio operaque Thomae Gatakeri Londinatis. Huic secundae editioni accessere annotationes selectiores A. D'Acerii Latinitate donatae, necnon Marci Antonini Vita, passim aucta, & idoneis scriptorum veterum testimoniis firmata à Geo. Stanhope, Coll. Reg. apud Cantabr. quondam Socio. Londini, 1697.

The Emperor Marcus Antoninus His Conversation with Himself: Together with the Preliminary Discourse of the Learned Gataker. As Also, the Emperor's Life, Written by Monsieur Dacier, and Supported by the Authorities Collected by Dr. Stanhope. To Which Is Added the Mythological Picture of Cebes the Theban. Translated into English from the respective originals, by Jeremy Collier, M.A. London, 1701.

Markou Antoninou tou Autokratoros tōn eis heauton biblia 12 = Marci Antonini Imperatoris eorum quae ad seipsum libri XII. Recogniti et notis illustrati [R.I.]. Oxoniae, 1704.

Markou Antoninou tou Autokratoros tōn eis heauton biblia 12 = Marci Antonini Imperatoris eorum quae ad seipsum libri XII. Glasguae, 1744.

The Thoughts of the Emperor Marcus Aurelius Antoninus. Translated by George Long. London: Bell & Daldy, 1862.

Marcus Aurelius Antoninus to Himself: An English Translation with Introductory Study on Stoicism and the Last of the Stoics. Translated by Gerald H. Rendall. London: Macmillan, 1898.

The Communings with Himself of Marcus Aurelius Antoninus Emperor of Rome, Together with His Speeches and Sayings. Edited and translated by C. R. Haines. London: Heinemann, 1916.

The Meditations of the Emperor Marcus Antoninus. Edited by A. S. L. Farquharson. 2 vols. Oxford: Clarendon Press, 1944.

The Meditations of Marcus Aurelius Antoninus. Translated by A. S. L. Farquharson with introduction and notes by R. B. Rutherford. Oxford: Oxford University Press, 1990.

Other Works Referred to in the Text and Notes

"Account of the Life and Writings of William Robertson, D.D." In *Biographical Memoirs of Adam Smith, L.L.D., William Robertson, D.D., and Thomas Reid, D.D.,* edited by Sir William Hamilton. Edinburgh, 1858.

Aesop. *Fables.* Edited by Emile Chambry. Paris: Société d'édition "Les Belles Lettres," 1960.

Aesop. *Fables of Aesop.* Translated by S. A. Handford. Harmondsworth, Eng.: Penguin Books, 1954.

Antisthenes. *Antisthenis fragmenta.* Edited by F. D. Caizzi. Milano, Varese: Instituto Editionale Cisalpino, 1966.

Apuleius. *The Apologia and Florida of Apuleius of Madura.* Translated by H. E. Butler. Oxford: Clarendon Press, 1909.

Aristides, P. Aelius. *The Complete Works.* Translated by Charles A. Behr. 2 vols. Leiden: E. J. Brill, 1981–86.

Aristotle. *The Complete Works of Aristotle.* Edited by Jonathan Barnes. 2 vols. Princeton, N.J.: Princeton University Press, 1984.

Athenagoras. *Legatio and De resurrectione.* Edited and translated by William R. Schoedel. Oxford: Clarendon Press, 1972.

Bentley, Richard. *A Dissertation upon the Epistles of Phalaris with an Answer to the Objections of the Honourable Charles Boyle.* London, 1699.

Bernard of Clairvaux. *Sancti Bernardi Opera.* Edited by Jean Leclercq, C. H.

Talbot, and Henri M. Rochais. 8 vols. in 9. Rome: Editiones Cistercienses, 1957–77.

Birley, Anthony R. *Marcus Aurelius, A Biography.* Rev. ed. London: Batsford, 1987.

[Blair, Hugh.] *Dissertatio philosophica inauguralis de fundamentis et obligatione legis naturae.* Edinburgh, 1739.

———. "Hutcheson's Moral Philosophy." *Edinburgh Review,* no. 1 (1755): 9–23.

———. *Sermons.* 5 vols. London: T. Cadell and W. Davies, 1814–15.

Brill's New Pauly: Encyclopaedia of the Ancient World. Edited by Hubert Cancick and Helmuth Schneider, English translation supervised by C. F. Salazar and D. E. Orton. Leiden: Brill, 2002–.

Brunt, P. A. "Marcus Aurelius and the Christians." In *Studies in Latin Literature and Roman History,* edited by Carl Deroux. Collection Latomus v. 164. Bruxelles: Latomus, 1979.

Cambridge Ancient History. Vol. 11: *The High Empire,* A.D. *70–192.* Edited by Alan K. Bowman, Peter Garnsey, and Dominic Rathbone. 2nd ed. New York: Cambridge University Press, 2000.

Carmichael, Gershom. *Natural Rights on the Threshold of the Scottish Enlightenment.* Edited by James Moore and Michael Silverthorne. Indianapolis: Liberty Fund, 2002.

Cicero, Marcus Tullius. *De finibus bonorum et malorum* [*On the Ends of Good and Evil*]. Translated by H. Rackham. Loeb Classical Library. 2nd ed. Cambridge, Mass.: Harvard University Press, 1931.

———. *De officiis* [On Duties]. Edited and translated by Walter Miller. Loeb Classical Library. London: Heinemann, 1913.

Clement of Alexandria. *Stromateis.* In *Clemens Alexandrinus,* vol. 3, edited by Otto Stählin. 2nd ed. Berlin: Akademie-Verlag, 1970.

Diels, H. *Die Fragmente der Vorsokratiker.* 12th ed. Revised by W. Kranz. 3 vols. Dublin: W. Weidmann, 1966–67.

Dio Cassius. *Dio's Roman History.* Edited and translated by Herbert B. Foster and Earnest Cary. 9 vols. Loeb Classical Library. Cambridge, Mass.: Harvard University Press, 1914–27.

Diogenes Laertius. *Lives of Eminent Philosophers.* Edited and translated by R. D. Hicks. 2 vols. Loeb Classical Library. London: Heinemann, 1925.

Dio of Prusa, *Dionis Prusaensis quem vocant Chrysostomum quae extant omnia.* Edited by J. de Arnim. 2 vols. (1893). Berlin: Weidmann, 1962.

Duncan, William James. *Notices and Documents Illustrative of the Literary History of Glasgow during the Greater Part of the Last Century.* Glasgow: T. D. Morison, 1886.

Epictetus. *The Discourses as Reported by Arrian, the Manual, and Fragments.* Edited and translated by William A. Oldfather. 2 vols. Loeb Classical Library. London: Heinemann, 1925–28.

Epicurus. *Epicurea.* Edited by Hermann Usener. Rome: "l'Erma" di Bretschneider, 1963.

Euripides. *Suppliant Women, Electra, Heracles.* Edited and translated by David Kovacs. Loeb Classical Library. Cambridge, Mass.: Harvard University Press, 1998.

Eusebius. *The Ecclesiastical History.* Edited and translated by H. Kirsopp Lake and J. E. L. Oulton. 2 vols. Loeb Classical Library. Cambridge, Mass.: Harvard University Press, 1926–32.

———. *Eusebiou tou Pamphilou ekklesiastikē historia = Eusebii Pamphili Ecclesiasticae historiae libri decem.* Edited by H. Valesius. Parisiis, 1659.

———. *The History of the Church from Christ to Constantine.* Translated by G. A. Williamson. Harmondsworth, Eng.: Penguin Books, 1965.

Fénelon, François de Salignac de la Mothe-. *Fables and Dialogues of the Dead.* London, 1723.

Fordyce, David. *Dialogues Concerning Education.* 2 vols. London, 1745–48.

Frederick II, king of Prussia. *Anti-Machiavel: or, An Examination of Machiavel's* Prince, *with notes historical and political. Published by Mr. de Voltaire. Translated from the French.* London, 1741.

Fronto, Marcus Cornelius. *Correspondence.* Edited and translated by C. R. Haines. 2 vols. Loeb Classical Library. London: Heinemann, 1919.

Gibbon, Edward. *The History of the Decline and Fall of the Roman Empire.* Edited by J. B. Bury. 7 vols. London: Methuen, 1909–26.

Hadot, Pierre. *The Inner Citadel: The Meditations of Marcus Aurelius.* Cambridge, Mass.: Harvard University Press, 1998.

Herodian. *Herodian.* Edited and translated by C. R. Whittaker. 2 vols. Loeb Classical Library. Cambridge, Mass.: Harvard University Press, 1969–70.

Hesiod. *Theogony, Works and Days, Testimonia.* Edited and translated by Glenn W. Most. 2 vols. Loeb Classical Library. Cambridge, Mass.: Harvard University Press, 2006.

Homer. *The Iliad.* Translated by Richmond Lattimore. Chicago: University of Chicago Press, 1951.

———. *The Odyssey.* Translated by A. T. Murray, revised by G. E. Dimock. 2 vols. Loeb Classical Library. Cambridge, Mass.: Harvard University Press, 1995.

Horace (Quintus Horatius Flaccus). *Satires, Epistles, and Ars Poetica.* Edited and translated by H. Rushton Fairclough. Rev. ed. Loeb Classical Library. Cambridge, Mass.: Harvard University Press, 1929.

Hume, David. *Essays Moral, Political, and Literary.* Edited by Eugene Miller. Indianapolis: Liberty Fund, 1985.

———. *The Philosophical Works of David Hume.* Vols. 3 and 4. Edited by T. H. Green and T. H. Grose. London: Longmans, Green, 1875.

———. *A Treatise of Human Nature.* Edited by L. A. Selby-Bigge. New York: Oxford University Press, 1978.

———. *A Treatise of Human Nature.* Edited by David Fate Norton and Mary J. Norton. Oxford: Oxford University Press, 2000.

Hutcheson, Francis. *An Essay on the Nature and Conduct of the Passions and Affections, with Illustrations on the Moral Sense.* London, 1728. (For a modern edition, see *An Essay on the Nature and Conduct of the Passions and Affections, with Illustrations on the Moral Sense,* edited by Aaron Garrett. Indianapolis: Liberty Fund, 2002.)

———. *An Inquiry into the Original of Our Ideas of Beauty and Virtue.* Edited by Wolfgang Leidhold. Indianapolis: Liberty Fund, 2004.

———. Letter to the Reverend Mr. Thomas Drennan in Belfast. From Glasgow, May 31, 1742. In Glasgow University Library MS Gen 1018, no. 11.

———. *Logic, Metaphysics, and the Natural Sociability of Mankind.* Edited by James Moore and Michael Silverthorne. Indianapolis: Liberty Fund, 2006.

———. *On Human Nature.* Edited by Thomas Mautner. Cambridge: Cambridge University Press, 1993.

———. *Philosophiae moralis institutio compendiaria. Libris III. Ethices et jurisprudentiae continens.* Editio altera auctior et emendatior. Glasgow, 1745. (For a modern edition, see *Philosophiae Moralis Institutio Compendiaria, with A Short Introduction to Moral Philosophy,* edited by Luigi Turco. Indianapolis: Liberty Fund, 2007.)

———. *A Short Introduction to Moral Philosophy, in Three Books; Containing the Elements of Ethicks and the Law of Nature.* Glasgow, 1747.

———. *A System of Moral Philosophy, in Three Books.* Glasgow and London, 1755.

Isidore of Pelusium, Saint. *Sancti Isidori Pelusiotae Epistolarum libri quinque.* Edited by J. P. Migne. *Patrologiae Graecae,* vol. 78. Paris, 1864.

Jebb, R. C. *Bentley.* London: Macmillan, 1889.

Justin Martyr, Saint. *The First Apology, The Second Apology, Dialog with Trypho, Exhortation to the Greeks, Discourse to the Greeks, The Monarchy or The Rule of God.* Edited and translated by T. B. Falls. Washington, D.C.: Catholic University of America in assoc. with Consortium Books, 1948.

———. *Justini Martyris Apologiae pro Christianis.* Edited by Miroslav Marcovich. Berlin: Walter de Gruyter, 1994.

King, William. *De origine mali.* Dublin: A. Crook, 1702.

Long, A. A. *Hellenistic Philosophy: Stoics, Epicureans, Sceptics.* London: Duckworth, 1974.

Long, A. A., and D. Sedley. *The Hellenistic Philosophers.* 2 vols. Cambridge: Cambridge University Press, 1987.

Lucan (Marcus Annaeus Lucanus). *The Civil War.* Edited and translated by J. D. Duff. Loeb Classical Library. Cambridge, Mass.: Harvard University Press, 1928.

Lucian. *Lucian.* Edited and translated by A. M. Harmon and M. D. Macleod. 8 vols. Loeb Classical Library. Cambridge, Mass.: Harvard University Press, 1913–2004.

Maximus Tyrius. *Maximus Tyrius Dissertationes.* Edited by M. B. Trapp. Leipzig: Teubner, 1994.

———. *The Philosophical Orations.* Translated with introduction and notes by M. B. Trapp. New York: Oxford University Press, 1997.

Menander. *Menander.* Edited by W. Geoffrey Arnott. 3 vols. Loeb Classical Library. Cambridge, Mass.: Harvard University Press, 1979–2000.

Moore, James. "Hutcheson's Theodicy: The Arguments and the Contexts of *A System of Moral Philosophy.*" In *The Scottish Enlightenment: Essays in Reinterpretation,* edited by Paul Wood. Rochester, N.Y.: University of Rochester Press, 2000.

Moore, James, and Michael Silverthorne. "Hutcheson's LLD." *Eighteenth-Century Scotland* 20 (2006): 10–12.

More, Henry. *Enchiridion ethicum* (1666). Translated as *An Account of Virtue: or, Dr. Henry More's Abridgment of Morals, Put into English.* London, 1690.

The Oxford Classical Dictionary. 3rd ed. rev. Edited by Simon Hornblower and Antony Spawforth. Oxford: Oxford University Press, 2003.

Persius. *Satires.* In *Juvenal and Persius,* edited and translated by Susanna Morton

Braund. Loeb Classical Library. Cambridge, Mass.: Harvard University Press, 2004.

Philostratus, Lucius Flavius, and Eunapius. *The Lives of the Sophists.* Edited and translated by W. C. F. Wright. Loeb Classical Library. Cambridge, Mass.: Harvard University Press, 1921.

Plato. *Euthyphro, Apology, Crito, Phaedo, Phaedrus.* Edited and translated by Harold North Fowler. Loeb Classical Library. Cambridge, Mass.: Harvard University Press, 1914.

———. *Laws.* Edited and translated by Robert G. Bury. 2 vols. Loeb Classical Library. London: Heinemann, 1926.

———. *Lysis, Symposium, Gorgias.* Edited and translated by W. R. M. Lamb. Loeb Classical Library. London: Heinemann, 1925.

———. *Republic.* Edited and translated by Paul Shorey. 2 vols. Loeb Classical Library. Cambridge, Mass.: Harvard University Press, 1930–35.

———. *Theaetetus and Sophist.* Edited and translated by H. N. Fowler. Loeb Classical Library. London: Heinemann, 1921.

———. *Timaeus, Critias, Cleitophon, Menexenus, Epistles.* Edited and translated by Robert G. Bury. Loeb Classical Library. Cambridge, Mass.: Harvard University Press, 1929.

Pliny the Younger (Gaius Plinius Caecilius Secundus). *Letters and Panegyricus.* Translated by Betty Radice. 2 vols. Loeb Classical Library. Cambridge, Mass.: Harvard University Press, 1969.

Plutarch. *Plutarch's Lives.* Translated by Bernadotte Perrin. 11 vols. Loeb Classical Library. Cambridge, Mass.: Harvard University Press, 1914–26.

———. *Plutarch's Moralia.* Edited and translated by F. C. Babbitt et al. 16 vols. Loeb Classical Library. London: Heinemann; and Cambridge, Mass.: Harvard University Press, 1922–2004.

Polybius. *The Histories.* Edited and translated by W. R. Paton. 6 vols. Loeb Classical Library. London: Heinemann, 1922–27.

Real-Encyclopädie der classischen Altertumswissenschaft (Pauly-Wissowa), vol. 4. Stuttgart: Druckenmüller, 1901.

Reid, Thomas. MS entry in *The Meditations of the Emperor Marcus Aurelius Antoninus.* Glasgow, 1764. In Bodleian Library, Oxford Vet A4f, 505 (9).

Rivers, Isabel. *Reason, Grace, and Sentiment: A Study of the Language of Religion and Ethics in England, 1660–1780.* Vol. 2: *Shaftesbury to Hume.* Cambridge: Cambridge University Press, 1991–2000.

Robertson, William. Untitled MS translation of *The Meditations* of Marcus Aurelius Antoninus, bks. 1–8. In National Library of Scotland MS 3955.

Scott, William Robert. *Francis Hutcheson: His Life, Teaching, and Position in the History of Philosophy.* Cambridge: Cambridge University Press, 1900.

The Scriptores historiae Augustae [Writers of the History of the Caesars]. Edited and translated by David Magie. 3 vols. Loeb Classical Library. London: Heinemann, 1922–32.

Seneca, Lucius Annaeus. *Ad Lucilium epistulae morales.* Edited and translated by Richard M. Gummere. 3 vols. Loeb Classical Library. London: Heinemann, 1917–25.

Shaftesbury, Anthony Ashley Cooper, third earl of. *Characteristics of Men, Manners, Opinions, Times.* Edited by Lawrence Klein. New York: Cambridge University Press, 1999.

Sher, Richard. *Church and University in the Scottish Enlightenment: The Moderate Literati of Edinburgh.* Princeton, N.J.: Princeton University Press, 1985.

Smith, Adam. *The Theory of Moral Sentiments.* Edited by D. D. Raphael and A. L. Macfie. New York: Oxford University Press, 1976. Reprinted Indianapolis: Liberty Fund, 1982.

Sophocles. *Sophocles: Ajax, Electra, Oedipus Tyrannus.* Edited and translated by Hugh Lloyd-Jones. Loeb Classical Library. Cambridge, Mass.: Harvard University Press, 1994.

Stephen, James. "Francis Hutcheson and the Early History of the Foulis Press: Some Overlooked Evidence." *Bibliographical Society of Australia and New Zealand Bulletin* 8, no. 4 (1984): 213–14.

Tertullian (Quintus Septimius Florens Tertullianus). *Apology, De spectaculis.* Edited and translated by T. R. Glover. Loeb Classical Library. Cambridge, Mass.: Harvard University Press, 1966.

Tragicorum Graecorum fragmenta. Edited by Richard Kannicht and Bruno Snell. 5 vols. Göttingen: Vandenhoeck & Ruprecht, 1971–2004.

Virgil (Publius Vergilius Maro). *Georgics.* Edited by R. A. B. Mynors. Oxford: Clarendon Press, 1990.

———. *Virgil.* Edited and translated by H. Rushton Fairclough. 3rd ed. Revised by G. P. Goold. 2 vols. Loeb Classical Library. Cambridge, Mass.: Harvard University Press, 1999–2000.

Von Arnim, H. F. A. *Stoicorum veterum fragmenta.* Leipzig: Teubner, 1905–24.

INDEX

This book is set in Adobe Garamond, a modern adaptation by Robert Slimbach of the typeface originally cut around 1540 by the French typographer and printer Claude Garamond. The Garamond face, with its small lowercase height and restrained contrast between thick and thin strokes, is a classic "old-style" face and has long been one of the most influential and widely used typefaces.

Printed on paper that is acid-free and meets the requirements of the American National Standard for Permanence of Paper for Printed Library Materials, z39.48-1992. ♾

Book design by Louise OFarrell
Gainesville, Florida
Typography by Apex Publishing, LLC
Madison, Wisconsin
Printed and bound by Edwards Brothers, Inc.
Ann Arbor, Michigan